THE IDEA OF COMMUNISM

THE IDEA OF COMMUNISM

EDITED BY COSTAS DOUZINAS
AND
SLAVOJ ŽIŽEK

VERSO

London • New York

First published by Verso 2010
© the collection Verso 2010
© individual contributions the contributors
Translator © Andrew Gibson, Chapter 2 (with author)
Translator © Arianna Bové, Chapter 10

3 5 7 9 10 8 6 4 2

Verso
UK: 6 Meard Street, London W1F 0EG
US: 20 Jay Street, Suite 1010, Brooklyn, NY 11201
www.versobooks.com

Verso is the imprint of New Left Books

ISBN-13: 978-1-84467-459-6 (pbk)
ISBN-13: 978-1-84467-455-8 (hbk)

British Library Cataloguing in Publication Data
A catalogue record for this book is available from the British Library

Library of Congress Cataloging-in-Publication Data
A catalog record for this book is available from the Library of Congress

Typeset in Cochin by Hewer Text UK Ltd, Edinburgh
Printed and bound by CPI Group (UK) Ltd, Croydon, CR0 4YY

Contents

Introduction: The Idea of Communism   vii

1   The Idea of Communism   1
    Alain Badiou

2   To Present Oneself to the Present. The Communist
    Hypothesis: a Possible Hypothesis for Philosophy, an
    Impossible Name for Politics?   15
    Judith Balso

3   The Leftist Hypothesis: Communism in the Age of Terror   33
    Bruno Bosteels

4   The Second Time as Farce . . . Historical Pragmatics and
    the Untimely Present   67
    Susan Buck-Morss

5   *Adikia*: On Communism and Rights   81
    Costas Douzinas

6   Communism: Lear or Gonzalo?   101
    Terry Eagleton

7   'Communism of the Intellect, Communism of the Will'   111
    Peter Hallward

8   The Common in Communism   131
    Michael Hardt

9   Communism, the Word   145
    Jean-Luc Nancy

10 Communism: Some Thoughts on the Concept and Practice   155
    Antonio Negri

11 Communists Without Communism?   167
    Jacques Rancière

12 Did the Cultural Revolution End Communism?
    Eight Remarks on Philosophy and Politics Today   179
    Alessandro Russo

13 The Politics of Abstraction: Communism and Philosophy   195
    Alberto Toscano

14 Weak Communism?   205
    Gianni Vattimo

15 How to Begin From the Beginning   209
    Slavoj Žižek

Index   227

Introduction: The Idea of Communism

The long night of the left is drawing to a close. The defeat, denunciations and despair of the 1980s and 1990s, the triumphalist 'end of history', the unipolar world of American hegemony – all are fast becoming old news. In Europe, in the year 2000, Jürgen Habermas and Ulrich Beck enthused about the European Union and its common currency, prophesying that it would become the model for the future of humanity. How different the reality is today! The Union is no longer a model but a dysfunctional organization of fanatical right-wing governments and supine social democrats imposing unprecedented austerity measures, unemployment and poverty on working people in order to return to 'fiscal discipline'.

All pretence of social solidarity and justice, always an exaggerated assertion of the EU, has been abandoned. The 2008 'bail-out' of banks to the tune of over one trillion dollars socialized the losses of neo-liberal casino capitalism, asking the multitude to pay for the speculation of hedge funds, derivative markets and an economic system based on consumption and debt. Socialism for the banks, capitalism for the poor became the modus vivendi of the 2000s. People around the world learnt, to paraphrase Brecht, that you go to prison if you fiddle your benefit payments, but receive huge bonuses if you bankrupt a bank.

At the beginning of the second decade of the new century, the post-Cold War complacency is over. The economic crisis has matured into a full-fledged political crisis which is de-legitimizing political systems and distancing people from capitalist ideology. New antagonisms and struggles are developing over the defence of the welfare state in the West, the programmatic exclusion of large groups of people from economic activity and political participation, and ecological fears. A new militancy evident at the beginning of the new decade in, amongst other places, Greece, France, India and Thailand is introducing wide sections of the population and, critically, young people to ideas of resistance, rebellion and emancipation. If 1989 was the inaugural year of the new world order, 2001 announced its decline, and the collapse of the banking system in 2008 marked the beginning of a return to full-blown history. If that was our 'new world order', it is the shortest the world has even seen.

The return of history has led to a renewed interest in radical ideas and politics. The twenty-first century left can finally leave behind the introspection, contrition and penance that followed the fall of the Soviet Union. The left which aligned itself with 'actually existing socialism' has disappeared or turned into a historical curiosity. New forms of radical militancy and mobilization have marked the return to politics. In Latin America, the different new lefts in Bolivia, Venezuela and Brazil are developing unprecedented and imaginative national paths to socialism. In the United States, the election of Barack Obama was a symbolic moment hailed throughout the world as a sign of historical progress. In India, China and Africa, dissent, resistance and rebellion have replaced the somnolent and fearful 1990s.

In this context, the conference 'The Idea of Communism', organized by the Birkbeck Institute for the Humanities in March 2009, had huge political importance. When we first planned it, in the summer of 2008, we expected only a limited audience and booked a room capable of holding 180. But when, in early 2009, we opened for registration, the interest was such that we had twice to move to larger rooms, eventually ending in the main auditorium at the Institute of Education accommodating 900 people, with an adjacent video-link room holding another 300. Julia Eisner, who administered the conference, was deluged with messages and pleading voices from individuals, campaigns and political organizations all over the world who came to London to listen and participate. Julia's efficient, calm and elegant presence made this event possible.

The participants at the conference – now the contributors to this volume – have developed new theoretical and political radicalisms that have a particular resonance amongst younger people. But the conference was the first occasion for bringing together some of the most interesting philosophers on the left under the name of communism – a word that has recently received more bad press than perhaps any other. The key question addressed then, is whether 'communism' is still the name to be used to designate radical emancipatory projects. The conference participants, although coming from different perspectives and projects, shared the thesis that one should remain faithful to the name 'communism'. It is a name that can not only express the Idea which guides radical activity, but can also help expose the catastrophes of the twentieth century, including those of the left.

By de-demonizing the signifier 'communism' – by asserting in Alain Badiou's felicitous words that 'from Plato onwards, Communism is the only political Idea worthy of a philosopher' – the conference opened the way for a reactivation of the strong link between radical philosophy and politics. The massive participation, the amazing buzz that propelled the conference (strangers greeting each other like old friends), the good-humoured and non-sectarian question and answer sessions (something rather rare on the left), all indicated that the period of guilt is over. If this conference was a major intellectual encounter, it was an even greater political event.

Left theory has been always linked with political practice. Thinking in action is the left's key weapon. At this critical turning point, where all bets on the outcome of the crisis are off and the best and worst stand in close proximity, the idea of communism has the potential to revitalize theoretical thinking and reverse the de-politicizing tendency of late capitalism.

The energy, dynamism and pluralism that characterized the conference is evident in this collection. We have edited the lectures minimally in order to preserve the vitality of a political event. It goes without saying that the speakers did not all agree on the meaning of communism, its relevance today, or the ways in which it may mark a new political beginning. But despite some disagreement, certain common themes emerged. Without any particular priority, these were the shared premises that brought most people together.

1. Recent politics has attempted to ban and foreclose conflict. The idea of communism confronts widespread de-politicization by inducing new political subjectivities and returning to a popular voluntarism.

2. 'Communism' is the idea of radical philosophy and politics. As the precondition of radical action, communism must be thought today by taking its distance from statism and economism and becoming informed by the political experiences of the twenty-first century.

3. Neo-liberal capitalist exploitation and domination takes the form of new enclosures of the commons (language and communication, intellectual property, genetic material, natural resources and forms of governance). Communism, by returning to the concept of the 'common', confronts capitalist privatizations with a view to building a new commonwealth.

4. Communism aims to bring about freedom and equality. Freedom cannot flourish without equality and equality does not exist without freedom.

As Slavoj Žižek suggested during the closing session, we have to start again and again and beginnings are always the hardest. But it may be that the beginning has already happened, and it is now a question of fidelity to that beginning. This then is the task ahead.

Costas Douzinas and Slavoj Žižek

1   The Idea of Communism

Alain Badiou

My aim today is to describe a conceptual operation to which, for reasons that I hope will be convincing, I will give the name 'the Idea of communism'. No doubt the trickiest part of this construction is the most general one, the one that involves explaining what an Idea is, not just with respect to political truths (in which case the Idea is that of communism) but with respect to any truth (in which case the Idea is a modern version of what Plato attempted to convey to us under the names of *eidos*, or *idea*, or, even more precisely, the Idea of the Good). I will leave a good deal of this generality implicit,[1] in order to be as clear as possible regarding the Idea of communism.

Three basic elements – political, historical and subjective – are needed for the operation of 'the Idea of communism'.

First, the political element. This concerns what I call a truth, a political truth. Regarding my analysis of the Chinese Cultural Revolution (a political truth if ever there was one), one reviewer for a British newspaper remarked – merely from noting my positive account of this episode of Chinese history (which *he* of course regards as a sinister, bloody catastrophe) – that it was 'not hard to feel a certain pride in workaday Anglo-Saxon empiricism, which inoculates us [the readers of the *Observer*] against the tyranny of pure political abstraction'.[2] He was basically taking

---

1   The theme of the Idea appears gradually in my work. It was no doubt already present in the late 1980s from the moment when, in *Manifesto for Philosophy*, I designated my undertaking as a 'Platonism of the multiple', which would require a renewed investigation into the nature of the Idea. In *Logics of Worlds*, this investigation was expressed as an imperative: 'true life' was conceived of as life lived in accordance with the Idea, as opposed to the maxim of contemporary democratic materialism, which commands us to live without any Idea. I examined the logic of the Idea in greater detail in *Second Manifesto for Philosophy*, in which the notion of ideation, and thus of the operative, or working, value of the Idea is introduced. This was backed up by a multifaceted commitment to something like a renaissance of the use of Plato. For example: my seminar, which for the past two years has been entitled 'For today: Plato!'; my film project, *The Life of Plato*; and my complete translation (which I call a 'hypertranslation') of *The Republic*, renamed *Du Commun(isme)* and divided into nine chapters, which I hope to complete and publish in 2010.
2   Rafael Behr, 'A Denunciation of the "Rat Man"', *Observer*, 1 March 2009. *Translator's note.*

pride in the fact that the dominant imperative in the world today is 'Live without any Idea'. So, to please him, I will begin by saying that a political truth can, after all, be described in a purely empirical way: it is a concrete, time-specific sequence in which a new thought and practice of collective emancipation arise, exist and eventually disappear.[3] Some examples of this can even be given: the French Revolution, from 1792 to 1794; the People's War of Liberation in China, from 1927 to 1949; Bolshevism in Russia, from 1902 to 1917; and – unfortunately for the *Observer*'s critic, although he probably won't like my other examples all that much either – the Great Cultural Revolution, at any rate from 1965 to 1968. That said, formally, that is, philosophically, I am speaking about a truth procedure here, in the sense that I have been giving this term since *Being and Event*. I'll come back to this shortly. But let's note right away that every truth procedure prescribes a Subject of this truth, a Subject who – even empirically – cannot be reduced to an individual.

Now for the historical element. As the time frame of political sequences clearly shows, a truth procedure is inscribed in the general becoming of Humanity, in a local form whose supports are spatial, temporal and anthropological. Designations such as 'French' or 'Chinese' are the empirical indices of this localization. They make it clear why Sylvain Lazarus (cf. note 3) speaks of 'historical modes of politics', not simply of 'modes'. There is in fact a historical dimension of a truth, although the latter is in the final analysis universal (in the sense that I give this term in my *Ethics* book, for example, or in my *Saint Paul: The Foundation of Universalism*) or eternal (as I prefer to put it in *Logics of Worlds* or in my *Second Manifesto for Philosophy*). In particular, we will see that, within a given type of truth (political, but also amorous, artistic or scientific), the historical inscription encompasses an interplay between types of truth that are different from one another and are therefore situated at different points in human time in general. In particular, there are retroactive effects of one truth on other truths that were created before it. All this requires a transtemporal availability of truths.

---

3   The rarity of politics, in the guise of sequences destined for an immanent end, is very powerfully argued by Sylvain Lazarus in his book *Anthropologie du nom* (Paris: Seuil, 1996). He calls these sequences 'historical modes of politics', which are defined by a certain type of relationship between a politics and its thought. My philosophical elaboration of a truth procedure would appear to be very different from this (the concepts of event and genericity are completely absent from Lazarus's thought). I explained in *Logics of Worlds* why my philosophical enterprise is nevertheless compatible with Lazarus's, which puts forward a thought of politics elaborated from the standpoint of politics itself. Note that for him, too, obviously, the question of the time frame of the modes is very important.

And finally, the subjective element. What is at issue is the possibility for an individual, defined as a mere human animal, and clearly distinct from any Subject, to decide[4] to become part of a political truth procedure. To become, in a nutshell, a militant of this truth. In *Logics of Worlds*, and in a simpler manner in the *Second Manifesto for Philosophy*, I describe this decision as an incorporation: the individual body and all that it entails in terms of thought, affects, potentialities at work in it, and so forth, becomes one of the elements of another body, the body-of-truth, the material existence of a truth in the making in a given world. This is the moment when an individual declares that he or she can go beyond the bounds (of selfishness, competition, finitude . . .) set by individualism (or animality – they're one and the same thing). He or she can do so to the extent that, while remaining the individual that he or she is, he or she can also become, through incorporation, an active part of a new Subject. I call this decision, this will, a subjectivation.[5] More generally speaking, a subjectivation is always the process whereby an individual determines the place of a truth with respect to his or her own vital existence and to the world in which this existence is lived out.

I call an 'Idea' an abstract totalization of the three basic elements: a truth procedure, a belonging to history, and an individual subjectivation. A formal definition of the Idea can immediately be given: an Idea is the subjectivation of an interplay between the singularity of a truth procedure and a representation of History.

In the case that concerns us here, we will say that an Idea is the possibility for an individual to understand that his or her participation in a singular political process (his or her entry into a body-of-truth) is also, in a certain way, a *historical* decision. Thanks to the Idea, the individual, as an element of the new Subject, realizes his or her belonging to the movement of History. For about two centuries (from Babeuf's 'community of equals' to the 1980s), the word 'communism' was the most important name of an Idea located in the field of emancipatory, or revolutionary, politics. To be a communist was of course to be a militant of a Communist

---

4   This aspect of decision, of choice, of the Will, in which the Idea involves an individual commitment, is increasingly present in the works of Peter Hallward. It is telling that, as a result, references to the French and Haitian Revolutions, in which these categories are the most visible, should now haunt all his work.

5   In my *Théorie du sujet*, published in 1982, the couple formed by subjectivation and the subjective process plays a fundamental role. This is an additional sign of my tendency, as Bruno Bosteels contends in his work (including his English translation of the book, published by Continuum, 2009), to return little by little to some of the dialectical intuitions of that book.

Party in a given country. But to be a militant of a Communist Party was also to be one of millions of agents of a historical orientation of all of Humanity. In the context of the Idea of communism, subjectivation constituted the link between the local belonging to a political procedure and the huge symbolic domain of Humanity's forward march towards its collective emancipation. To give out a flyer in a marketplace was also to mount the stage of History.

So it is clear why the word 'communism' cannot be a purely political name: for the individual whose subjectivation it supports, it effectively connects the political procedure to something other than itself. Nor can it be a purely historical term. This is because, lacking the actual political procedure, which, as we shall see, contains an irreducible element of contingency, History is but empty symbolism. And finally, it cannot be a purely subjective, or ideological, word either. For subjectivation operates 'between' politics and history, between singularity and the projection of this singularity into a symbolic whole and, without such materialities and symbolizations, it cannot attain the status of a decision. The word 'communism' has the status of an Idea, meaning that, once an incorporation has taken place, hence from within a political subjectivation, this term denotes a synthesis of politics, history and ideology. That is why it is better understood as an operation than as a concept. The communist Idea exists only at the border between the individual and the political procedure, as that element of subjectivation that is based on a historical projection of politics. The communist Idea is what constitutes the becoming-political Subject of the individual as also and at the same time his or her projection into History.

If only so as to move towards the philosophical turf of my friend Slavoj Žižek,[6] I think it might help to clarify things by formalizing the operation of the Idea in general, and of the communist Idea in particular, in the register of Lacan's three orders of the Subject: the Real, the Imaginary and the Symbolic. First, we will posit that the truth procedure itself is the Real on which the Idea is based. Next, we will allow that History exists

---

6   Slavoj Žižek is probably the only thinker today who can simultaneously hew as closely as possible to Lacan's contributions and argue steadfastly and vigorously for the return of the Idea of communism. This is because his real master is Hegel, of whom he offers an interpretation that is completely novel, inasmuch as he has given up subordinating it to the theme of Totality. There are two ways of rescuing the Idea of communism in philosophy today: either by abandoning Hegel, not without regret, incidentally, and only after repeated considerations of his writings (which is what I do), or by putting forward a different Hegel, an unknown Hegel, and that is what Žižek does, based on Lacan (who was a magnificent Hegelian – or so Žižek would claim – at first explicitly and later secretly, all along the way).

only symbolically. In effect, it cannot appear. In order to appear, belonging to a world is necessary. However, History, as the alleged totality of human becoming, has no world that can locate it in an actual existence. It is a narrative constructed after the fact. Finally, we will grant that subjectivation, which projects the real into the symbolic of a History, can only be imaginary, for one major reason: no real can be symbolized as such. The real exists, in a given world, and under very specific conditions that I will come back to later. However, as Lacan said over and over, it is unsymbolizable. So the real of a truth procedure cannot be 'really' projected into the narrative symbolism of History. It can be so only imaginarily, which doesn't mean – far from it – that this is useless, negative or ineffective. On the contrary, it is in the operation of the Idea that the individual finds the capacity to consist 'as a Subject'.[7] We will therefore assert the following: the Idea exposes a truth in a fictional structure. In the specific case of the communist Idea, which is operative when the truth it deals with is an emancipatory political sequence, we will claim that 'communism' exposes this sequence (and consequently its militants) in the symbolic order of History. In other words, the communist Idea is the imaginary operation whereby an individual subjectivation projects a fragment of the political real into the symbolic narrative of a History. It is in this sense that one may appropriately say that the Idea is (as might be expected!) ideological.[8]

It is essential today to understand that 'communist' can no longer be the adjective qualifying a politics. An entire century of experiences both epic in scope and appalling was required to understand that certain phrases produced by this short-circuiting between the real and the Idea were misconceived, phrases such as 'communist party' or 'communist state' – an oxymoron that the phrase 'socialist state' attempted to get around. The long-term effects of the Hegelian origins of Marxism are evident in this short-circuiting. For Hegel, in fact, the historical exposure of politics was not an imaginary subjectivation, it was the real as such. This was because the crucial axiom of the dialectic as he conceived of it was: 'The

---

7   To live 'as a Subject' can be taken in two ways. The first is like 'to live as an Immortal', a maxim translated from Aristotle. 'As' means 'as if one were'. The second way is topological: incorporation in effect means that the individual lives 'in' the subject-body of a truth. These nuances are clarified by the theory of the body-of-truth on which *Logics of Worlds* concludes, a decisive conclusion but, I must admit, one that is still too condensed and abrupt.
8   Basically, if you really want to understand the tired-out word 'ideology', the simplest thing to do is to stay as close as possible to its derivation: something can be said to be 'ideological' when it has to do with an Idea.

True is the process of its own becoming' or – what amounts to the same – 'Time is the being-there of the concept.' As a result, in line with the Hegelian philosophical heritage, we are justified in thinking that, under the name of 'communism', the historical inscription of revolutionary political sequences or of the disparate fragments of collective emancipation reveals their truth: to move forward according to the meaning of History. This latent subordination of truths to their historical meaning entails that we can speak 'in truth' of communist politics, communist parties and communist militants. It is clear, however, that we need to avoid any such adjectivation today. To combat such a thing, I have many times had to insist that History does not exist, which is in keeping with my conception of truths, namely, that they have no meaning, and especially not the meaning of History. But I need to clarify this verdict. Of course, there is no real of History and it is therefore true, transcendentally true, that it cannot exist. Discontinuity between worlds is the law of appearance, hence of existence. What *does* exist, however, under the real condition of organized political action, is the communist Idea, an operation tied to intellectual subjectivation and that integrates the real, the symbolic and the ideological at the level of the individual. We must bring this Idea back, by uncoupling it from any predicative usage. We must rescue the Idea, but also free the real from any immediate fusion with it. Only political sequences that it would ultimately be absurd to label as communist can be recovered by the communist Idea as the potential force of the becoming-Subject of individuals.

So we must begin with truths, with the political real, in order to define the Idea in terms of the threefold nature of its operation: politics-real, history-symbolic and ideology-imaginary.

Let me begin by reminding you of a few of my usual concepts, in a very abstract, simple form.

I call an 'event' a rupture in the normal order of bodies and languages as it exists for any particular situation (if you refer to *Being and Event* [1988] or *Manifesto for Philosophy* [1989]) or as it appears in any particular world (if you refer instead to *Logics of Worlds* [2006] or the *Second Manifesto for Philosophy* [2009]). What is important to note here is that an event is not the realization of a possibility that resides within the situation nor is it dependent on the transcendental laws of the world. An event is the creation of new possibilities. It is located not merely at the level of objective possibilities but at the level of the possibility of possibilities. Another way of putting this is: with respect to a situation or a world, an event paves the way for the possibility of what – from the limited perspective of the make-up of this situation or the legality of this world – is strictly impossible. If we keep in mind here that, for Lacan, the real = the impossible, the intrinsically real aspect of the event will be readily seen. We might also say that an event is the occurrence of the real as its own future possibility.

I call a 'State' or 'state of the situation' the system of constraints that limit the possibility of possibilities. By the same token, we will say that the State is that which prescribes what, in a given situation, is the impossibility specific to that situation, from the perspective of the formal prescription of what is possible. The State is always the finitude of possibility, and the event is its infinitization. For example, what is the State comprised of today with regard to its political possibilities? Well, the capitalist economy, the constitutional form of government, the laws (in the juridical sense) concerning property and inheritance, the army, the police . . . Through all these systems, all these apparatuses, including, of course, those that Althusser called 'ideological State apparatuses', which could be defined by their one common goal – preventing the communist Idea from designating a possibility – we can see how the State organizes and maintains, often by force, the distinction between what is possible and what isn't. It follows clearly from this that an event is something that can occur only to the extent that it is subtracted from the power of the State.

I call a 'truth procedure' or a 'truth' an ongoing organization, in a given situation (or world), of the consequences of an event. It will be noted at once that a fundamental randomness, that of its evental origins, partakes in every truth. I call 'facts' the consequences of the existence of the State. It will be observed that intrinsic necessity is always on the side of the State. So it is clear that a truth cannot be made up of pure facts. The non-factual element in a truth is a function of its orientation, and this will be termed subjective. We will also say that the material 'body' of a truth, in so far as it is subjectively oriented, is an exceptional body. Making unabashed use of a religious metaphor, I will say that the body-of-truth, as concerns what cannot be reduced to facts within it, can be called a glorious body. With respect to this body, which is that of a new collective Subject in politics, of an organization composed of individual multiples, we will say that it shares in the creation of a political truth. In the case of the State of the world in which this creation is at work, we will speak of historical facts. History as such, made up of historical facts, is in no way subtracted from the power of the State.

History is neither subjective nor glorious. History should instead be said to be the history of the State.[9]

So we can now return to our subject, the communist Idea. If, for an individual, an Idea is the subjective operation whereby a specific real truth is imaginarily projected into the symbolic movement of a History, we can say that an Idea presents the truth as if it were a fact. In other words, the Idea presents certain facts as symbols of the real of truth. This was how the Idea of communism allowed revolutionary politics and its parties to be inscribed in the representation of a meaning of History the inevitable outcome of which was communism. Or how it became possible to speak of a 'homeland of socialism', which amounted to symbolizing the creation of a possibility – which is fragile by definition – through the magnitude of a power. The Idea, which is an operative mediation between the real and the symbolic, always presents the individual with something that is located between the event and the fact. That is why the endless debates about the real status of the communist Idea are irresolvable. Is it a question of a regulative Idea, in Kant's sense of the term, having no real efficacy but able to set reasonable goals for our understanding? Or is it an agenda that must be carried out over time through a new post-revolutionary State's action on the world? Is it a utopia, perhaps a plainly dangerous, and even criminal, one? Or is it the name of Reason in History? This type of debate can never be concluded, for the simple reason that the subjective operation of the Idea is not simple but complex. It involves real sequences of emancipatory politics as its essential real condition, but it also presupposes marshalling a whole range of historical facts suitable for symbolization. It does not claim that the event and its organized political consequences are reducible to facts, as this would amount to subjecting the truth procedure to the laws of the State. But neither does it claim that the facts are unsuitable for any historical trans-scription (to make a Lacanian sort of play on words) of the distinctive characters of a truth. The Idea is an historical anchoring of everything elusive, slippery and evanescent in the becoming of a truth. But it can only be so if it admits as its own real this aleatory, elusive, slippery, evanescent dimension. That is why it is incumbent upon the communist Idea to respond to the question 'Where do just ideas come from?' the way Mao

---

9   That history is the history of the State is a thesis introduced into the field of political speculation by Sylvain Lazarus, but he has not yet published all its consequences. Here, too, one could say that my ontologico-philosophical concept of the State, as it was introduced in the mid-'80s, is distinguished by a different (mathematical) point of departure and a different (metapolitical) destination. However, its compatibility with Lazarus's is confirmed in one major regard: no political truth procedure can be confused, in its very essence, with the historical actions of a State.

did: 'Just ideas' (and by this I mean what constitutes the path of a truth in a situation) come from practice. 'Practice' should obviously be understood as the materialist name of the real. It would thus be appropriate to say that the Idea that symbolizes the becoming 'in truth' of just (political) ideas in History, that is to say, the Idea of communism, therefore comes itself from the idea of practice (from the experience of the real) in the final analysis, but nevertheless cannot be reduced to it. This is because it is the protocol not of the existence but rather of the *exposure* of a truth in action.

All of the foregoing explains, and to a certain extent justifies, why it was ultimately possible to go to the extreme of exposing the truths of emancipatory politics in the guise of their opposite, that is to say, in the guise of a State. Since it is a question of an (imaginary) ideological relationship between a truth procedure and historical facts, why hesitate to push this relationship to its limit? Why not say that it is a matter of a relationship between event and State? *State and Revolution* is the title of one of Lenin's most famous texts. The State and the Event are indeed what are at stake in it. Nevertheless, Lenin, following Marx in this regard, is careful to say that the State in question after the Revolution will have to be the State of the withering away of the State, the State as organizer of the transition to the non-State. So let's say the following: the Idea of communism can project the real of a politics, subtracted as ever from the power of the State, into the figure of 'another State', provided that the subtraction lies within this subjectivating operation, in the sense that the 'other State' is also subtracted from the power of the State, hence from its own power, in so far as it is a State whose essence is to wither away.

In this context that it is necessary to think and endorse the vital importance of proper names in all revolutionary politics. Their importance is indeed both spectacular and paradoxical. On the one hand, in effect, emancipatory politics is essentially the politics of the anonymous masses; it is the victory of those with no names,[10] of those who are held

---

10   Those who have 'no name', those who have 'no part' and ultimately, in all current political actions, the organizing role of the workers 'without papers' are all part of a negative, or rather stripped down, view of the human terrain of emancipatory politics. Jacques Rancière, starting in particular with his in-depth study of these themes in the nineteenth century, has specifically highlighted, in the philosophical field, the implications for democracy of not belonging to a dominant societal category. This idea actually goes back at least as far as to the Marx of the *Manuscripts of 1844*, who defined the proletariat as generic humanity, since it does not itself possess any of the properties by which the bourgeoisie defines (respectable, or normal, or 'well-adjusted', as we would say today) Man. This idea is the basis of Rancière's attempt to salvage the word 'democracy', as is evident in his essay *The Hatred of Democracy* (London: Verso, 1996). I am not sure that the word can so easily be salvaged, or, at any rate, I think that making a detour through the Idea of communism is unavoidable. The debate has begun and will go on.

in a state of colossal insignificance by the State. On the other hand, it is distinguished all along the way by proper names, which define it historically, which represent it, much more forcefully than is the case for other kinds of politics. Why is there this long series of proper names? Why this glorious Pantheon of revolutionary heroes? Why Spartacus, Thomas Münzer, Robespierre, Toussaint-L'Ouverture, Blanqui, Marx, Lenin, Rosa Luxemburg, Mao, Che Guevara and so many others? The reason is that all these proper names symbolize historically – in the guise of an individual, of a pure singularity of body and thought – the rare and precious network of ephemeral sequences of politics as truth. The elusive formalism of bodies-of-truth is legible here as empirical existence. In these proper names the ordinary individual discovers glorious, distinctive individuals as the mediation for his or her own individuality, as the proof that he or she can force its finitude. The anonymous action of millions of militants, rebels, fighters, unrepresentable as such, is combined and counted as one in the simple, powerful symbol of the proper name. Thus, proper names are involved in the operation of the Idea, and the ones I just mentioned are elements of the Idea of communism at its various stages. So let us not hesitate to say that Khrushchev's condemnation of 'the cult of personality', apropos Stalin, was misguided, and that, under the pretence of democracy, it heralded the decline of the Idea of communism that we witnessed in the ensuing decades. The political critique of Stalin and his terrorist vision of the State needed to be undertaken in a rigorous way, from the perspective of revolutionary politics itself, and Mao had begun to do as much in a number of his writings.[11] Whereas Khrushchev, who was in fact defending the group that had led the Stalinist State, made no inroads whatsoever as regards this issue and, when it came to speaking of the Terror carried out under Stalin, merely offered an abstract critique of the role of proper names in political subjectivation. He himself thereby paved the way for the 'New Philosophers' of reactionary humanism a decade later. Whence a very precious lesson: even though retroactive political actions may require that a given name be stripped of its symbolic function, this function as such cannot be eliminated for all that. For the Idea – and the communist Idea in particular, because it refers directly to the infinity of the people – needs the finitude of proper names.

---

11   Mao Zedong's writings on Stalin were published in the short book *Mao Tsé-Toung et la construction du socialisme*, clearly subtitled 'Modèle soviétique ou voie chinoise', translated and presented by Hu Chi-hsi (Paris: Le Seuil, 1975). Guided by the idea of the eternity of the True, I wrote a commentary on this book, in the preface to *Logics of Worlds*.

Let's recapitulate as simply as possible. A truth is the political real. History, even as a reservoir of proper names, is a symbolic place. The ideological operation of the Idea of communism is the imaginary projection of the political real into the symbolic fiction of History, including in its guise as a representation of the action of innumerable masses via the One of a proper name. The role of this Idea is to support the individual's incorporation into the discipline of a truth procedure, to authorize the individual, in his or her own eyes, to go beyond the Statist constraints of mere survival by becoming a part of the body-of-truth, or the subjectivizable body.

We will now ask: why is it necessary to resort to this ambiguous operation? Why do the event and its consequences also have to be exposed in the guise of a fact – often a violent one – that is accompanied by different versions of the 'cult of personality'? What is the reason for this historical appropriation of emancipatory politics?

The simplest reason is that ordinary history, the history of individual lives, is confined within the State. The history of a life, with neither decision nor choice, is in itself a part of the history of the State, whose conventional mediations are the family, work, the homeland, property, religion, customs, and so forth. The heroic, but individual, projection of an exception to all the above – as is a truth procedure – also aims at being shared with everyone else; it aims to show itself to be not only an exception but also a possibility that everyone can share from now on. And that is one of the Idea's functions: to project the exception into the ordinary life of individuals, to fill what merely exists with a certain measure of the extraordinary. To convince my own immediate circle – husband or wife, neighbours and friends, colleagues – that the fantastic exception of truths in the making also exists, that we are not doomed to lives programmed by the constraints of the State. Naturally, in the final analysis, only the raw, or militant, experience of the truth procedure will compel one or another person's entry into the body of truth. But to take him or her to the place where this experience is to be found – to make him or her a spectator of, and therefore partly a participant in, what is important for a truth – the mediation of the Idea, the sharing of the Idea, are almost always required. The Idea of communism (regardless of what name it might otherwise be given, which hardly matters: no Idea is definable by its name) is what enables a truth procedure to be spoken in the impure language of the State, and thereby for the lines of force by virtue of which the State prescribes what is possible and what is impossible to be shifted for a time. In this view of things, the most ordinary action is to take someone to a real political meeting, far from their home, far from their predetermined existential parameters, in a hostel of workers from Mali, for example, or at the gates of a factory. Once they have come to the place where politics is occurring, they will make a decision about whether to incorporate or withdraw. But in order for them to come to that place, the Idea – and for two centuries, or perhaps since Plato, it has been the Idea of communism – must have already shifted them in the order of representations, of History and of the State. The symbol must imaginarily come to the aid of the creative flight from the Real. Allegorical facts must ideologize and historicize the fragility of truth. A banal yet crucial discussion among four workers and a student in an ill-lit room must momentarily be enlarged to the dimensions of Communism and thus be both what it is and what it will have been as a moment in the local construction of the True. Through the enlargement of the symbol, it must become visible that 'just ideas' come from this practically invisible practice. The five-person meeting in an out-of-the-way suburb must be eternal in the very expression of its precariousness. That is why the real must be exposed in a fictional structure.

The second reason is that every event is a surprise. If this were not the case, it would mean that it would have been predictable as a fact, and so would be inscribed in the history of the State, which is a contradiction in terms. The problem can thus be formulated in the following way: how can we prepare ourselves for such surprises? And this time the problem really exists, even if we are already currently militants of a previous event's consequences, even if we are included in a body-of-truth. Granted, we are proposing the deployment of new possibilities. However, the event to come will turn what is still impossible, even for us, into a possibility. In order to anticipate, at least ideologically or intellectually, the creation of new possibilities, we must have an Idea. An Idea that of course involves the newness of the possibilities that the truth procedure of which we are the militants has brought to light, which are real-possibilities, but an Idea that also involves the formal possibility of *other* possibilities, ones as yet unsuspected by us. An Idea is always the assertion that a new truth is historically possible. And since the forcing of the impossible into the possible occurs via subtraction from the power of the State, an Idea can be said to assert that this subtractive process is infinite. It is always formally possible that the dividing line drawn by the State between the possible and the impossible may once again be shifted, however radical its previous shifts – including the one in which we as militants are currently taking part

– may have been. That is why one of the contents of the communist Idea today – as opposed to the theme of communism as a goal to be attained through the work of a new State – is that the withering away of the State, while undoubtedly a principle that must be apparent in any political action (which is expressed by the formula 'politics at a distance from the State' as an obligatory refusal of any direct inclusion in the State, of any request for funding from the State, of any participation in elections, etc.), is also an infinite task, since the creation of new political truths will always shift the dividing line between Statist, hence historical, facts and the eternal consequences of an event.

With this in mind, I will now conclude by turning to the contemporary inflections of the Idea of communism.[12] In keeping with the current reassessment of the Idea of communism, as I mentioned, the word's function can no longer be that of an adjective, as in 'communist party', or 'communist regimes'. The party-form, like that of the socialist State, is no longer suitable for providing real support for the Idea. This problem moreover first found negative expression in two crucial events of the 1960s and 1970s: the Cultural Revolution in China and the amorphous entity called 'May '68' in France. Later, new political forms, all of which are of the order of politics without a party, were – and are still being – tried out.[13] Overall, however, the modern, so-called democratic form of the bourgeois State, of which globalized capitalism is the cornerstone, can boast of having no rivals in the ideological field. For three decades now, the word 'communism' has been either totally forgotten or practically equated with criminal enterprises. That is why the subjective situation of politics has everywhere become so incoherent. Lacking the Idea, the popular masses' confusion is inescapable.

Nevertheless, there are many signs – this book, and the conference on which it is based, for example – suggesting that this reactionary period is coming to an end. The historical paradox is that, in a certain way, we are closer to problems investigated in the first half of the nineteenth century than we are to those we have inherited from the twentieth century. Just

---

12   On the three stages of the Idea of communism, especially the one (the second stage) during which the Idea of communism attempted to be overtly political (in the sense of the programme, of both the party and the State), see the final chapters of my *Circonstances 4*, published in English as *The Meaning of Sarkozy* (London: Verso, 2008).

13   There have been numerous, fascinating experiments with new political forms over the past three decades. The following could be mentioned: the Solidarity movement in Poland in 1980–81; the first sequence of the Iranian Revolution; the *Organisation Politique* in France; the Zapatista movement in Mexico; the Maoists in Nepal. This list is not intended to be exhaustive.

as in around 1840, today we are faced with an utterly cynical capitalism, which is certain that it is the only possible option for a rational organization of society. Everywhere it is implied that the poor are to blame for their own plight, that Africans are backward, and that the future belongs either to the 'civilized' bourgeoisies of the Western world or to those who, like the Japanese, choose to follow the same path. Today, just as back then, very extensive areas of extreme poverty can be found even in the rich countries. There are outrageous, widening inequalities between countries, as well as between social classes. The subjective, political gulf between Third World farmers, the unemployed, and poor wage-earners in our so-called developed countries, on the one hand, and the 'Western' middle classes on the other, is absolutely unbridgeable and tainted with a sort of indifference bordering on hatred. More than ever, political power, as the current economic crisis with its single slogan of 'rescue the banks' clearly proves, is merely an agent of capitalism. Revolutionaries are divided and only weakly organized, broad sectors of working-class youth have fallen prey to nihilistic despair, the vast majority of intellectuals are servile. In contrast to all this, though just as isolated as Marx and his friends were at the time when the retrospectively famous *Manifesto of the Communist Party* came out in 1848, there are nonetheless more and more of us involved in organizing new types of political processes among the poor and working masses and in trying to find every possible way to support the re-emergent forms of the communist Idea in reality. Just as at the beginning of the nineteenth century, the victory of the communist Idea is not at issue, as it would later be, far too dangerously and dogmatically, for a whole stretch of the twentieth century. What matters first and foremost is its existence and the terms in which it is formulated. In the first place, to provide a vigorous subjective existence to the communist hypothesis is the task those of us gathered here today are attempting to accomplish in our own way. And it is, I insist, a thrilling task. By combining intellectual constructs, which are always global and universal, with experiments of fragments of truths, which are local and singular, yet universally transmissable, we can give new life to the communist hypothesis, or rather to the Idea of communism, in individual consciousnesses. We can usher in the third era of this Idea's existence. We can, so we must.

2   To Present Oneself to the Present
The Communist Hypothesis: A Possible Hypothesis
for Philosophy, an Impossible Name for Politics?

Judith Balso

I shall begin with the paradox of my presence at this philosophical meeting.[1]

Unlike most of those who are speaking here, until now I have not written about politics from a philosophical point of view. My relationship to philosophy is constituted by an exploration of the possible relationship between poetry and philosophy. More precisely by an exploration of what poetry may teach philosophy.[2]

Again, unlike most of those speaking here, since the 1970s I have been uninterruptedly involved in researching an altogether new thought and practice of a politics worthy of being called a 'politics of emancipation', a name I use provisionally here, and only because I have no better one.

It is from this singular place that I accepted the invitation to consider a question which (I insist) is asked only by philosophers, and only in the field of philosophy: whether the communist hypothesis remains valid or not. I propose to speak in my own name on this issue.

Firstly, a proposal regarding method: if philosophy wishes to pronounce on the question of the communist hypothesis, it cannot ignore the fact that this has been a political hypothesis.

It existed formerly as a utopian hypothesis, a will to equality and an act of establishing a distance from the State internal to revolts and rebellions of all kinds. But when it actually regulated a politics – in a sequence which begins in 1847 (with the *Communist Manifesto*) and ends between 1966 and 1968 (between the Shanghai Commune in China and the political singularity of May 1968 in France) – it emerged as a decisive question for a certain politics. This politics necessarily defined its task as that of putting an end to domination – that is, it aimed to be positive and

---

1   Many thanks to Andrew Gibson for co-translating this with me.
2   Judith Balso, *Pessoa, le passeur métaphysique* (Paris: Seuil, 2006).

emancipatory, not for one class or group of people, but 'for the whole of humanity', or, to put it more simply, 'for everybody'.

With Marx, Lenin and Mao, politics closely allied itself with communism and communism closely allied itself with politics. It is therefore this pair – 'politics/communism' – that needs to be examined if we want to be able to pronounce on whether or not the communist hypothesis should be maintained today.

My first proposition will thus be as follows: the communist hypothesis has been a central political hypothesis; and this hypothesis failed. Or rather, since I do not like failure as either a word or a category, the communist hypothesis did not attain its objective, which was to invent an emancipatory political capacity. The evidence bears this out. I do not say this in order to renounce the political will within such a politics. On the contrary, I want to explain the conditions for continuing with this political will, with reference to the following three points, which will form the substance of the first part of my talk:

- The communist hypothesis is a political hypothesis.
- This hypothesis has not found the path it was searching for, namely, a political capacity that exists for all.
- Acknowledging this political impasse is not to return to political impotence or to already established structures of submission and domination. On the contrary, it aims at opening up new paths for the political will toward a 'politics for all'.

In the second part, I will examine two figures of the 'suturing' of philosophy and politics internal to philosophy (this is one of Alain Badiou's categories): the first figure, attached to the name of Heidegger, puts the question of national socialism at stake. At stake in the second figure, attached to the name of Althusser, is the possibility of explaining Stalinism.

We must identify these two forms of suture, and work as hard as possible to undo them, because they prevent the appearance of new relations between philosophy and politics. I mean relations freed from a disastrous equivocation, which takes philosophy for a politics or (I do not know which is worse) subordinates politics to a philosophical proposition: it takes philosophy as a condition for, or a source of, politics. I want to propose a different relationship between philosophy and politics, on the basis of a necessary double separation:

- the separation of philosophy from politics, and
- the separation of politics from philosophy.

I will conclude that, in the field of philosophy, philosophy's investigations of its relationship with politics should be displaced, because from now on, whether we like it or not, we are working in the 'aftermath' of the communist hypothesis as a political hypothesis. This will be my position, and I hope to show you why I hold to it.

1

In what sense should we assert that the communist hypothesis was a political hypothesis? Firstly, politics consists in a set of singular organized processes, with their own disposition of thought, for which for a long time communism was the referent, sustained by both parties and States.

It was a double hypothesis: it articulated a historical part – the constitution of the proletariat as a guiding political figure – and an 'economist' hypothesis about the State – the withering away of the State and the transition to communism through the suppression of private property, beginning with the suppression of the private ownership of the means of production.

This vision guided a vast political sequence running from the *Communist Manifesto* (1847) to the Chinese Cultural Revolution (let us say, 1967), representing over a century of struggle and major political inventions, the final assessment of which matters in the highest degree to those wishing to practice politics today.

At the centre of the communist hypothesis lies the possible relationship between two elements: under what conditions can the constitution of the workers as a directing political figure (the 'proletariat' as its first element) prove capable of taking politics towards real communism (as the second element)? The history of this long sequence – or rather curve – indicates that the question refers mainly to the transformations necessary in the first element in order to advance towards the second.

In the inaugural vision of the *Manifesto*, the category of class is political. This is why 'the communists do not form a separate party opposed to other working-class parties'.[3]

The *Manifesto* insists that they distinguish themselves in two respects only. They are 'the most resolute section of the working-class parties of

---

3   Karl Marx and Friedrich Engels, *The Communist Manifesto* (Harmondsworth: Penguin, 1967), p. 95.

every country'; their subjective consistence relates to the fact that, theoretically, 'they have the advantage of clearly understanding the line of march, the conditions, and the ultimate general results of the proletarian movement'.[4] The communists are a section of a larger movement by means of which the working class constitutes itself into a political class, through workers' insurrections. Here 'communism' is the name of 'a historical movement going on under our very eyes'. I quote again from the *Manifesto*: 'The theoretical conclusions of the communists are in no way based on ideas or principles that have been invented, or discovered, by this or that would-be universal reformer. They merely express, in general terms, actual relations springing from an existing class struggle, from a historical movement going on under our very eyes.'[5]

What demonstrates the 'ruling' political capacity of the proletariat, for Marx and Engels? They deduce it from the thesis that the working class is a singular class in so far as, via the 'modern working class', capitalism fabricates people who are 'the spontaneous movement of the immense majority, in the interest of the immense majority'. This vision is nourished by the whole of nineteenth-century workers' history, and the name 'proletariat' inscribes the immanence of this general political capacity as belonging to the 'modern working class'. In fact, Marx's conviction is that, unlike all other classes, 'the proletarians cannot become masters of the productive forces of society, except by abolishing their own previous mode of appropriation, and thereby also every other previous mode of appropriation'. It therefore seems possible to derive from the deployment of capital itself, not only the announcement of the collapse and end of capital, but also their logic.

Nevertheless, Marx does not develop a purely historical thesis. The demand is that the proletariat be able to master capital through singular, political acts which put an end to the private ownership of productive forces. If the historical movement is of the essence and develops towards a new proletarian political capacity, the point is also that the State is thought of as 'open to attack'. It is a question of taking power and 'breaking the machine of the State', as Marx expresses the point when he describes the invention of the Commune. To break up the machine of State will firstly be to transform it into an instrument of the political hegemony of the proletariat, the dictatorship of the proletariat, so as to change the regime of property; and the abolition of private property will mean the possibility

---

4   Ibid.
5   Ibid., pp. 95–96.

of the 'extinction of the State', to be replaced by the plain 'administration of things'. This is why 'the theory of the communists', according to the *Manifesto*, may 'be summed up in the single sentence: abolition of private property'.[6]

As far as the first point is concerned, Lenin places us in a quite different element: that of the necessity of an organized, political consciousness which is no longer either consubstantial with, or immanent to, the class, since workers may also organize themselves into trade unions, which manifests their adherence to the social and political order, instead of opposing it.

As Sylvain Lazarus has shown,[7] the invention of the Leninist party is the invention of modern politics itself, in the sense that for the first time, Lenin subjects politics to the condition of its own 'conditions of possibility': for politics to exist, the fact that there are workers is not enough, class struggle is not enough; politics must have built a place, a space, that is proper to it. Opposition to the whole social and political order is neither a given of consciousness nor of class. It is subject to the condition of organization, a new type of organization, that of the Leninist party, the members of which must possess the capacities of 'popular tribunes', as *What Is to Be Done?* puts it.

The Leninist hypothesis concerning the establishment of communism, on the other hand, adopts Marx and Engels's hypothesis just as it stands. The bloody crushing of the Paris Commune and the failure of the 1905 Revolution in Russia left open the capacity of the newly organized institution (the Leninist party) to take over State power and hold on to it. Remember the joy of Lenin dancing in the snow when the 1917 Revolution had lasted a day longer than the Paris Commune.

In *The State and Revolution* – a text Lenin was working on in the days leading up to the 1917 Revolution at a moment when, as he insisted, 'the question of the attitude towards the State takes on a practical importance' – the question is that of restoring the main Marxist theses regarding the State, reviving them in all their vigour and radical nature (as against Kautsky's revisionism): 'The State is the product and manifestation of this fact that classes are irreconcilable';[8] it is a matter of establishing the dictatorship of the proletariat as the only possible means towards the withering away of the State and the advent of communism. Lenin shares

---

6   Ibid., p. 96.
7   Sylvain Lazarus, 'Lénine et le temps', *Conférence du Perroquet*, March 1989.
8   V. I. Lenin, *The State and Revolution: The Marxist Theory and the Tasks of the Proletariat in the Revolution* (Mosco: Progress, 1949), p. 10.

with Marx a kind of extraordinary optimism about the transformation and the destiny of the State. Firstly, both suppose that capitalism has 'simplified' the great majority of the functions of the former State, so that these functions can easily be restricted to mere registration, administration and control, operations 'absolutely within the reach of every one who benefited from primary school education', and 'with every one being given the salary of a simple worker to do that work'. Lenin also has the certitude, in Engels's words, of a rapid obsolescence of the State: 'The society which will reorganize production on the basis of a free and egalitarian association of producing people will send back the whole machine of the State to the place where the spinning wheel and the bronze axe are already: the Antiquities museum.'

In this vision of things, the State is thought of, on the one hand, as a special repressive power – a power that can be turned against the bourgeoisie – and, on the other hand, as strictly functional: 'The more the functions of State power are exercised by all the people, the less this power becomes necessary.' This is how 'the public functions will lose their political nature and will transform themselves into mere administrative functions'. Or again: 'A moment arrives when the State en route to extinction can be called a non-political State.'[9] This transformation of the State into a non-State, or a purely functional State, will be the product of 'the proletariat organized as a dominant class'.

The extreme importance of the Chinese Cultural Revolution and of Maoism was to reopen the question of the socialist State, of its identification, in terms quite other than those of the Stalinist party/State. On Mao's initiative, two things are made starkly evident: the emergence of the proletariat once organized as a dominant class will not signify the disappearance of classes, and will not coincide with the rapid extinction of the State. Or again, in Mao's words, 'the dictatorship of the proletariat' does not signify an 'integral dictatorship relative to the bourgeoisie'. On the contrary, in a country like socialist China, one experiences a very difficult struggle 'between two orientations and two classes', 'between the capitalist orientation and the socialist orientation', even inside the Communist Party itself. During the Cultural Revolution, Mao several times draws the attention of everyone to this point: 'China is a socialist country. Before the Liberation, it was more or less like capitalism. From now on, we have a salary system based on eight scales, what is given to people depends on their work, we

---

9   Ibid., pp. 60–61; and Engels, quoted from 'On Authority', in *The Marx–Engels Reader*, ed. by R.C. Tucker (London: Norton, 1972), p. 732.

still use money, and all these things are not very different from the former society. The only difference lies in the fact that the property system was changed.' A major tension exists here between these three realities signified in three phrases : 'a socialist country'; 'not very different from the former society'; 'the property system was changed'. As Mao emphasizes, even when the property system has been changed, it does not prevent 'apparitions of the bourgeois way of life among the proletariat as well as among the people working for State or other organizations'.

In a situation like this, which Mao describes with a political acuteness and clarity that resemble Lenin's, the effort to follow the road to communism is aimed at the party. The Cultural Revolution is an attempt to transform the Communist Party in opening up a large debate about the fact that the struggle between bourgeoisie and proletariat is going on within socialism, and that the Communist Party itself is exposed to the possibility of becoming a bourgeois space dominated by the will to restore capitalism. Transforming the party by placing it under the political control of the masses – students, workers, peasants – was the means by which Mao sought to resist this.

We should note that the category of 'the masses' here replaces the category of 'class' as the category of true politics, so that the workers are no longer the unique representatives of a communist political capacity. But with reference to the State, the frame of thought remains that of the Marxist and Leninist hypothesis: to finish with the State is to finish with private property, even when doing so appears complicated and difficult. Here politics remains 'the concentrated expression of the economy', even if Mao elsewhere explores the question of the effects of what he calls the 'superstructure' (art, culture, ideas . . .) on the properly material structure. When one reads texts from the Cultural Revolution from today's point of view, from the point of view of the current homogeneity of the Chinese party/State and global capitalism, there is something deeply disturbing in seeing how the hypothesis regarding the question of the State and communism, followed through to its conclusion, remained that of the total suppression of the law of the bourgeoisie and private property.

The dictatorship of the proletariat existed, private property was abolished, yet to continue on that path leads only to an impasse. The two guiding ideas of the communist hypothesis as a political hypothesis – the idea that politics had an appointment with history, via the proletariat, and the idea that it was necessary to address the question of the State via the question of the collective ownership of the means of production – showed themselves to be false or insufficient. False not because they could not be realized, but because even their realization turned out to be an impasse.

The point I wish to draw your attention to is that it is possible today to argue this, and to argue it in a political space that is not the reactive space of the 1980s, forged as that was in response to the category of totalitarianism and the wish to establish the supremacy of parliamentarianism. And what makes that possible is a political advance regarding the question of the State, the principles of which I will try to give you.

In 1966, the Shanghai Commune had opened up the possibility of another path. It separated the workers from the State and from the party by making visible the fact that such categories as class, party and State, fall, even in socialism, under certain conditions. Thousands of workers organized themselves, creating independent organizations, posing the question of the true nature of socialist factories. In this crucial political episode, all links between the working class and the socialist State that was supposed to express their interests were broken; as they were between the workers and the party supposed to represent them. Even more important was the exposure of the truth that the factory itself exists under certain conditions, that it cannot be separated from the State if the factory as a political question does not exist among the workers, apart from the objective existence of the socialist State. I would emphasize here the importance of Alessandro Russo's studies, which decisively identify and characterize this political episode.

My view is that the singularity of May 1968 in France, and even more of what happened in the following years, was that it separated and distinguished workers and Communist Party, workers and trade unionism, and opened up the question of the political capacity of the workers, of their true contemporary condition.

Within the broad historical span we have considered (1847–8 to 1967–70) – in which revolution remained the key word, the guiding word for politics – political thought circulates between politics, history and philosophy. Marx himself is sometimes an activist, sometimes a historian or an economist, and sometimes a philosopher, even if he decides that his own task will be to put an end to philosophy, since the question is no longer that of interpreting the world but of changing it. Lenin, too, engages closely with philosophy. In 1908, he declares that he is a *'philosophical researcher'* and confronts the question of materialism while criticizing what he calls 'empiriocriticism'. In the first months of the First World War, facing the question of war and imperialism, he studies, meditates and carefully annotates Hegel's *Science of Logic*. So, too, Mao wrote *On Contradiction* and *On Practice* in the summer of 1937, to sustain the political processes of popular war.

The circulation between history and politics is comprehensible, since the political capacity of the working class has a historical foundation. In Marx, of course, attentive as he was to the strikes and insurrectional episodes of his time. But Lenin and Mao also maintain the hypothesis of the historical singularity of the working class as a political figure, even if subordinated to the party in Lenin and extended to the masses in Mao.

One can hypothesize that the circulation between philosophy and politics derives from the fact that the working-class political capacity is in fact not strictly immanent to historic movements, but actually also receives external contributions. Even in Marx, in reality, there is a tiny difference between communists and proletariat, and this difference rests on a theoretical foundation: a clear intelligence of the conditions, progress and ends in general of historical movement.

2

What authorizes the declaration that this historical epoch is closed from the political point of view? For to declare it closed signifies that one can no longer think within its political categories, and that all political questions must be taken up afresh.

First, I would like to quote someone who would certainly have been among us, if his death had not prevented it. Antoine Vitez, at a conference dedicated in 1990 to the crisis in communism, declared:

> The collapse, the catastrophe, are real . . . the collapse has indeed taken place, it continues, not everything has fallen as yet. The collapse is that of the idea. One cannot separate the idea from the material disaster; it does not float intact above the ruins. Ideas exist only in their incarnation; if the incarnation disappears, the idea itself is mortally wounded. So communism has entered into its final phase.[10]

Words that were, in his mouth, deeply sad. But words of reason to which I subscribe.

What does this historical closure lay bare? I want to try to reflect on this closure. I should say at once that in my view there exist two assessments

---

10   Antoine Vitez, 'Ce qui nous reste', in *Le Théâtre des idées* (Paris: Gallimard, 1991), p. 162.

of this closure of the communist political hypothesis, both internal to philosophy, to which I do not subscribe.

First, there is an assessment which I would call 'hyper-historicism'. This assessment pursues and aggravates the superimposition of the possibility of political emancipation onto the historical process of capitalism. The thesis of the possibility – absolutely contradicted by experience – of resorting to the progress of capitalism itself as an emancipatory figure becomes in effect, purely and simply, an erasure of politics as a singular and separate project. In this vision of things, communism appears not at the end of the gun, but at the end of capital. The circumstances of the current global crisis do not inspire confidence in this idea. To the contrary, capitalism regains its force in the present systemic crisis, and by no means grows weaker. It is a crisis for capital, but not of capital. In itself, it will not develop into a promising situation. If any positive political figures are constituted in this conjuncture, they will be the product of new political and organizational capacities. They will certainly not appear as the result of any simple reactions to the crisis and its effects, devastating as those may be for the great majority of people.

The second assessment, which also tries to break through the impasse of the communist hypothesis, consists in what I would call 'hyper-valorization of the worker'. By this, I mean the attempt to separate the worker from politics, or to separate the worker from the proletariat, while continuing to identify the worker with the communist hypothesis, on condition that the figure of the worker be granted no political identity. This is an assessment which finally seeks to promote the category of the 'social' over that of the political, or that of a 'movement' over any new thought about organization. The intrinsic weakness of this position is that it does not address the question of the State, as if the social existence or lives of people were in themselves a real alternative to the State. This is indeed a problem today, when we find ourselves in a world where only the State exists, where the category of society is a trick, a deceit, an illusion constructed by the State itself, and where the life of people is entirely demarcated, delimited, even destroyed by the operation of constraining laws, of laws which no longer define rights but which serve to place whole populations outside the realm of rights. In France, this is the case with the CESEDA laws regarding foreigners, with the Perben laws against the youth of the suburbs, and all the policing laws which give the police total power to criminalize entire sections of the population.

My own assessment is quite different. It can be summed up in two sentences, which I will try to develop further:

- Politics proceeds on its own.
- The question of the State is to be rethought from the ground up.

Politics proceeds on its own: I want to unpack that statement with reference to several points.

Politics proceeds on its own because it has no appointment with history. If it is still true that the history of humanity has been the history of class struggle, politics is not to be confused with class struggle, and revolution is no longer the vector of politics. In my view, we have arrived at the end – not only necessary but salutary – of the idea that one carries out political work in order to see better days tomorrow. Today, the cynical reverse of this is the democratic practice of apologizing and expressing regrets for past times. As an African *sans-papiers* friend told me: 'What we want is for people to be treated well right now. Not that apologies are made tomorrow for the harm it has done to people today.' There is no rendezvous of politics with history. Politics takes as a guiding principle that it is the present that matters, a principle which imposes upon it the obligation of having always to begin again.

Politics proceeds on its own because it must be organized without reference to a party. The Stalinist party-State and the democratic State parties are proof of the fact that party fuses with State, and politics grows corrupt and criminal when it fuses with the State. Mao's project continued to search for a political space defined by the party and the State. It gave organized forms to their dialectic and conflictual opposition, rather than their Stalinist fusion. But it did not establish a principle of disjunction and a distance between the State and politics. On this point, I refer you to Sylvain Lazarus's forthcoming text: 'Chercher ailleurs et autrement'.[11]

Politics proceeds on its own because it is not expressive of a class nor does it take, as its point of reference, an already constituted people nor groups already in existence. Today, it is strictly a matter of decisions that are both personal and voluntary. Any political capacity belongs to those who have volunteered themselves for politics, and this is as true of the workers as of anyone else.

---

11   Sylvain Lazarus, 'Chercher ailleurs et autrement: Sur la doctrine des lieux, l'économie, l'effondrement du socialisme', *Conférence du Perroque*, 35 May 1992.

Politics proceeds on its own because it must proceed at a distance from State politics, but also at a distance from people who have been captured by ideas and categories created by the State. Neither the social nor the movement or the struggle can provide the categories proper to politics.

Politics proceeds on its own because its thought must be intrinsic to itself, and because this thought can derive no knowledge from any assessment of previous political processes unless, at the same time, it thinks each question anew.

Politics proceeds on its own because pronouncing on the State is not a matter of objective analysis, but is only possible from a perspective of a new political space that has been instituted at a distance from the State. The State is politically mobile. It is not only a 'system' or a 'machine'; it is also involved in a political process of constant change and readjustment. Marx asserted that the Commune was the direct antithesis of Empire. This is true, but one has to add that the Third Republic was, in its turn, the direct antithesis of the Commune; similarly the Welfare State was the corollary of the Stalinist State.

Politics proceeds on its own, but it has multiple and variable sites: hostels for foreign workers (*foyers ouvriers*), popular neighbourhoods (*quartiers*), factories, schools . . . This is the case not only because these are places where people live. It is also because these are the places where people organize themselves in order to declare what it means for each to count for what he is, where he is. And what each individual counts for must be articulated through different names and different norms from those supplied by the State. One doesn't exchange the workers for 'the people' as one changes one's clothes. It is a matter of constituting political sites other than those organized by the State, and doing so among the people themselves. This is the condition for a politics organized as interior to people rather than from above.

Finally, politics proceeds on its own because we are in an era when American and European war is devastating the world. The war in Gaza is a distillation of this new kind of war, which followed the 'Cold War'-era war. War today asserts the principle of pure power, of the State against people; it is an endless war, because it is not accompanied by a concept of peace. What does facing up to war in this new mode of existence entail, when no revolution can any longer hope to conjure war away, and when no State desires peace any longer?

This question leads to my second assertion: the question of the State must be rethought from the ground up. It is possible to maintain from experience that we should not shelter behind the idea that politics might have developed better or more fruitfully from within the same frame, on the basis of the same hypothesis. The communist hypothesis of the withering away of the State was in fact a hypothesis which actually de-politicized the question of the State. Or rather, it was a hypothesis which, on the one hand, hyper-politicized the question of the State – the seizing of State power being the central question for politics (an assumption the proletariat actually shared with the bourgeoisie and all the other dominant classes) – while, on the other, it de-politicized it, in so far as the question of the political development of the State was presented in purely instrumental or technical terms. It was necessary to dispose of the repressive apparatus, in order to be able to transform the function of the State. The dictatorship of the proletariat would make it possible to pass from 'governing people' to 'administering things and directing the productive operations', in Engels's terms.

Experience has shown that, far from withering away, the political capacity of the State merely mutated and took new forms. At the same time, whilst calling itself socialist, the State hugely corrupted political will and subjectivity. In other words, it was not at all a neutral political space, nor was it easily neutralized, nor was it simply a space that one could take over with impunity. On the contrary, it increasingly appeared as the site specifically of a State politics, determined by its own normative principles, rules and values, which were quite heterogeneous to the hypothetical assumption that it would wither away.

If the question of the State must be rethought from the ground up, it is because its political capacity appears today not only as an authoritarian bureaucratic capacity for repression, but as an awesome capacity for organization. The singularly massive and pressing problem that the obsolescence of the communist hypothesis leaves behind consists in the fact that the State is a power which organizes people politically, and does so as much when it is socialist as when its foundation is parliamentary democracy. Furthermore, it is clear that this power of State organization has grown exponentially as a result of the collapse of the communist hypothesis regarding the withering away of the State.

It is from this point, and not from the question of capitalism, that we must set out again. This is why I would maintain that we are working in the 'aftermath' of the communist hypothesis. Setting out again defines a framework for research, thought, labour, that is absolutely without precedent in politics, but of which I will here provide a few preliminary indications.[12]

First, in these circumstances, establishing a distance from State politics is a condition of any possible new political capacity. It is from the point of view of a new political space different from that of the State in all its forms that the workings of the State can be identified and named. The State should not be conceived of as reduced to the government and its repressive and administrative institutions (police, army, justice). The State creates many different modes of organizing people: parties, trade unions, associations, the media, votes, elections, public opinion . . .

'Establishing a distance from the State' cannot be brought back to a dialectical figure of politics, nor does it mean that it is sufficient to negate the workings of the State to discover the principles and declarations animating a different politics. The first condition is the institution of a political site organized according to different ideas, principles and values.

At the same time, at the furthest possible remove from 'withdrawal' or 'retreat', 'at a distance' means working to constitute a political will, capacity and force facing the State.

As far as the question of the State is concerned, the major political weakness today is adherence to the names, terms, categories and sites of State politics. Let us take law as our example. Today in almost every country there exist 'laws of exception' and special statutes regarding workers of foreign origin which regulate their tracking and persecution. Why do so few people demand the repeal of these laws? Because the question of law is thought of as inseparable from parties and State processes, and thus from elections and parliamentary power relations. To think the question of law at a distance from the State, by contrast, opens up the following questions: What do these laws want of us? What are their consequences for our neighbours? Should we accept the existence of such laws? They must be repealed, but they will not be, unless people themselves demand it.

The work of breaking with the State requires not a binary opposition, as in Marxism and Leninism, but the deployment of three altogether new terms. A place for politics (to be instituted) at a distance from everything that is the State, creating a new political organization. Declarations and principles (to be formulated in specific situations) of a politics which counts everyone for what he is, where he is. Finally, identifications (to be

---

12   See *Le Journal politique*, from 2005 to the present, and *La Distance politique* from 1992 to 2002.

produced) of the State as the site of a singular politics, whose power and monopoly derives from its capacity to propagate the idea that no politics other than State politics is practicable or possible.

It is imperative that we succeed in thinking through an identification of the State as a singular political site. This requires us to make evident what constitutes the political space of the State as such. The attachment to wealth, in particular in so far as it is an attachment to national wealth, whatever the price to be paid (appalling colonial wars, the American war on terror, internal wars against workers without papers, young people from the *quartiers*, working families, the poor, the unemployed . . .). The erosion of institutions representing the general interest (hospitals, schools, the judiciary, housing . . .) and their replacement by the break-up of people into separate categories, and the refusal to count everyone for what he is, where he is. The pervasive regulation of social tensions by military and police power. The power granted to the police to impose State order amongst people and, in international relations, the deployment of armies, the military regulation of civil matters, such as the foundation of a legitimate government, the existence or non-existence of a nation-State or the circulation of migrants . . .

3

I suggested earlier that I would consider the question of the suturing of philosophy to politics which goes by the name of Heidegger, on the one hand, and that of Althusser on the other. I shall have to proceed rather swiftly through my argument here, but it is nonetheless crucial to my account of what is at stake for philosophy today.

Heidegger's involvement with Nazism in the 1930s has led to his being linked with various theses concerning the criminalization of philosophy. On the one hand, profoundly reactionary theses on the criminal character of philosophy itself, of all philosophy. On the other, theses which suture philosophy to politics by suggesting that philosophy, or a certain type of philosophy, was the very matrix of Nazism, particularly in relation to art and poetry. These last theses were allegedly progressive. But we should insist that they are false, for they share the confusion of philosophy with politics – of the space proper to philosophical thought with that of political thought (understood as a form of thought in itself) – which it is vital that we leave behind us today. In the confused vision of things, philosophy is like Lady Macbeth: it has all political blood on its hands and cannot conceivably wash them clean. But it seems to me that we must leave this blood to politics because if there is one thing we should understand about Nazism it is its political capacity to organize people in the service of horror, extermination and total war. I shall not comment on this point here, but I would want to emphasize that we should give an account of Nazism from a political point of view, in terms of what, politically, it teaches us about politics.[13]

Althusser represents another form of suture of philosophy to politics, linked to the question of the French Communist Party and Stalin. It works as follows. Marx founded a new science, that of history or 'historical materialism'. Althusser does not attribute the deficiency of the communist parties and socialist States to the communist hypothesis in itself and the relationship between politics and the State that was played out in it. He imputes their political weakness, evident in the 1960s, to a lack in philosophy, to a philosophical deficiency at the heart of politics. This lack stems from the fact that there has been no contemporary renewal of the figure of Marx as a figure capable, precisely, of circulating between politics, the science of history, and philosophy. Philosophy, thereby, reveals itself to be belated with respect to politics, and, in this sense, responsible for its erring ways and imperfections.

It seems to me that, in Althusser, the name of this suture of philosophy to politics is 'theory'. According to him, philosophy is charged with 'representing politics in the field of theory', and, symmetrically, representing science (that is, history, economics, the sciences of historical materialism) in politics. If philosophy is belated or absent, politics will then be weak in the theoretical and blind in the scientific field.

The Althusserian distinction between theory and practice is symptomatic in his work of the exteriority of the thought of politics to politics itself. Thought comes to politics from outside, alternately from science and/or from philosophy. The Althusserian thesis is therefore that, without science and philosophy, politics necessarily goes astray. It follows that philosophy and science are necessary for the orientation of politics. In fact, this thesis is not incompatible with Stalinist politics, since Stalin ensured that the State party produced the philosophy and science necessary to orient and justify his own State politics.

I would therefore insist that, intellectually, if we are to find a positive mode of exiting from the communist hypothesis, we must also break

13   Martine Leruch, 'Qu'en est-il de la pensée du nazisme aujourd'hui?', *Conférence du Rouge-Gorge* 9, April 2004.

with the structure of thought initiated by Althusser. In the first instance, this means identifying politics as an absolutely singular thought, one wholly internal to the organized processes of politics itself; abandoning the *dispositif* which consists in asking philosophy questions which only politics can answer; ceasing to think that it is possible to proceed from philosophy (or science) to politics. Above all, ceasing to require of philosophy that it provide new foundations or a completed form for politics, or that it serve as a palliative for the seeming absence or weakness of politics. I address this proposition to you, my audience at this conference, because your presence here testifies to the extraordinary and continuing confusion between philosophy and the singularity of political thought and political processes.

But I also address my proposition to the philosophers present here. This will be the theme of my conclusion. It seems to me that, like everyone else, you philosophers can see how far the possible resources of contemporary politics are complex and difficult to formulate, to invent, to think through and put into practice. Thus, you say to yourselves: let us bring the word 'communism' back to life. We need this word to indicate that the politics in which philosophy can take an interest is not in any respect identifiable with the dominant politics. For my part, I would want finally to propose, by way of addition, two further paths for philosophical investigation in the aftermath of communism:

- Within philosophy, to work for the disjunction or separation of philosophy and politics, to give politics back to politics itself. Because any confusion on this point delays the progress of a new politics, by displacing the site of investigation.
- To investigate the word 'politics' itself instead of just sticking the word 'communism' on to the hypothesis of an emancipatory politics. Can one continue to preserve this word, which today belongs to the State as completely as it does to politics? If we assume that it is possible to institute new sites for a politics that remains at a distance from the State, that is because there is politics and politics.

For my part, I think that the time for adjectives is behind us. We have entered a time for nouns. If a politics apart from State politics, which is at present groping its way forward, succeeds in flowering, it may even find a name other than 'politics' for itself in the future. Indeed, it may be 'politics' that ends up in the Museum of Antiquities, and not the State as Engels thought. But that can only be a distant hypothesis. It is also the only one I allow myself with reference to the future. Essentially, I have sought to confine myself to the demand of the present. Politics is always about beginning to begin. Let us present ourselves to the present. I am convinced that this is the best principle in our difficult but politically lively and enlivening times.

3   The Leftist Hypothesis:
Communism in the Age of Terror

Bruno Bosteels

Communism is for us not a *state of affairs* which is to be established, an *ideal* to which reality [will] have to adjust itself. We call communism the *real* movement which abolishes the present state of things. The conditions of this movement result from the now existing premise.
Karl Marx and Friedrich Engels, *The German Ideology*

Communism cannot be reached unless there is a communist movement.
Mao Zedong, 'Critique of Stalin's
Economic Problems of Socialism in the USSR'

Don't ask: What would Jesus do? Ask: What would Žižek do?
Anonymous bathroom graffiti, Birkbeck College

Spectres of Lenin

In his well-known 1920 pamphlet, Lenin denounced what he called 'leftism' or 'left-wing communism' as an 'infantile disorder' of a 'fully expanded and mature communism'.[1] Almost fifty years later, in 1968, the brothers Danny 'the Red' and Gabriel Cohn-Bendit would cleverly turn this diagnostic around by announcing tongue-in-cheek that, instead of the spectre of the *Communist Manifesto*, it is the spectre of 'leftism' that is henceforth roaming the streets of Europe as the 'remedy' for the 'senile disorder' of communism.[2] Today, around forty years later, what are we to

---

1   Vladimir I. Lenin, *'Left-Wing' Communism, an Infantile Disorder*, in *Selected Works* (Moscow: Foreign Languages Publishing House, 1961), vol. 3, pp. 371–460.
2   Daniel and Gabriel Cohn-Bendit, *Obsolete Communism: The Left-Wing Alternative*, trans. Arnold Pomerans (New York: McGraw-Hill, 1968). This book's original French title conveys much better the intended inversion of Lenin's pamphlet: *Le Gauchisme remède à la maladie sénile du communisme* (Paris: Seuil, 1968).

make of this pseudo-dialectical inversion in the midst of a global economic crisis and a never-ending war of terror upon terror? Should we revert to Lenin's orthodox denunciation of the leftist 'disorder' in favour of a return to the original idea of communism, however much we may want to 'deconstruct', 'retreat' or 'weaken' this idea today so as to soften the blow of orthodoxy? Or should we throw in our voice with the crowd to expand on the paean to 'leftism' as the only idea that will save us from the historical failure of 'really existing' communism, that is, the 'bureau-cratic', 'totalitarian', or downright 'criminal', 'worthy-of-black-books' communism of the Soviet Union and from the worldwide fate of the official Communist Parties – now almost all bankrupt, extinct, or buried under the mystification of a new name? Finally, at what point do these two options risk becoming indiscernible so that our return to the ethereal 'Idea' of communism, cleansed of every compromising trace of Marxism, Leninism, Trotskyism, Stalinism or Maoism, actually passes over into just another form of leftism?

Prior to all these questions, can we even come to an agreement about the need to separate the communist hypothesis from the history and theory of leftism? By tackling this history and theory, which beyond a rapidly growing number of journalistic or confessional accounts and testimonies for the most part still remains to be written, can we hope to strengthen rather than take away from the part of the common in communism? In other words, if 'communism named the effective history of "we"', as Alain Badiou wrote a decade ago in *Of an Obscure Disaster: On the End of the Truth of State*, and if, according to this same account of the so-called 'death' of communism after the collapse of the Berlin Wall, 'there is no longer a "we", there hasn't been for a long time', is there hope that it might become possible once again, albeit on a modest scale, to speak as 'we', or even as 'we communists'?[3] Or, to follow a slightly different trajectory that on this topic at least might lead to a point of convergence, is now perhaps a good occasion to repeat the gesture that brought together Félix Guattari and Antonio Negri, more than two decades ago, when they wrote *Communists Like Us*?[4] To be more precise, is there a chance for a 'we' or 'us' to emerge

3   Alain Badiou, *D'un désastre obscur: Sur la fin de la vérité d'État* (Tour d'Aigues: Éditions de l'Aube, 1990; 1998), pp. 7–8; partially translated as 'Philosophy and the "death of communism"', in *Infinite Thought: Truth and the Return of Philosophy*, trans. and ed. Oliver Feltham and Justin Clemens (London: Continuum, 2003), pp. 126–7.

4   Félix Guattari and Toni Negri, *Communists Like Us: New Spaces of Liberty, New Lines of Alliance*, trans. Michael Ryan (New York: Semiotext(e), 1990). Originally published as *Les Nouveaux espaces de liberté* (Gourdon: D. Bedou, 1985).

that would not be prisoner to the imaginary schemes of like and dislike or to the militarized ideal of 'us' and 'them'? As Badiou also concludes in *The Century*: 'From the seventies onwards, the century has bequeathed to us the following question: What is a "we" that is not subject to the ideal of an "I", a "we" that does not pretend to be a subject? The problem is not to conclude from this that every living collective is over, that the "we" has purely and simply disappeared.'[5] This would then be the problem for communism as a common horizon for thinking and acting in the twenty-first century.

In mainstream media, all such talk is of course easily dismissed and cast aside as yet another case of 'ultraleftism', or of that 'extreme left' which always serves journalists so well in their search for an ideological mirror image of the 'extreme right', to be rejected on a par with the latter for being equally dogmatic and fundamentalist: one of those items out of a cabinet of political curiosities usually restricted to academics and activists on the fringes of the public sphere though now, ironically, seen as threatening enough so as to warrant public rebuttals in the press if not, as is also happening ever more frequently under our very own noses, violent repression by the police and military state apparatus. Does not then the attempt to demarcate the communist hypothesis from various forms of leftism fall in line with this tried formula by which ideologues of the status quo time and again seek to keep at arm's length the extremism of the real movement which abolishes the present state of things? What is more, is not the accusation of 'leftism' or 'ultraleftism' responsible for some of the worst kinds of sectarianism and internecine strife within communist circles, comparable in this regard to the related and equally nefarious split between 'revolution' and 'reformism'? Even among participants at this conference, the leftist epithet in one guise or another has been thrown around with surprising ease and insouciance. In effect, the allegation of 'leftism' over the past few decades has produced in the realm of politics a chain effect that is similar to the accusation of lingering 'logocentrism' in the realm of the destruction of metaphysics from Nietzsche to Heidegger to Derrida. 'This is what allows these destroyers to destroy each other reciprocally – for example, Heidegger regarding Nietzsche, with as much lucidity and rigor as bad faith and misconstruction, as the last metaphysician, the last "Platonist"', Jacques Derrida himself wrote in one of his most anthologized pieces: 'One could do the same for Heidegger himself,

---

5   Badiou, *The Century*, trans. Alberto Toscano (London: Polity Press, 2007), p. 96.

for Freud, or for a number of others. And today no exercise is more widespread.'[6] Equally widespread is the exercise of laying the criticism of leftism back at the doorstep of the latest critic of leftist deviations. Thus, to restrict myself for the time being to a small French genealogy of this trend: Louis Althusser and his followers were accused of 'authoritarian' or 'speculative leftism' early on by the rebellious disciple Jacques Rancière; Rancière, in turn, is accused of radical 'apoliticism' by his older classmate Alain Badiou; and, closing the circle in the style of a winged Ouroboros, Slavoj Žižek goes on to accuse the ex-Althusserians Badiou, Rancière and Balibar of dreaming up, in typical leftist fashion, a form of 'pure politics'.[7] My intention with regard to these internal contradictions, which otherwise are perhaps little more than domestic fights of a dysfunctional family, is not to prolong and aggravate them by throwing salt in open or freshly healed wounds but rather to clarify the underlying tensions and render them explicit so as to avoid finding relief in the quick fix of a superficial consensus that at bottom is inexistent. This is after all how Marx, in one of his letters to Arnold Ruge, defines our task, namely as 'self-clarification (critical philosophy) to be gained by the present time of its struggles and desires'. He continues: 'This is a work for the world and for us. It can be only the work of united forces. It is a matter of a *confession*, and nothing more. In order to secure remission of its sins, mankind has only to declare them for what they actually are.'[8]

Did Somebody Say Left-Wing Communism?

Unlike Marx, Lenin at first prefers a medical over a theological-confessional mode. Left-wing communism for him is not so much a 'sin', even

---

6   Jacques Derrida, 'Structure, Sign, and Play in the Discourse of the Human Sciences', in *Writing and Difference*, trans. Alan Bass (Chicago: University of Chicago Press, 1978), p. 182.

7   Jacques Rancière, *La Leçon d'Althusser* (Paris: Gallimard, 1974), pp. 86 and 146; Badiou, 'Rancière and Apolitics', *Metapolitics*, trans. Jason Barker (London and New York: Verso, 2005), pp. 114–23; Slavoj Žižek, *The Ticklish Subject: The Absent Centre of Political Ontology* (London and New York: Verso, 1999), pp. 171–244; and 'Against Pure Politics', in *Revolution at the Gates: Selected Writings of Lenin from 1917* (London and New York: Verso, 2002), pp. 271–2.

8   Marx, letter to Arnold Ruge, September 1843. See 'Letters from *Deutsch-Französische Jahrbücher*', in Karl Marx and Friedrich Engels, *Collected Works* (New York: International Publishers, 1975), vol. 3, p. 145. I must confess that, in spite of original plans for a collective statement and debate, my impression was and still is that many of the underlying discrepancies behind the London conference 'On the Idea of Communism' were never fully addressed or even openly stated. If communism is to provide a common horizon, there is still a work of philosophical self-clarification to be done that so far remains painfully incomplete. Lenin's advice in this regard would have been a welcome reminder: 'At all events, a split is better than confusion' (*'Left-Wing' Communism*, p. 451).

though his pamphlet does mention 'the opportunist sins of the working-class movement', so much as a 'disease' to be diagnosed on the basis of a set of recurring 'symptoms', and 'cured' or 'eradicated' with the appropriate treatments. In fact, in so far as leftism is described as a 'childhood illness', we would have to conclude that in the era prior to mass vaccinations such as those against measles or rubella, it may very well be beneficial for communists like us to catch the disease at least once while we are still young: 'The illness does not involve any danger', Lenin admits, 'and after it the constitution becomes even stronger'.[9] On the other hand, in addition to this clinical history, the notion of 'childishness' and sometimes of 'puerility' also comes to be diagnosed in moral and pedagogical terms, with leftism revealing a dangerous lack of maturity combined with an impatient desire to skip the intermediate stages in the gradual process of growth and development, by leaping all at once to the highest phase of communism. Here Lenin uses an analogy that should be to the liking of the Platonists among us: 'To attempt in practice today to anticipate this future result of a fully developed, fully stabilized and formed, fully expanded and mature communism would be like trying to teach higher mathematics to a four-year-old child.'[10] In our era of self-anointed pedagogues and supernannies, we might say that this second image presents leftists as communists with an attention deficit disorder. For Lenin, in any case, the remedy for leftist immaturity is no joke and requires a great deal of all-round training and guidance, for example, in 'the schools of socialism' that are the trade unions and syndicates for Marx and Engels.

All irony and clinical-pedagogical rhetoric aside, Lenin's conceptual effort at defining the phenomenon itself will be familiar enough: leftism, or left-wing communism, involves a principled stance against any and all participation in parliamentary or bourgeois electoral politics, in unions, and even or especially in party discipline. The upshot of this repudiation of all compromises is a doctrinal 'repetition of the truths of "pure" communism', reduced to a frenzied, incendiary and semi-anarchist type of radicalism, also called 'petty-bourgeois revolutionism' or 'massism', in the sense of a clamorous appeal to the direct action of the masses over and

9   Lenin, 'Left-Wing' Communism, p. 396.
10   Ibid., p. 400. The reader is left to wonder, of course, what happened to Lenin's enthusiasm for the leaps and breaks in Hegel's Logic, profusely annotated with exclamations in the margin of his Philosophical Notebooks, Collected Works, vol. 38, p. 123. See Daniel Bensaïd, 'Leaps! Leaps! Leaps!', in Sebastian Budgen, Stathis Kouvelakis and Slavoj Žižek (eds), Lenin Reloaded: Toward a Politics of Truth (London and New York: Verso, 2007), pp. 148–63.

against the organizational structures of the party, unions and parliaments. Subjective impatience, in a characteristic oscillation between exuberance and dejection, between fanaticism and melancholy, thus takes the place of the arduous and persistent work of party organization. 'Repudiation of the party principle and of party discipline – such is the opposition's *net result*'; Lenin concludes: 'It is tantamount to that petty-bourgeois diffuseness, instability, and incapacity for sustained effort, unity and organized action, which, if indulged in, must inevitably destroy any proletarian revolutionary movement.'[11] It is then only logical that in order to overcome the leftist trend, Lenin as a good pedagogue and anything-but-ignorant schoolmaster would roll out what he calls 'the ABC of Marxism', according to which masses are divided into classes, classes are usually led by parties, and parties are run by more or less stable groups of their most influential and experienced members, called leaders: 'All this is elementary. All this is simple and clear', Lenin writes, adding the bite of sarcasm to the repertoire of his teacherly mode. 'Why replace this by some kind of rigmarole, by some new Volapük?'[12]

Lenin obviously was neither the first nor the last to hurl abuse against some form or other of leftism. As he acknowledges, Marx and Engels long before him already struggled with the uncompromising radicalism of the Blanquist Communards, about whom Engels writes:

The thirty-three Blanquists are Communists just because they imagine that, merely because *they* want to skip the intermediate stations and compromises, that settles the matter, and if 'it begins' in the next few days – which they take for granted – and they come to the helm, 'communism will be introduced' the day after tomorrow. If that is not immediately possible, they are not Communists. What childish innocence it is to present one's own impatience as a theoretically convincing argument![13]

Long after Lenin, on the other hand, the battle against the twin deviations of left-wing 'adventurism' and right-wing 'opportunism' also was to define the stakes of ideological struggle in Maoist China, before spreading to various Maoisms worldwide, especially during and right after the

---

11   Lenin, *'Left-Wing' Communism*, pp. 394–5.
12   Ibid., p. 393.
13   Engels, 'Programme of the Blanquist Communards' (1874), quoted by Lenin, *'Left-Wing' Communism*, pp. 414–15.

Cultural Revolution. 'We are also opposed to "Left" phrase-mongering', Mao had written in 'On Practice':

> The thinking of 'Leftists' outstrips a given stage of development of the objective process; some regard their fantasies as truth, while others strain to realize in the present an ideal which can only be realized in the future. They alienate themselves from the current practice of the majority of the people and from the realities of the day, and show themselves adventurist in their actions.[14]

The model was thereby set for a struggle on two fronts against the mirroring extremes of leftism and rightism, with Mao notoriously invoking the need for a communist to be a centrist!

As indicated in the title of the book by the Cohn-Bendit brothers, however, leftism underwent a dramatic role reversal precisely around the late 1960s and early '70s, in part as a perverse and unexpected consequence of the Maoist struggle on two fronts and in part as the long-term outcome of anarchist, Trotskyist and Situationist criticisms of Stalinist orthodoxies and bureaucratic dogmas. In fact, the leftist hypothesis from this moment onward becomes so dominant, not to say consensual, both in Marxist-inspired political circles and in the non-Marxist or openly anti-Marxist cultural politics of everyday life, that in order to define ever more radical forms of revisionism and extremism, new epithets come to be coined such as 'ultraleftism' or 'pseudoleftism'. Such labels, of course, are not the monopoly of the conservative powers that be; they are also frequently used by run-of-the-mill liberals or social democrats, who in this way can at least serve up the illusion that they, too, are knights in shining armour coming to the rescue of genuine leftism.

The Two Sources of Contemporary Leftism

With the inversion of Lenin's indictment, what I would call the leftist hypothesis can be said to have taken two basic forms. Both of these can be illustrated with respectable quotes and ideas from the orthodox canon and, in this sense, they remain anchored in the history and theory of Marxism. This is even the reason why, if the term is not used pejoratively in the midst of internal strife and polemical mud-slinging, leftists can also

---

14   Mao Zedong, 'On Practice' (1937), in *Five Philosophical Essays* (Beijing: Foreign Languages Press, 1977), p. 18.

positively claim to embody the genuine movement of communism in the wake of the decline and fall of the Soviet Union. The logic behind the Marxist-Leninist or Maoist usage is thus turned inside out, to the point where leftism comes to be used as part of a conceptual machinery aimed against the whole 'master discourse' of Marxism-Leninism-Maoism itself. As a matter of fact, such role reversals, too, were anticipated in Lenin's pamphlet on left-wing communism: 'The surest way of discrediting and damaging a new political (and not only political) idea is to reduce it to absurdity on the plea of defending it.'[15]

The first great figure of leftism involves a purification of the central Marxist idea of contradiction, now reduced to an unmediated and often explicitly anti-dialectical opposition such as the one that pits the masses directly against the State. In the *Communist Manifesto* we are taught that 'our epoch, the epoch of the bourgeoisie', if that is still our epoch, 'has simplified class antagonisms. Society as a whole is more and more splitting up into two great hostile camps, into two great classes directly facing each other.'[16] Yet for leftists in the 1970s, this split or scission, in which a prior generation of militants still gladly heard echoes of Freud's or Lacan's splitting of the ego as well, no longer sets the bourgeoisie against the proletariat but rather, in a heroic and ultimately inoperative face-to-face confrontation, the formless masses against the oppressive and corrupt machinery of the State. Especially among French so-called New Philosophers, almost all of them ex-communist and more specifically ex-Maoist renegades, this purification of the Marxist contradiction is often phrased in terms of the plebs against the State, with the latter being modelled upon the generalized image of Solzhenitsyn's Gulag.

Politics, even when labelled the class struggle, then perennially opposes the same vitally creative masses to the same deadly repressive system. 'In this regard, the "massist" ideology that came out of 1968 excels in flattening out the dialectical analysis', Badiou remarks in his *Theory of Contradiction*: 'Always the same exalted masses against the identical power, the invariable system'.[17] Not only does this view fail to take into account how political and ideological struggles proceed through internal splits between the old and the new: 'It is never "the masses", nor the "movement" that as a whole carry the principle of engenderment of the new,

---

15   Lenin, *'Left-Wing' Communism*, p. 411.
16   Marx and Engels, *The Communist Manifesto. A Modern Edition*, Introduction by Eric Hobsbawn (London and New York: Verso, 1998), p. 35.
17   Badiou, *Théorie de la contradiction* (Paris: François Maspero, 1975), p. 69.

but that which in them divides itself from the old.'[18] But what is more, far from signalling a radically new discovery, the fascination with the mass figure of leftism as an extreme form of generic communism was already a prime target of urgent attacks, more than a century earlier, in the eyes of Marx and Engels:

> All these daring revisions, which are supposed to raise up the strik- ing novelty of the marginal and dissident masses against 'totalitarian' Marxism-Leninism – are word for word that which Marx and Engels, in *The German Ideology*, had to tear to pieces – around 1845! – in order to clear the terrain for a finally coherent systematization of the revolu- tionary practices of their time.[19]

Finally, we should not forget that the actual target of this anti-dialecti- cal disjunction of masses/State as bandied about by the New Philosophers is totalitarianism, the critique of which is overdetermined by an implicit defence of Western-style liberal democracy that will eventually lead to explicit support for a whole range of military-humanitarian interventions from the Balkans to Iraq. This should warn us about the fact that the anti-repressive obsession ultimately contradicts what may appear to be an initial pledge of allegiance to the wildly creative force of popular resist- ance: 'It is inconsistent to read in history the omnipresent contradiction of the masses and the State, to affirm that one is on the side of the plebs, and then to pontificate exclusively about the force and the multiform victori- ous ruses of the State.'[20]

In an important collection of essays from 1977 titled *The Current Situation on the Philosophical Front*, the Maoist Union of French Communists Marxist-Leninist (UCFML) argues that all revisionist tendencies in French thought of the '70s, not only on the part of New Philosophers such as André Glucksmann, Christian Jambet or Guy Lardreau but also among Deleuzians and even among Althusserians and Lacanians, can be seen as presupposing such a categorical opposition. 'Everywhere to substitute the couple masses/State for the class struggle: that is all there is to it', the introduction reads. 'The political essence of these "philosophies"

---

18   Ibid.
19   Ibid., p. 72. On the notion of 'generic communism', as related to the 'anti-statist drive' of 'mass democracy', see also Badiou, 'A Speculative Disquisition on the Concept of Democracy', in *Metapolitics*, pp. 88–9.
20   Badiou, *Théorie de la contradiction*, p. 53.

is captured in the following principle, a principle of bitter resentment against the entire history of the twentieth century: "In order for the revolt of the masses against the State to be good, it is necessary to reject the class direction of the proletariat, to stamp out Marxism, to hate the very idea of the class party."[21] The result of such arguments is then either the complete denial of antagonistic contradictions or else the jubilatory recognition of a hyper-antagonism, raised to the power of a grandiose, almost mystical experience of twoness. 'They dream of a formal antagonism, of a world broken in two, with no sword other than ideology. They love revolt, proclaimed in its universality, but they are secondary in terms of politics, which is the real transformation of the world in its historical particularity.'[22] The primacy of politics, which in the Maoist reformulation of the theory of contradiction often received the name of antagonism, in this first figure of leftism thus becomes reduced to the postulate of an absolute dissidence or a radical exteriority with regard to an equally absolute understanding of the state apparatus – socialist no less than capitalist – as oppressive system.

At the level of what we might call its aesthetic form of appearance, such a mode of understanding politics is frequently under the sway of a melodramatic presentation, including the sense in which Louis Althusser, in what is perhaps is his most breathtaking and least outdated text in *For Marx*, defines melodramatic consciousness as a false dialectic of good/ bad conscience. 'In this sense, melodrama is a foreign consciousness as a veneer on a real condition', Althusser writes: 'One makes oneself "one of the people" by flirtatiously being above its own methods; that is why it is essential to play at being (not being) the people that one forces the people to be, the people of popular "myth", people with a flavour of melodrama.'[23] This phenomenon is not limited to the literal soap operas of the Sarkozys and Berlusconis of this world. The left, too, frequently falls for a melodramatic figuration of politics by presenting itself in the guise of a radical disjunction between, on the one hand, a pure social force such as the poor or the powerless, and, on the other, the corrupt machinery of the rich and powerful, protected by the State. This became perhaps nowhere more painfully evident than during the 2006 electoral process in

---

21   Groupe Yénan-Philosophie, 'Etat de front', *La situation actuelle sur le front philosophique* (Paris: François Maspero, 1977), p. 12.
22   Ibid., p. 10.
23   Louis Althusser, 'The "Piccolo Teatro": Bertolazzi and Brecht. Notes on a Materialist Theatre', in *For Marx*, trans. Ben Brewster (London: Verso, 1990), p. 139.

Mexico, where the candidate of the left, Andrés Manuel López Obrador, was immediately caught up in the dilemma of demanding official recognition from those same juridical and electoral state apparatuses that his populist discourse had univocally reviled in the months running up to the alleged fraud that brought to power his rival Felipe Calderón.

Expanding on well-known interpretations of the original role of the melodramatic imagination in nineteenth-century Europe as a morally reassuring answer to the turmoil caused by the French Revolution, I would argue that melodrama, with its image of an eternal struggle of Good and Evil, has now become the privileged genre in which contemporary forms of post-politics nonetheless give themselves an aura of left-wing radicalism after the alleged decline or death of the revolutionary ideal of communism. The profoundly de-politicizing and disastrous consequences of this tendency can be gauged by reflecting upon another contemporary phenomenon in the moralization of politics, namely, the so-called white marches. Comparable to the *mani pulite* ('clean hands') campaign of the 1990s against political corruption in Italy, these are massive manifestations such as the 1996 *witte mars* ('white march') against paedophilia in Belgium or the 2008 *marcha* against violence and insecurity in Mexico City, in which protesters typically dress in all-angelical white clothes and, often wearing no signs at all, loudly or quietly proclaim their indignation, impatience or shame over the current state of affairs. 'Protesters', though, is perhaps saying too much, since the causes to which these large masses of crisp white shirts and waving clean hands respond typically involve such incontestable forms of evil – violence, corruption, paedophilia – that nobody in his or her right mind would want to make an argument against them. In fact, it is frequently the government itself through public television and radio channels that summons citizens to join these marches in the first place. Who then is being interpellated? Marching through the streets of the capital, often with the largest gatherings these countries have seen in all of their history, no longer exerts a properly political or divisive effect. Instead, these events become gigantic festivals of self-congratulatory good conscience, the spectacular pseudocollective counterpart of all those *pentiti* or 'repented' leftists who, in one bestselling confession after another, beg for forgiveness from civil society for their youthful mistakes and excesses in the '60s and '70s. Better yet: are we not witnessing here the endpoint of a long process of de-politicization, starting in the late '60s, in which a certain leftist political aesthetic more often than not has been complicit with the melodramatic moralization of politics?

Rancière proposes a similar reading of leftism's melodramatic portrayal of the logic of contradiction, in a review of Glucksmann's *La Cuisinière et le mangeur d'hommes*: 'The whole book is an organized effect based on a purification of the contradiction: on one hand, power and the discourse of the masters (philosophers, kings, Jacobins, Marxists . . .) organized according to the rules of state constraint; on the other, the class of nonpower, the plebs, pure generosity, whose discourse expresses the sole desire of not being oppressed.'[24] Such simple contradictions that pit the wretched of the earth directly against a fascistoid State power, however, are nowhere to be found in reality. Nor can the plebs be depicted purely as those excluded from power, or as pure nonpower: 'Nowhere is the conflict of power and nonpower played out. Everywhere the task of the State stumbles upon, not the plebs but classes, corporations, collectives and their rules, their forms of recognition and democracy, but also of exclusion and even oppression.'[25] Rancière draws an important lesson from this reading of the developments of leftism in the 1970s: 'Lesson perhaps of this confrontation: that there is never any pure discourse of proletarian power nor any pure discourse of its nonpower', he concludes, hearkening back to an unfinished task bequeathed to us by Marx: 'The force of Marx's thought – but perhaps also its untenable character – resides no doubt in the effort to hold on to these contradictions, which since then have been stripped bare into the police fictions of proletarian powers or the pastoral dreams of plebeian nonpower.'[26] In other words, instead of purifying the logic of contradiction into a strict exteriority for the benefit of a melodramatic sensation of moral good conscience, the task would consist in finding the specific points of articulation where power and resistance, or power and nonpower, are tied together into a single knot, with each strand reciprocally feeding on the strength of the other.

This brings us to the second great figure of contemporary leftism, the main source of which lies precisely in a principle of strict immanence, or reciprocal presupposition, between power and resistance. In other words, instead of postulating the idea of a radical break, this figure proposes

---

24   Jacques Rancière, 'La bergère au Goulag', in *Les Scènes du peuple (Les Révoltes logiques*, 1975/1985) (Lyon: Éditions Horlieu, 2003), pp. 317–18. This collection of essays in general provides an indispensable building block towards a reconstruction of the history of the left and of leftism in France.
25   Ibid., p. 319.
26   Ibid. In the French, Rancière plays on the difficulty of 'holding on to' or 'holding together' (*tenir*) what is otherwise 'untenable' (*intenable*). See also the 'Préface: Les gros mots': 'To hold on steady to the all-too-big words of the people, the worker and the proletariat meant to hold on to their difference from themselves, to the space of dissensual discussion opened up by this difference' (ibid., p. 16).

to sketch the latent outline of communism from within capitalism. We might even say that, against the corrupt forms of 'really existing' communism, this paradigm of leftism traces the contours of a 'virtually existing' communism within the current state of affairs, arguing with Marx and Engels that the conditions of the communist movement result from the now existing premise. This second figure, too, can indeed present solid orthodox credentials. Besides the famous passages in the *Communist Manifesto* which describe how 'the development of modern industry . . . cuts from under its feet the very foundation on which the bourgeoisie produces and appropriates products', to the point where 'what the bourgeoisie therefore produces, above all, are its own grave-diggers', we can invoke Marx's well-known 1859 Preface to his *Contribution to the Critique of Political Economy*, according to which

> new, higher relations of production never appear before the material conditions of their existence have matured in the womb of the old society itself. Therefore mankind always sets itself only such tasks as it can solve; since, looking at the matter more closely, it will always be found that the task itself arises only when the material conditions of its solution already exist or are at least in the process of formation.[27]

All these passages, in part as a compensation for the absence of an actual grave for capitalism, have been buried under a mountain of orthodox and heretical glosses.

Perhaps the most eloquent passage in this regard can be found in another of Marx's striking letters to Ruge, which shows how the conditions for the new society are already present within the old one. 'The reform of consciousness consists *only* in making the world aware of its own consciousness, in awakening it out of its dream about itself, in *explaining* to it the meaning of its own actions', Marx writes to his friend, shortly before breaking his theoretical and political ties with the Young Hegelians:

> It will then become evident that the world has long dreamed of possessing something of which it has only to be conscious in order to possess it in reality. It will become evident that it is not a question of drawing a great mental dividing line between past and future, but of *realizing*

---

27   Marx, Preface, *A Contribution to the Critique of Political Economy*, in Marx and Engels, *Collected Works*, vol. 29, pp. 261–5.

the thoughts of the past. Lastly, it will become evident that mankind is not beginning a *new* work, but is consciously carrying into effect its old work.[28]

The image of time according to this scenario of immanence no longer responds to the theological and quasi-mystical notion of the absolute break or rupture, but to that of a paradoxical fold or wrinkle. It is not a matter of skipping ahead by leaping over all intermediate stages but of seizing the new warped into the old; a matter no longer of breaking the history of humankind in two, with a great mental line between a before and an after, according to some Nietzschean-style grand politics, but rather to track down the latent counterfinalities within the existing state of affairs in order to awaken them and empower their potential for resistance, subversion or destruction.

In fact, after the melodramatic purification and eventual de-politicization of antagonism, based on an absurd version of the principle according to which 'One divides into two', we can see that pure immanence as the philosophical source of a second form of left-wing communism ironically finds support in another Maoist principle, namely, the one according to which 'Where there is oppression, there is rebellion.'[29] To be more precise, rebellion in this orientation is said to be ontologically prior to oppression. Such is indeed the paradoxical mode of reasoning about power and rebellion that we can find in different guises from Michel Foucault to Gilles Deleuze to Antonio Negri. 'Even more, the last word on power holds that resistance comes first', as Deleuze writes in his book on Foucault: 'Thus, there is no diagram that does not contain, aside from those points it connects, other relatively free or unbound points, elements of creativity, mutation, resistance; and we should start from these, perhaps, to under-

---

28   Marx, 'Letters from *Deutsch-Französische Jahrbücher*', p. 144.

29   See Badiou, 'One Divides into Two', *The Century*, pp. 58–67. Guattari and Negri, in *Communists Like Us*, also quote the Maoist slogan: 'It is right to revolt' (p. 71). Elsewhere, Michael Hardt and Negri very freely paraphrase another Maoist directive: '"It is not the two that recompose in one, but the one that opens into two", according to the beautiful anti-Confucian (and anti-Platonic) formula of the Chinese revolutionaries' (*Empire* [Cambridge: Harvard University Press, 2000], p. 48). Here, the liberty taken with the formula 'One divides into two' is reminiscent of Gilles Deleuze and Félix Guattari's own creative rewriting of the phrase: 'One becomes two: whenever we encounter this formula, even stated strategically by Mao or understood in the most "dialectical" way possible, what we have before us is the most classical and well reflected, oldest and weariest kind of thought' (*A Thousand Plateaus: Capitalism and Schizophrenia*, trans. Brian Massumi [Minneapolis: University of Minnesota Press, 1987], p. 5). In both cases, the goal seems to be above all to dilute the violence of the dialectic as the thought of *division* into an anti-dialectical process of *becoming* or *opening*.

stand the whole.'[30] Badiou himself points out this link with one of the guiding principles of the Cultural Revolution, in his early take on Deleuze and Guattari's collaborative work in *Capitalism and Schizophrenia*: 'Where there is oppression, there is revolt', Badiou quotes from Chairman Mao. 'But it is the revolt that, at its own hour, passes judgement on the fate of the oppression, not the other way around.'[31] Even Glucksmann, who is never far behind when it comes to stepping in the shadow of genuine emancipatory thinkers, makes this principle his own in *La Cuisinière et le mangeur d'hommes* when he posits: 'In the beginning there was resistance.'[32] From this primacy of resistance, however, as its gospel-like rephrasing might have foretold us, the attention of the New Philosopher quickly turns to the overwhelming power of repression displayed by an awe-inspiring State. 'This is why Glucksmann's political conclusions are properly despairing', Badiou argues in *Of Ideology*, co-authored with the late François Balmès: 'He tells us "There where the State ends, the human being begins", but of the popular combat against the State, he retraces only the morose and repetitive duration, the infinite obstinacy, while nowhere marking any accomplishment whatsoever in this continued accumulation of forces. Upon reading him, it would seem that the human being is not ready to begin.'[33] Nor would there seem to be any real urgency for the capitalist State to end, since in a common ideological reversal of prior leftist radicalism – an about-face whose law is studied by Lardreau and Jambet – the likes of Glucksmann quickly would come to the rescue of the Washington consensus and its war-mongering allies in Europe.

By contrast, it belongs to Toni Negri, including in his collaborative work first with Guattari and then with Michael Hardt, to have developed the most articulate view of what we might call the left-wing communism of pure immanence. 'Communism is already alive within the capitalist and/or socialist societies of today, in the form of a secret order dedicated to cooperation in production', Negri writes in the 'Postscript' to *Communists Like Us*, taking up the argument from the *Communist Manifesto*: 'As Marx teaches us, communism is born directly from class antagonism, from the refusal of both work and the organization of work, whether in the bourgeois form or the socialist form.'[34] Hardt and Negri's collaborative work,

---

30   Gilles Deleuze, *Foucault* (Paris: Minuit, 1986), pp. 95 and 51.

31   Badiou, 'Le flux et le parti', in *La Situation actuelle sur le front philosophique*, p. 25.

32   André Glucksmann, *La Cuisinière et le mangeur d'hommes* (Paris: Éditions du Seuil, 1975), p. 21.

33   Badiou and François Balmès, *De l'idéologie* (Paris: François Maspero, 1976), pp. 52–3.

34   Negri, 'Postscript, 1990', trans. Jared Becker, in *Communists Like Us*, pp. 166 and 168.

then, is the greatest expression of this potential for resistance of the multitude already present, without the need for any dialectical mediations or
sublations, within the power and command of Empire. Instead of relying
on some version or other of the logic of the constitutive outside of all
order, in other words, the relation between power and resistance must
be conceived in terms of an immanent reversibility: power is not some
monstrous Leviathan or totalitarian Gulag oppressing the masses or the
plebes from above, nor must resistance rely on the weakest link as an
external point of articulation for the struggle. Instead, power and resistance appear as the recto and verso of a single Möbius strip. The point
is only to push far enough so that one may surreptitiously turn into the
other: 'The multitude, in its will to be-against and its desire for liberation,
must push through Empire to come out the other side.'[35] In addition to
the principle of absolute immanence, therefore, to recognize this latent
potential of the multitude within the new imperial order also requires that
we adopt the principle of the ontological primacy of resistance, already
defined by Deleuze and Foucault:

> From one perspective Empire stands clearly over the multitude and
> subjects it to the rule of its overarching machine, as a new Leviathan.
> At the same time, however, from the perspective of social productivity
> and creativity, from what we have been calling the ontological perspec-
> tive, the hierarchy is reversed. The multitude is the real productive
> force of our social world, whereas Empire is a mere apparatus of
> capture that lives only off the vitality of the multitude – as Marx would
> say, a vampire regime of accumulated dead labour that survives only
> by sucking off the blood of the living.[36]

Inside and against the logic of imperial command, like its photographic
negative yet without allowing any of the familiar dialectical topics of the
outside within, there thus inevitably emerges the spectre of the multitude.

Empire, in fact, has never been anything more than an impossible project
to capture and control the creative mobility and desire of the multitude,
whose vital constituent force should therefore be considered anterior to all
the attempts at mediation on behalf of constituted power – whether in terms
of the market and globalization, the people, or the modern State. What
springs from this inexhaustible fountain is not so much a melodramatic

35   Hardt and Negri, *Empire*, p. 218.
36   Ibid., p. 62.

good conscience as the unmistakable politico-ontological optimism that characterizes Hardt and Negri's brand of materialism: 'The creative forces of the multitude that sustain Empire are also capable of autonomously constructing a counter-Empire, an alternative political organization of global flows and exchanges'.[37] Based on the principle of immanent reversibility between power and resistance, we would almost have to conclude that the more capitalism there is, the better are the chances for communism to emerge: 'Perhaps the more capital extends its global networks of production and control, the more powerful any singular point of revolt can be.'[38] We are, after all, still within a familiar scheme, the one that contrasts the pure potential for insurrection and immanence to the equally pure power of transcendence and the established order – except that now the two extremes are folded into a thoroughly materialist and nondialectical one.

In sum, a certain leftist and ex-Maoist renegacy on the one hand regurgitates the melodrama of the world broken in two. This is not 'One divides into two' so much as 'Two times one', based on a principle of absolute exteriority and dissidence between the 'good' masses and the 'evil' Gulag. On the other hand, we find a left-wing communism based on the immanent reversibility of power and resistance, of capitalism and communism, or even of Empire and multitude, as two sides of one and the same flippable coin. There is then no more outside, but neither is there the protective safe haven of a preconstituted inside, since both inside and outside are nothing but the illusory extremes of an older dialectic which has now, in the new global order, become completely obsolete except in the form of nostalgic, if not senile, regressions. 'Another world is possible', without ever having to rely on an idealist, utopian or transcendent *Hintenwelt*, a 'world behind the world'. If there is still a two from this point of view, it no longer requires division so much as the folding and unfolding of a small wrinkle in time itself. Thus far, we could also say, philosophers have only attempted variously to construct communism as a utopian ideal or future horizon; the point, however, is to express it as already being at work within the present state of affairs.

The Current Situation and Our Tasks, or, Communism in Cochabamba?

Thus, at the end of this cursory look into the struggle between left-wing communism and the ABC of Marxism, everything would seem to indicate

---

37   Ibid., p. xv.
38   Ibid., p. 58.

that, in an era marked by the worldwide crisis of capitalist parliamentarianism and of the party-form of politics in general, all that is left is the
unlimited and spontaneous affirmative energy of 'pure' communism, i.e.,
leftism, purged of all its historically compromising ties that once invoked
the now infamous names of Marx, Lenin, Stalin or Mao.

Badiou, for one, as late as in his 1982 *Theory of the Subject* still included
communism among what he called, in a playful allusion to one of Lacan's
seminars, the 'four fundamental concepts of Marxism', together with the
class struggle, the dictatorship of the proletariat, and revolution. But then
what happens when of these four fundamental ideas, only that of communism is retained – moreover raised to the status of a Platonic or Kantian
Idea? Can we still legitimately tie such an 'Idea' of communism to the
history and theory of Marxism as politics? More generally, if we consider
as closed or saturated the sequence in which politics could historically be
referred to Marxism, what are we to make of Badiou's recent calls for the
complete separation of the communist hypothesis both from the party-
form of politics and from the figure of the State?

With regard to the question of communism and the State, Badiou
indeed sees an urgent need for the complete delinking of the two. As he
writes after the collapse of the Soviet Union, in *Of an Obscure Disaster*:
'At the level of subjectivity, the concrete history of communisms (I refer
to them this time in their common identity, that of parties, groups and
militants, whether official or dissident) does not rely upon the "paradisia-
cal" State, which serves solely as a random objectification', to which he
later adds: 'There is a hypothesis which is both stronger and simpler: it
is that the political and thus subjective history of communisms is essentially divided from their State history.'[39] In fact, the seeds for this view are
already sown in *Theory of the Subject*, in which the combined experience
of Maoism and the Cultural Revolution in particular is retrospectively

---

39   Badiou, *Infinite Thought*, pp. 136–7. Elsewhere, in a section of *D'un désastre obscur* not included
in *Infinite Thought* but translated, though very badly, in *lacanian ink*, Badiou enunciates a general
principle of the separation of politics and the State: 'Now politics, inasmuch as it is a condition of
philosophy, is a subjective procedure of truth. It finds in the State neither its primary stake nor its
incarnation'; 'The history of politics, made of decisions of thought and of risky collective engage-
ments, is entirely different, I repeat, from the history of the State' (*D'un désastre obscur*, pp. 54–5; 'Of
an Obscure Disaster', trans. Barbara P. Fulks, *lacanian ink* 22 [2003]: 85–6). On this topic Negri is
in strict agreement with Badiou: 'The State is only a cold monster, a vampire in interminable agony
which derives vitality from those who abandon themselves to its simulacra'; 'What is contested by
communism are all types of conservative, degrading, oppressive reterritorialization imposed by the
capitalist and/or socialist State, with its administrative functions, institutional organs, its collective
means of normalization and blockage, its media, etc.' (See Negri, 'Postscript, 1990', in *Communists
Like Us*, pp. 144–5 and 140–1.)

assessed as having put a definitive end to the guaranteeing of communism through a reference to the socialist State. 'We declare that, socialist or not, and though invariably needed for the intelligibility of action, the State guarantees nothing with regard to the subjective effectuation of communism', writes Badiou.

> In order to believe the contrary, one must imagine this socialist State as an exception – as state of the exception, capable by itself of an algorithm for its own withering away, whereas Lenin already knew that any modern State, including the socialist one, is intrinsically bourgeois and hence pertains, with regard to the communist topology, to the category of the structure and the obstacle.[40]

This also means that great care must be given to separate communism from anything pertaining to the problematic of socialism as the transition to an ever farther receding communist society. 'Socialism doesn't exist. It is a name for an obscure arsenal of new conditions in which the capitalism/communism contradiction becomes somewhat clarified', Badiou boldly proclaims from the very beginning of *Theory of the Subject*: 'If there is a major point in Marxism, which this century confirms almost to the level of disgust, it is that we should certainly not inflate the question of "socialism", of the "construction of socialism". The serious affair, the *precise* affair, is communism. This is why, all along, politics stands in a position of domination over the State, and cannot be reduced to it.'[41]

With regard to the Leninist party, on the other hand, Badiou concludes the last chapter of his book *The Meaning of Sarkozy*, also published separately in *New Left Review*, with a brief sketch of the history of the communist Idea. In this periodization, most elements of which can already be found, sometimes verbatim, in *Theory of the Subject*, the party-form of political organization proves to be as pivotal as the negative assessment of the theory of the State from which, furthermore, the party seems to have

---

40 Badiou, *Theory of the Subject*, trans. Bruno Bosteels (London and New York: Continuum, 2009), p. 235. Negri also writes: 'All statist manipulations, the ingratiating as well as the disgraceful, must be relentlessly combated. Statism and corporatism are two faces of the same obstacle to the development of autonomies and of singularities' (*Communists Like Us*, p. 116).

41 Badiou, *Theory of the Subject*, pp. 7–8. Again, Negri affirms the same principle in nearly identical terms: 'The need to distinguish between "socialism" and "communism" has once again become obvious: but this time not because of the blurred boundaries between them, but because they are so opposed. Socialism is nothing other than one of the forms taken by capitalist management of the economy and of power, whereas communism is an absolutely radical political economic democracy and an aspiration to freedom' (*Communists Like Us*, p. 167).

become inextricable. 'The party had been an appropriate tool for the overthrow of weakened reactionary regimes, but it proved ill-adapted for the construction of the "dictatorship of the proletariat" in the sense that Marx had intended – that is, a temporary state, organizing the transition to the non-state, its dialectical "withering away"', Badiou claims. 'Instead, the party-state developed into a new form of authoritarianism'.[42] As a result of this lack of adaptation between the party and the task it is supposed to fulfil, the last historical realization of the communist hypothesis, towards the end of the sequence that runs from October 1917 to 1976, targets the very party-form that had been capable of solving the problems left hanging in the wake of the first sequence, the one that runs from the 1848 riots or even from the 1792 French Revolution to the 1871 Paris Commune: 'The last great convulsions of the second sequence – the Cultural Revolution and May '68, in its broadest sense – can be understood as attempts to deal with the inadequacy of the party'.[43]

But then, I repeat, what are we to make of a communist hypothesis from which all the traditional mediating terms – the party, unions, parliaments and other electoral-democratic mechanisms or compromise formations, to use Lenin's ABC of Marxism – have been subtracted or punched out so as to leave in place only the autonomous action of the masses as the direct effectuation of the communist invariants, albeit this time not *against* so much as *at a distance from* the State?

In his 1976 booklet *Of Ideology*, Badiou had first introduced the idea of communist invariants as a recurring set of ideological anti-property, anti-authority and anti-hierarchy principles. Part of the aim of this first presentation of the communist hypothesis, though, also involved a plea for a historical dialectic between the communist invariants at the level of ideology and the various class actors, organized by a party of a new type, which with varying degrees of success actualized these invariants at the level of politics. Between the final seminars from *Theory of the Subject* and *The Meaning of Sarkozy*, however, the communist hypothesis is gradually

---

42   Badiou, 'The Communist Hypothesis', *New Left Review* 49 (2008): 36.

43   Ibid. In *Theory of the Subject*, Badiou had given a similar periodization: 'The Leninist party is the historical answer to a problem that is wholly inscribed in the State/revolution contradiction. It treats of the victorious destruction. What happens then to this party with regard to the State/communism contradiction, that is, in relation to the process whereby the State – and classes – must no longer be destroyed but must wither, through an effect of transition? . . . The domain of Leninism makes no real place, when it comes to the party, for the problem of communism as such. Its business is the State, the antagonistic victory. The Cultural Revolution begins the forcing of this uninhabitable place. It invites us to name 'party of the new type' the post-Leninist party, the party for communism, on the basis of which to recast the entire field of Marxist practice' (p. 205).

shorn of the dialectic of masses, classes and party, so as to let the Idea in question appear once again in the naked beauty of its purely generic invariance, that is, as autonomous mass action against, or at a distance from, the coercive State. In the words of Badiou: 'As a pure Idea of equality, the communist hypothesis has no doubt existed in a practical state since the beginnings of the existence of the State. As soon as mass action opposes state coercion in the name of egalitarian justice, we have the appearance of rudiments or fragments of the communist hypothesis.'[44] The outcome of May '68 and its Maoist aftermath would only have heightened the separation of communism from the State: 'May '68, and still more so the five years that followed, inaugurated a new sequence for the genuine communist hypothesis, one that always keeps its distance from the state.'[45] Are we not back, then, in the scheme of left-wing communism as diagnosed not only by Lenin but also, ironically, by Badiou himself three decades ago?

Of course, in this age of terror and crisis, of crisis as terror, leftism always offers an attractive ethical-moral high ground. In fact, the appeal of the leftist hypothesis might very well be the result of an interiorization of defeat, one which at the same time seeks to bypass the scenarios of repentance and apostasy. In a worldwide situation of rampant conservatism and blunt reactionary policies, when new forms of political organization are either lacking or insufficiently articulated, the most tempting posture is indeed one of radical left-wing idealism. Leftism, in other words, appears today as the beautiful soul of communism, if it were not for the fact that, without this soul, the communist Idea is perhaps little more than an empty shell, a poor excuse of a body, if not a soothingly embalmed and

---

44   Badiou, *De quoi Sarkozy est-il le nom? Circonstances, 4* (Paris: Lignes, 2007), p. 133; *The Meaning of Sarkozy*, trans. David Fernbach (London and New York: Verso), p. 100 (I occasionally change this translation and use upper case to differentiate the political State from a given state of affairs).
45   Ibid., p. 136 (p. 102). In the written version of his talk at the London conference, no doubt as a subsequent addition in response to some of the polemics that barely came to the surface on the last day, Badiou directly addresses the question of the State by arguing that the Idea of communism – as the ideological triangulation between politics, history and subjectivity – may be capable of 'projecting the real of a politics, always subtracted from the power of the State, onto the historical figure of "another State", provided that the subtraction be internal to this subjectivizing operation, in the sense that "the other State" is also subtracted from the power of the State, and hence from its own power, in so far as it is a State whose essence is to wither away', and further along: 'This is why one of the contents of the communist Idea today – and this against the motif of communism as a goal to be attained by the labour of a new State – is that the withering of the State is no doubt a principle that must be visible within every political action (which is expressed in the formula "politics at a distance from the State", as the obligatory refusal of all direct inclusion in the State, of all demands for credits from the State, of all participation in elections, etc.)' (*L'Hypothèse communiste: Circonstances, 5* [Paris: Lignes, 2009], pp. 195–6 and 201–2).

mummified corpse. Conversely, whenever the question of organization is brought up, the old spectres of Leninism, of party discipline and the critique of mere economism and social-democratic reformism, as well as of adventurism, inevitably raise their ugly heads again. Perhaps we even got off on the wrong foot by taking as our point of departure Lenin's pamphlet on left-wing communism, with its impasse between social movement and party organization, between anarchism and statism?

I would like to test some of the presuppositions behind this alleged impasse by turning to the theoretical work of another major thinker of our time: Álvaro García Linera, Evo Morales's running mate for the 2005 elections and the current vice-president of Bolivia, author not only of important books on Marx and Marxism, including *De demonios escondidos y momentos de revolución* and *Forma valor y forma comunidad* – written under the pen name of Qhananchiri while locked up in the maximum security prison of Chonchocoro during the 1990s on charges of subversive activity – but also of a fundamental collection of political and sociological writings, published a few months ago in Argentina under the title *La potencia plebeya*.

This very title, to begin with, would seem to suggest a profound indebtedness to both forms of leftism as described earlier. (Besides, in several of these writings García Linera also throws some well-aimed punches at those whom he describes as sectarian, catastrophic, or mystical 'pseudoleftists', *pseudoizquierdistas*, which would confirm his own implicit self-identification as a presumably 'genuine' leftist.[46]) The reference to the 'plebes' (*la plebe armada, la plebe facciosa, las plebes insurrectas*, and so on), on the one hand, entails a sustained attempt to bypass the classical figure of the proletariat modelled on the workers in a large factory, in favour of a wider and much more flexible composition of the revolutionary subject. Linera calls this composition 'motley', or *abigarrada* in Spanish, borrowing a term from the famous Bolivian sociologist René Zavaleta Mercado. In actual fact, this concept and its name already appear in the Spanish translation of Lenin's pamphlet on left-wing communism:

---

46   García Linera's ex-partner and fellow guerrilla fighter in the Ejército Guerrillero Túpac Katari (EGTK), Raquel Gutiérrez Aguilar, writing under the pen name of Qhantat Wara Wara, also formulates a critique of creole 'bourgeois leftism', in *Los q'aras izquierdizantes: una crítica al izquierdismo burgués* (La Paz: Ofensiva Roja, 1988); conversely the positions of both García Linera and Raquel Gutiérrez are seen as leftist-revisionist, in Carlos M. Volodia, *Contribución a la crítica del revisionismo: Crítica de las posiciones ideológicas de Raquel Gutiérrez* (La Paz: Bandera Roja, 1999), and Fernando Molina, *Crítica de las ideas políticas de la nueva izquierda boliviana* (La Paz: Eureka, 2003).

Capitalism would not be capitalism if the 'pure' proletariat were not surrounded by a large number of exceedingly motley types intermediate between the proletarian and the semi-proletarian (who earns his livelihood in part by the sale of his labour-power), between the semi-proletarian and the small peasant (and petty artisan, handicraft worker and small master in general), between the small peasant and the middle peasant, and so on, and if the proletariat itself were not divided into more developed and less developed strata, if it were not divided according to territorial origin, trade, sometimes according to religion, and so on. And from all this follows the necessity, the absolute necessity, for the vanguard of the proletariat, its class-conscious section, the Communist Party, to resort to manoeuvres, agreements and compromises with the various groups of proletarians, with the various parties of the workers and small masters. It is entirely a case of *knowing how* to apply these tactics in order to *raise*, and not lower, the *general* level of proletarian class-consciousness, revolutionary spirit, and ability to fight and win.[47]

This is also how García Linera, drawing on his militant sociological investigations into the phenomena of re-proletarianization and the so-called extinction of the working class, describes the new class composition of that motley social formation of the 'plebs' in which socio-economical and cultural-symbolical aspects must be thought together.

More generally speaking, the plebeian reference is consistent with a leftist and/or populist appeal to various names for the formless or as yet unformed masses: from Hegel's 'rabble' to Deleuze's 'hordes' and 'packs' to Laclau's retrieval of Marx's 'lumpen'. As Jacques and Danielle Rancière explain in an important article on the trajectory of leftism in 1970s France, what many of these names but especially that of the plebs promise are ways of sidestepping the issue of representation as the principal obstacle against which all emancipatory politics run aground.

---

47 Lenin, *'Left-Wing' Communism*, p. 421. For the Spanish translation I have consulted *La enfermedad infantil del 'izquierdismo' en el comunismo* (Moscow: Progreso, n.d.). On the notion of 'formación social abigarrada', see René Zavaleta Mercado, *Las masas en noviembre* (La Paz: Juventud, 1983) and *Lo nacional-popular en Bolivia* (Mexico City: Siglo XXI, 1986; La Paz: Plural, 2008); the massive overview of Zavaleta's thought by Luis Tapia, *La producción del conocimiento local* (La Paz: Muela del Diablo, 2002); and the collection of essays *René Zavaleta Mercado: Ensayos, testimonios y re-visiones*, ed. Maya Aguiluz Ibargüen and Norma de los Ríos (Mexico City: FLACSO, 2006). This concept is also discussed in Toni Negri, Michael Hardt, Giuseppe Cocco and Judith Revel's seminar discussion with García Linera and Luis Tapia, *Imperio, multitud y sociedad abigarrada* (La Paz: CLACSO/Muela del Diablo/Comuna, 2008).

Thus, referring once again to the use of the notion on the part of New Philosophers such as Glucksmann, if not already on the part of Michel Foucault, they describe how

> the figure of a *plebs* appears whom the intellectual represents just as yesterday he represented the proletariat, but in a way that precisely denies representation, the plebs means both and at the same time all the positivity of suffering and popular laughter and the part of refusal, of negativity, that each carries with them, realizing the immediate unity of the intellectual and the people.[48]

Used in this sense, the plebeian reference is an integral part of the left-wing purification of antagonism as discussed above.

In *La potencia plebeya*, I might add, the unity of the intellectual and the people as sought after through the plebeian reference paradoxically also seeks to forego all figures of that mediating third who in Latin America usually comes in the guise of the white *letrado* ('man of letters') or *ladino* ('he who knows Latin'). Ironically, though, not only was *un hombre que sabe*, or 'a man who knows', a slogan used for posters in García Linera's 2005 electoral campaign, but Qhananchiri, the Aymara name with which he used to sign many of his prison writings, also means 'he who clarifies things', so that many of the stabs in *La potencia plebeya* against the representational figure of the intellectual can be read as prescient self-criticisms. No author writes more ardently and eloquently than García Linera himself against the risks that beset those 'committed intellectuals' who claim to speak 'for' or 'to' the subaltern masses, all the while having their eyes fixed high on the benefits, both moral and material, that derive from a privileged position near or inside the Hydra-headed apparatuses of the State. Nothing would be easier than to turn these criticisms against

---

48   Jacques Rancière (with Danielle Rancière), 'La légende des philosophes. Les intellectuels et la traversée du gauchisme', *Les Scènes du peuple*, pp. 307–8. I should add that this insight into the role of the figure of the plebs did not keep Rancière himself from presenting the work of Gabriel Gauny as that of a 'plebeian philosopher' or to delve into the history of 'plebeian' appropriations of 'heretical' workers' knowledge. Rancière's justification of this earlier use is helpful here: 'I use the adjective "plebeian" rather than "proletarian" in order to avoid equivocations. Some people, indeed, stubbornly insist on wanting "proletarian" to designate the worker of a certain type of modern industry. By contrast, it should be clear that "plebeian" designates a symbolical relation and not a type of work. Plebeian is the being who is excluded from history-making speech' ('Savoirs hérétiques et émancipations du pauvre', *Les Scènes du peuple*, p. 38). In the case of García Linera, another important reference is E. P. Thompson, 'The Patricians and the Plebs', *Customs in Common, Studies in Traditional Popular Culture* (New York: The New Press, 1993), pp. 16–96; this is a revised and expanded version of the famous article 'Patrician Society, Plebeian Culture', *Journal of Social History* 7 (1974): pp. 382–405.

their author and, nowadays, no enterprise is indeed more common.

On the other hand, leading back to immanence as the source for the second figure of contemporary leftism, this search for an overcoming of representation is further developed through the element of *potencia* in García Linera's title. This term is certainly as difficult to translate into English as is Negri's *potenza*: 'potentiality' sounds like an amputated Aristotelianism without actuality, à la Whitehead or Agamben; 'potency' is overly sexual and anxiously virile; and 'power' creates disastrous confusions with the customary translation of the Spanish *poder* or Italian *potere*, so that I will opt for 'potential' instead. Still, the English-speaking reader does well to keep in mind that in Spanish, a bonus feature of *potencia* is the ease with which this noun turns into a verb, *potenciar*, 'to empower', or literally, 'to potentialize', meaning both and at the same time to actualize that which otherwise remains as yet potential and to retrieve the potential that is latent within an existing state of affairs.

In fact, the most astonishing passages in *La potencia plebeya* are those that refer to the contemporary relevance of the *Communist Manifesto* in which Linera, also following Marx's *Grundrisse* and Negri's seminal rereading thereof, uncovers the immanent counterfinality of capitalism as the place that at the same time contains the still abstract potential for communism. 'Marx's attitude in the *Manifesto* towards this globalization of capital consists simply in understanding the emancipatory potentials [*potencias*] which are hidden therein but which until now appear deformed and distorted by the dominant capitalist rationality', Linera writes, so that a 'critical analysis must bring to light the counterfinalities, the emancipatory countertendencies of labour against capital that are nested materially in its midst and that Marxists must understand and empower [*potenciar*] by all the means at their disposal'.[49] This also means that the potential of the plebs, while currently still dormant and abstract, already lies within the power of capital, instead of opposing the latter from some utopian or imaginary outside with the dream of pure nonpower. Communism as

---

49   García Linera, 'El *Manifiesto comunista* y nuestro tiempo', in *El fantasma insomne: Pensando el presente desde el* Manifiesto Comunista (La Paz: Muela del Diablo, 1999), reprinted in *La potencia plebeya: Acción colectiva e identidades indígenas, obreras y populares en Bolivia*, ed. Pablo Stefanoni (Buenos Aires: Prometeo Libros/CLACSO, 2008), pp. 59–60. García Linera's work unfortunately is not yet extensively available in English. See 'State Crisis and Popular Power', *New Left Review* 37 (2006): 73–85; and 'The "Multitude"', in Oscar Olivera with Tom Lewis, *¡Cochabamba! Water War in Bolivia* (Cambridge: South End Press, 2004), pp. 65–86. A video of 'Marxismo e indianismo' ('Marxism and Indigenism'), García Linera's important 2007 inaugural speech at the 'Marx and Marxisms in Latin America' conference at Cornell University, is also available in English translation at http://www.cornell.edu/video.

the real movement which abolishes the present state of affairs, in other words, is not some speculative idealist dream but is linked in a properly materialist, critical if not dialectical way to the tendencies and counterfinalities inherent in capitalism.

And yet, the power of the plebs does not emerge spontaneously from the crisis and impotence of capitalism, since capital only produces ever more capital – even in, or especially thanks to, global crises such as the current one. As Marx used to say: 'Social reforms are never achieved because of the weakness of the strong but are always the result of the power of the weak.'[50] This empowering of the weak depends on a massive and often violent act of torsion or forcing, an act which García Linera – formally a mathematician by training who, like Badiou, no doubt believes that it *is* possible to teach higher mathematics to a four-year-old child – also names the curvature of communist self-determination. Linera concludes:

In other words, capital unfolds the potentials of social labour only as abstraction, as forces that are constantly subordinated and castrated by the rationality of value of the commodity. The fact that these tendencies may come to the surface is no longer an issue of capital, which while it exists will never allow that they flourish for themselves; it is an issue of labour over and against capital, on the basis of what capital thus far has done.

He adds: 'To break this determination, to *curve* in another direction the domain of classes, otherwise to define labour on the basis of labour itself, is a question of the construction of workers for themselves, of the determination of labour for itself in the face of capital's determination for itself: it is the historical–material problem of self-determination.'[51]

From these all too brief remarks about García Linera's recent work as a theorist, I derive two general conclusions in regard to the communist hypothesis in its never-ending dialectical struggle with the leftist

---

50   Marx, quoted in García Linera, *La potencia plebeya*, p. 65.
51   García Linera, ibid., pp. 79 and 114. For Linera, such curvature of determination corresponds precisely to Marx's definition of the political party: 'The party is then the large movement of historical constitution of the proletarian mass into a subject in charge of its destiny through the elaboration of multiple and massive practical forms capable of producing a reality different from the one established by capital. The *party*, in this sense, *is a material fact of the masses*, not of sects or vanguards; it is a movement of practical actions, not just theoretical acquisitions; it is the class struggle carried out by the working class itself, not a programme or "an *ideal* to which reality will have to adjust itself"' (ibid., p. 122).

hypothesis, that is, two tasks for self-clarification which in the end may bring about a common front in which arguments for the subtraction from party and the State hopefully no longer exclude our taking seriously – while neither idealizing nor prejudging – experiments such as the one unfolding today in Bolivia.

The first task requires that we actively continue to historicize the communist hypothesis. We need to go beyond the confines of Western Europe and/or the ex-Soviet Union with what is at once the beauty and disarming simplicity of the idea, or the second-degree idea about the idea, which remains a constant in Badiou's work from *Of Ideology* until most recently *The Communist Hypothesis*, according to which communism is defined, on one hand, by a series of axiomatic invariants that can be found whenever a mass mobilization directly confronts the privileges of property, hierarchy and authority, and, on the other hand, by the specific political actors who historically and with varying degrees of success or failure implement those same communist invariants. In other words, this first task amounts to writing, as it were, a history of communist eternity, in a counterfactually Borgesian sense. The key concept in this regard is not the orthodox one of *stages* and *transitions* in a linear dialectical periodization but rather that of the different *sequences* of the communist hypothesis in a strictly immanent determination, with all that this entails in terms of the assessment of failures, including an assessment of the very nature of what is called a failure, and of the legacy of unsolved problems handed down from one sequence to another.

Unless, however, the communist hypothesis is to be left to shine for eternity with all the untimely brilliance of a Platonic or Kantian regulative Idea, communism must also be actualized and organized as the real movement which abolishes the present state of things. In other words, communism must again find inscription in a concrete body, the flesh and thought of a political subjectivity – even if it may no longer be necessary for such an act of subjectivization to pass through the traditional form of the party for its embodiment. After the historicization of eternity, this would be the second task for the renewal of the communist hypothesis in our current situation. As Badiou writes in *Of an Obscure Disaster*: 'The point where an instance of thought subtracts itself from the State, inscribing this subtraction into being, constitutes the real of a politics. And a political organization has no other goal than to "hold onto the gained step", that is, to provide a *body* for that thought which, collectively re-membered, has been able to find the public gesture of the insubordination that founds it.'[52] But then, of course, the way in which communism can be organized and embodied is also precisely the place where all the major doubts and disagreements can be found, including among participants at this conference.

On several occasions in *La potencia plebeya*, García Linera interestingly enough draws our attention to a letter from Marx to Ferdinand Freiligrath, dated 29 February 1860, in which Marx writes that after the dissolution, at his behest, of the League of Communists in November 1852, he himself '*never* belonged to any society again, whether *secret* or *public*; that the *party*, therefore, in this wholly ephemeral sense, ceased to exist for me eight years ago . . . By party, I meant the party in the broad historical sense.'[53] Based on this letter, García Linera goes on to call for a retrieval and proper re-evaluation of the dialectic between these two senses of the party, the ephemeral and the grand historical, in ways that may well dovetail with some of Badiou's lesser-known pronouncements on the same subject, even as late as in his *Metapolitics*, a collection which otherwise pleads for a militant form of politics without a party. García Linera interprets Marx's letter as follows:

> *Historical sense and ephemeral sense of the party* form an historical dialectic of the party in Marx, which we must vindicate today in the face of a tragic experience of the party-state that prevails in the organized experiences of large parts of the Left worldwide. The party-state, in all cases, has been the miniature replica of hierarchical state despotism, which has alienated the militant will in the omnipotent powers of bosses and party functionaries; and no sooner do revolutionary social transformations appear than these apparatuses show an extraordinary facility to amalgamate themselves with the state machinery so as to reconstruct them in their exclusive function of expropriating the general will, which at the same time reinforces the rationality of capitalist reproduction from which it emerged.[54]

Can we not articulate this idea of retrieving the party in the grand historical sense with a rather surprising defence of the party-form of politics on

---

52   Badiou, *D'un désastre obscur*, p. 57. *Tenir le pas gagné* is an allusion to Arthur Rimbaud's *A Season in Hell*, just as the book's main title *D'un désastre obscur*, like that of Badiou's last novel *Calme bloc, ici-bas*, is an allusion to Stéphane Mallarmé's *The Tomb of Edgar Allan Poe*.

53   Marx to Ferdinand Freiligrath in London, *Collected Works*, vols. 41, 81 and 87, quoted in García Linera, *La Potencia plebeya*, p. 82.

54   García Linera, ibid., p. 130.

the part of Badiou in *Metapolitics*? 'It is crucial to emphasize that for Marx or Lenin, who are both in agreement on this point, the real characteristic of the party is not its firmness, but rather its porosity to the event, its dispersive flexibility in the face of unforeseeable circumstances', Badiou writes, with direct references to the *Communist Manifesto* and *What Is To Be Done?*

Thus, rather than referring to a dense, bound fraction of the working class – what Stalin will call a 'detachment' – the party refers to an unfixable omnipresence, whose proper function is less to represent class than to de-limit it by ensuring it is equal to everything that history presents as improbable and excessive in respect of the rigidity of interests, whether material or national. Thus, the communists embody the unbound multiplicity of consciousness, its anticipatory aspect, and therefore the precariousness of the bond, rather than its firmness. It is not for nothing that the maxim of the proletarian is to have nothing to lose but his chains, and to have a world to win.[55]

The party, in other words, would no longer be the incarnation of historical necessity running things behind our backs while we applaud in unison with the apparatchiks. Instead, it would simply name the flexible organization of a fidelity to events in the midst of unforeseeable circumstances.

With regard to the State, finally, García Linera obviously shares the idea already fully expressed by Marx and Engels after the experience of the Paris Commune and endlessly repeated today by Badiou and Negri, namely: 'The modern State, in whatever form it takes, is essentially a capitalist machinery, it is the State of capitalists, the ideal collective capitalist.'[56] This is why, in an earlier text written in prison under the pen

---

55 Badiou, *Metapolitics*, p. 74.
56 Engels, 'From Utopian Socialism to Scientific Socialism', quoted in García Linera, *La Potencia plebeya*, p. 101, n. 157. Marx's own point of view famously shifted in this regard after and as a result of the Paris Commune. For a commentary of this 'rectification' of the *Communist Manifesto* with regard to the State, García Linera refers to the study by Étienne Balibar, 'La "rectification" du *Manifeste communiste*', in *Cinq études du matérialisme historique* (Paris: François Maspero, 1974), pp. 65–101. Elsewhere, in his polemic with José Aricó's famous argument about Marx and Latin America, García Linera draws the conclusion: 'There is thus no social revolutionization possible nor therefore any national construction from within the old State. This task can only come into being as society's movement of self-organization, as a creative and vital impulse of civil society to organize itself as nation', and yet García Linera adds: 'This does not take away the possible role of the State in this task, as Marx signals in the case of absolute monarchism in Europe, or of the creole elites themselves, as in Mexico, but always as condensations, as orienting syntheses of the impulses of society' (see Qhananchiri, *De demonios escondidos y momentos de revolución: Marx y la revolución social en las extremidades del cuerpo capitalista, Parte I* [La Paz: Ofensiva Roja, 1991], pp. 255–6; also included in *La potencia plebeya*, p. 50).

name Qhananchiri, García Linera repeats the orthodox-leftist viewpoint that communism has nothing to do with an apparatus such as the parliament, except to smash it: 'Destroy it! Burn it! Make it disappear together with the government and the whole state apparatus!, propose instead the workers, tired of being used as servants by the bosses.'[57] And yet, just as he argues against the potential for corruption inherent in the State-form, years later the soon-to-become vice-president of Bolivia also warns against what he calls

> a kind of non-statehood dreamed of by primitive anarchism. The naivety of a society outside of the State would be no more than an innocent speculation, if it were not for the fact that it is thus 'forgotten' or hidden how the state 'lives off' the resources of the whole society, hierarchically assigning these goods in function of the strength of the totality of social fractions and consecrating the access to these powers by means of the coercion that it exerts and the legitimacy that it obtains from the totality of society's members. The state is thus a total social relation, not only the ambition of the 'capable' or of the 'power-thirsty'; the state in a certain way traverses all of us, which is where its public meaning stems from.[58]

Even the State, in other words, is ultimately built on and lives off nothing else than the plebeian potential, which can always manifest itself by expropriating the expropriators so as to take back what for the past five

---

57   Qhananchiri, *Crítica de la nación y la nación crítica naciente* (La Paz: Ofensiva Roja, 1990), p. 34. As the second half of this pamphlet's title indicates, even in what is perhaps his most radical text, García Linera already invokes not just a 'nascent critical nation' but also the possibility of an alternative, 'non-capitalist' State. On the one hand: 'The current struggle of Aymara and Quechua vindications remits us, therefore, to the problem of a non-capitalist national constitution' (pp. 18–19); on the other: 'Whether in this communal association there is place or not for the formation of a state of Aymara workers, a state of Quechua workers, a state of Bolivian workers, etc., in any case, will be the outcome of the collective decision and will imposed by the vitality of the natural-cultural-historical dimension in the context of the insurgency and of the communitarian links established in all this time between the workers of the city and the country in order to heal the scars of distrust borne from the capitalist national oppression' (pp. 28–9).

58   García Linera, 'Autonomía indígena y Estado multinacional' (2004), reprinted in *La potencia plebeya*, pp. 231–2, n. 277. The most succinct overview of the ongoing debate over the possible role of the State in popular, indigenous, proletarian and peasant uprisings in Bolivia's recent history can be traced in the articles by Jaime Iturri Salmón and Raquel Gutiérrez Aguilar, in the collection *Las armas de la utopía. Marxismo: Provocaciones heréticas* (La Paz: CIDES/UMSA, 1996), followed by García Linera's letters in response to the criticisms of his two *compañeros* (66–76); and 'La lucha por el poder en Bolivia', in *Horizontes y límites del estado y el poder* (La Paz: Muela del Diablo, 2005), partially reprinted in *La potencia plebeya*, pp. 350–73.

centuries has been the defining theft of modern power and sovereignty in Latin America.

In a more recent interview, taped when he had already moved on to occupy the post of second in command of his country's state apparatus, García Linera goes so far as to suggest the possibility that the State, provided that it is subjected to a new constituent power, might be one of the embodiments that 'potentialize' or 'empower' the communist hypothesis from within. Nobody for sure would have expected to hear anything less from a sitting vice-president who has gradually come to jettison his more doctrinaire autonomist allegiances to the work of Toni Negri in favour of a well-nigh classical Hegelian or Weberian view. Even so, García Linera's words as usual are both eloquent and provocative:

The general horizon of the era is communist. And this communism will have to be constructed on the basis of society's self-organizing capacities, of processes for the generation and distribution of communitarian, self-managing wealth. But at this moment it is clear that this is not an immediate horizon, which centres on the conquest of equality, the redistribution of wealth, the broadening of rights. Equality is fundamental because it breaks a chain of five centuries of structural inequality, that is the aim at the time, as far as social forces allow us to go, not because we prescribe it to be in that way but because that is what we see. Rather, we enter the movement with our expecting and desiring eyes set upon the communist horizon. But we were serious and objective, in the social sense of the term, by signalling the limits of the movement. And that is where the fight came with various *compañeros* about what it was possible to do. When I enter into the government, what I do is to validate and begin to operate at the level of the state in function of this reading of the current moment. So then, what about communism? What can be done from the State in function of this communist horizon? To support as much as possible the unfolding of society's autonomous organizational capacities. This is as far as the possibility can go in terms of what a leftist State, a revolutionary State, can do. To broaden the workers' base and the autonomy of the workers' world, to potentialize [*potenciar*] forms of communitarian economy wherever there are more communitarian networks, articulations and projects.[59]

59   García Linera, 'El "descubrimiento" del Estado', in Pablo Stefanoni, Franklin Ramírez and Maristella Svampa, *Las vías de la emancipación: Conversaciones con Álvaro García Linera* (Mexico City:

In response to this well-nigh complete turnaround in the interpretation of the relation between communism and the State – which in any
case should be no more scandalizing than the turnabouts we can find
in the work of other communist thinkers with regard to the question
of the party, to say nothing of the apostasies of the repentant that by
contrast always meet with the utmost sympathy and compassion on the
part of mainstream media – I would argue by way of conclusion that we
need to avoid two extreme and equally nefarious answers: on one hand,
the wholesale condemnation of all such articulations of the communist
hypothesis and the State in the name of a limited historicization focused
on Western Europe and on the debacles of both Soviet communism
and Eurocommunism; and, on the other, the relativist conclusion that
what may be bad for Paris or Bologna may be good for Kathmandu or
Cochabamba, or vice versa. We have use for neither arrogant universalism nor abject and ultimately patronizing culturalism. Instead, what we
need is a comprehensive and collective rethinking, without epic or apostasy, of the links between communism, the history and theory of the State,
and the history and theory of modes of political organization – with the
latter including not only the party but also the legacy of insurrectionary
mass action and armed struggle, which in the context of Latin America,
Asia and Africa is certainly at least as important as, if not more so than,
the old questions of party and State.

As for those of us who, like Badiou or Negri, want to have no dealings
with any state apparatus whatsoever, not to mention those communists

Ocean Sur, 2008), p. 75. There is no shortage of critics of this defence of the idea of empowering
communism from within the State. One of the most eloquent among these critics is Raquel Gutiérrez
Aguilar, who most recently studied with John Holloway in Mexico. See especially 'Cuatro reflex-
iones finales', in *Los ritmos de Pachakuti* (La Paz: Ediciones Yachaywasi/Textos Rebeldes, 2008), pp.
299–313. Among the array of movements and insurrections in Bolivia's recent history, she distinguishes two main trends, one communitarian and anti-statist; the other national-popular and always
aimed at taking over the power of the State. For a similar assessment, see Forrest Hylton and Sinclair
Thomson, *Revolutionary Horizons: Past and Present in Bolivian Politics* (London and New York: Verso,
2007), pp. 127–43. James Petras and Henry Veltmeyer are even more critical of MAS and the
Morales/García Linera electoral formula, in *Social Movements and State Power: Argentina, Brazil, Bolivia,
Ecuador* (London: Pluto Press, 2005), pp. 175–219. Finally, it should be noted that García Linera
himself lays out the possible options and outcomes of an 'indigenous' State for Bolivia, in 'Autonomía
indígena y Estado multinacional', pp. 240–2; and in 'Indianismo y marxismo. El desencuentro de
dos razones revolucionarias' (originally from 2005), reprinted in *La potencia plebeya*, pp. 373–92. He
soberly concludes: 'What remains to be seen about this varied unfolding of Indianist thought is if it
will be a worldview that takes the form of a dominant conception of the State or if, as seems to be
insinuated by the organizational weaknesses, political mistakes and internal fractures of the collectiv-
ities that vindicate it, it will be an ideology of a few political actors who merely regulate the excesses
of state sovereignty exercised by the same political subjects and social classes who habitually have
been in power' (p. 391).

like us who simply have too short an attention span to wait for the second or third coming of communism, perhaps the first and most basic task must be to abandon all images that would model the history of communism upon the life of an individual, from birth through infanthood and puberty to senility and death. All such imagery ultimately may well amount to a minimal historicization of communism in terms of its ages, at once individual and supposedly collective, but unlike a proper sequential presentation, it actually confirms the tacit assumption that communism is or was merely an episode, a passing fad or phase within the broader frame of capitalism, which by contrast appears to be eternal – or, in a vulgarization of the same argument, better adapted to an equally eternal human nature. Contrary to these modes of arguing for acquiescence to the status quo in the name of an underlying anthropology, one of Marx's most succinct definitions of the ideological work of communism comes to us by way of a quote from Jean-Jacques Rousseau's *The Social Contract*, in 'On the Jewish Question': 'Whoever dares undertake to establish a people's institutions must feel himself capable of *changing*, as it were, *human nature*.'[60] The problem with human nature, in other words, is not that it is human but that it is presented as natural. In spite of all of Althusser's best efforts at making the opposite argument, communism may very well be a humanism, or at least a subjectivism, so long as the underlying presupposition of an unchanging nature of the human subject is destroyed. As Rancière reminds us, referring to the effective political role of humanistic references in the nineteenth-century class struggle:

> The bourgeoisie proclaims: You want to stay together? That's fine, that's only 'human'. But the economy has its laws. The 'human' with which the workers' discourse replies to this has the same role as 'history' for Marx: to denounce the 'nature' that justifies capitalist domination, to overturn the bourgeois affirmation (it is impossible for the economy to function otherwise) into the revolutionary affirmation: another economy is possible.[61]

It is in this sense that the invocation of human nature, which to this day serves as the basest of ideological arguments in favour of the existing economy and which may even cast its shadow over Lenin's rhetoric of immaturity and childishness in his pamphlet against leftism, is the first

---

60   Marx, 'On the Jewish Question', *Collected Works*, vol. 3, p. 167.
61   Rancière, *La Leçon d'Althusser*, pp. 172–3.

thing that needs to be tackled on the level of ideology as part of the practice of communism – of communism not as an ideal to come but as the destruction of the current state of affairs.

The only trouble I foresee with this is that the ideological struggle, while flattering and soothing to the teachers, academics and intellectuals that most of us are, might be setting too low a common denominator, merely calling for the umpteenth repetition of a generic communism that in actual fact does not contribute to the construction of a common horizon – beyond leftism yet also in dialogue with its invaluable lessons – in which it might be possible to take stock of and learn from the most radical political experiments of our present.

4 The Second Time as Farce . . .
Historical Pragmatics and the Untimely Present

Susan Buck-Morss

1

Time and Space are forms that structure all our understandings of the world. Kant, with reason, asserted that experience is impossible without them. But in presuming that, as forms pre-existing content, they are a priori in an absolute sense – impervious to socio-historically particular spaces and times – he failed to recognize (to recall Lukács's early critique of reification) that even this idea of separating form from content is historically concrete, reflecting the formalism of mathematics that, in Kant's own space-time of the European, science-inspired Enlightenment, was the highest mode of epistemological legitimation.

By means of sophisticated critiques of progress – Eurocentricity, theories of development, and modernity's 'homogeneous, empty time' – we consider our times to have exposed and transcended this bias. Indeed, we claim to have *progressed* beyond it, our rhetoric ironically returning to the teleological mode of history-telling that we mean to leave behind. Any attempt to escape from the historical limits of our perspectives stumbles on theory's necessary relation to praxis. It is not enough to expose critically the constructedness of modernity's space-time forms without acknowledging the fact that our forms of critique are actions that themselves affect history. Our critical performances have pragmatic implications.

Marx, a European fully embedded in the history-producing, progress-believing nineteenth century, did not have our problem. Being a part of it, he placed his trust not only in historical progress, but also in the scientific status of his inquiry, its ability to rise above time. Nevertheless, with the practical success of socialist revolution in the self-proclaimed 'backward' country of Russia, theory had to bend to fact. Lenin's early death spared him from having to confront this unexpected situation in any more than provisional terms (after signing the treaty of Brest-Litovsk in 1918, he spoke of the anomalous condition of socialism succeeding in Russia but not yet in industrially advanced Germany, hence the provisional need to cede space to Germany – the territory of the Ukraine – in order to gain time[1]).

Stalin's thesis of 'socialism in one country' and his discussion of underdeveloped countries as capitalist imperialism's 'weakest link' accommodated reality in ways that encouraged the atavistic return of imperialist and autocratic Russian ghosts, now clothed in socialist garb. Trotsky's theories of uneven development and permanent revolution have proven pragmatically more fruitful, opening up paths of analysis of the global economy in terms of centre and periphery, development's own production of underdevelopment, and the progressive potential of multiple forms of resistance – insights that are still being mined for their practical, political implications.[2]

The point is not to present Marxist theory in a self-correcting, teleological narrative, but to insist that the dialectic of theory and practice passes through time. This is another way of saying, with Adorno and against Hegel, that while the truth is not *in* history (in terms of the unfolding of reason), 'history is in the truth'[3] – history, hence temporal change, is at play in the pragmatics of truth, which can never be understood as a foundational ground untouched by time. The transient nature of experience excludes an ontological foundation for theory, which necessarily builds its phenomenology on moving ground.

We can see now that it matters who owns time. If it is appropriated by the so-called West, if Europe's internal development – from ancient to feudal, to modern, to post-modern – monopolizes time's meaning, then the existence of others in space *and* time loses relevance. Indeed, their as yet unlived time has already been superseded, relegated to the baggage

---

1   See Susan Buck-Morss, *Dreamworld and Catastrophe: The Passing of Mass Utopia in East and West* (Cambridge, MA: MIT Press, 2000), p. 24. 'In his report to the Congress of Soviets in 1921, Lenin admitted: "We imagined . . . that future developments would take a more simple, more direct form," but instead "a strange situation" had developed, whereby the Revolution occurred and was possible to sustain in Russia, "one of the most backward and very weak states." Lenin's response to this anomaly in history was to picture "two worlds" that, while they might temporarily be distinguished geographically, actually referred to two stages of history, "the old world of capitalism that is in a state of confusion . . . and the rising new world, which is still very weak, but which will grow, for it is invincible"' (ibid., p. 36, quoting V. I. Lenin, cited in Myron Rush, ed., *The International Situation and Soviet Foreign Policy: Key Reports by Soviet Leaders from the Revolution to the Present* [Columbus: Merrill Publishing Co., 1970], pp. 29 and 32).

2   See the work of Justin Rosenberg (for example, 'Globalization Theory: A Post Mortem', *International Politics* 42 (2005): 2–74), and the debate on globalization theory that it sparked.

3   Theodor W. Adorno, Husserl ms., 'Zur Philosophie Hursserls' (1934–37), Frankfurt am Main, Adorno Estate, p. 141, cited in Buck-Morss, *The Origin of Negative Dialectics* (New York: The Free Press, 1979), p. 46; again: 'History enters into constellation of truth' (Adorno, 'Reaktion und Fortschritt' [1930], *Moments Musicaux*, Frankfurt am Main, p. 159, cited in Buck-Morss, ibid., p. 52).

car of the train of history.[4] The others are backward, belated, behind the times, and their co-temporality, their mere materiality within the present, can tell us nothing of historical significance.

The power-political effects of this structuring of time have not been limited to conditions of capitalist hegemony. The legitimacy of the Soviet Union depended on it as well. Socio-economic policy – the Five-Year Plans, peasant collectivization, Stakhanovite work speedups, the forced unveiling of Muslim women, the obliteration of the pre-modern cultures of the 'small peoples of the north' – all of these were justified by the same temporal structuring of time as progress, expressed vividly by one Soviet anthropologist who concluded that if the Russian people, as Stalin said, had to traverse ten years in the time of one, then the other ethnic groups, the 'indigenous people', needed to 'race like the wind' to catch up.[5] Stalin declared a war on time; as 'master of time', he decided when it needed to speed up and when it should slow down, or even come to a stop. Dictatorial power in state socialism hinged on monopoly ownership of time.[6]

If both sides in the Cold War were engaged in a struggle to appropriate time's meaning, if both relegated primitive peoples to another time than the anthropological present, this implied, by inference, the backwardness of the entire Third World – against the original meaning of that term which, as Aijaz Ahmad reminds us, was a self-chosen nomenclature by the non-aligned countries at the 1955 Bandung Conference to indicate their autonomy from both sides in the Cold War (following Mao, who had already defined the US *and* the USSR as imperialist), initiating nation-building projects that sought instead a third way to modernity.[7]

Some have suggested that the antidote to this denial of co-temporality is to multiply time, allowing for diverse, culturally particular experiences of modernity. But a purely descriptive, phenomenological approach to alternative modernities needs to be resisted for the following reasons:

1. The mere multiplicity of times distorts political judgement by placing the idea of progress too far out of play. In fact social progress *has* occurred in history, and even if the gains cannot be presumed to be secure,

---

4   For a critique of the Bolshevik *avant-garde* conception of time, which included this formulation by Trotsky, see Buck-Morss, *Dreamworld and Catastrophe*, pp. 60–7.

5   'The advanced peoples are tearing along in the fast locomotive of history . . . At the same time, the backward peoples have to "race like the wind" . . . in order to catch up' (Ibid., pp. 38–39, quoting S. M. Dimanshtein, official of the Commissariat of Nationalities [1930], cited in Yuri Slezkine, *Arctic Mirrors* [New York: Cornell, 1994], pp. 220).

6   Ibid., p. 37.

7   Aijaz Ahmad, 'Three Worlds Theory: End of a Debate', in *In Theory: Classes, Nations, Literatures* (London: Verso, 1992), pp. 287–318.

the legacy of these events is part of collective memory: the revolution in Saint-Domingue that, for the first time, radically abolished the institution of slavery; or the long century of international labour activism; or women's global activism for rights that are still held back by patriarchal, nation-state forms. What is questionable is the claim that a certain collective *owns* these progressive historical events as its exclusive possession. It is this right to inheritance that the communist spirit must challenge (illustrating Benjamin's warning that 'even the dead will not be safe' from appropriation by present rulers[8]). Such moments of historical progress belong to no one because they belong to everyone. In terms of historical pragmatics, the logic of their after-life is socialist: their memory increases in value by being shared.

2. The ontological assertion of multiplicities distorts political understanding by glorifying foundational narratives of cultural/civilizational authenticity when in fact people today are living culturally porous lives under the far more universal subjective conditions of capitalism, urbanism and hybridity, so that the conception of authenticity underpinning much indigenous and fundamentalist politics tends to promote mythical constructs and ideological obfuscations – in short, *in*authentic political subjectivities.[9] As a pragmatic by-product of such theorizing, cultural production is made to bear the brunt of political responsibility. It leads, for example, to the current pressure on artists to *do* the work of politics for us. Their ubiquitous spectacular performances expose both the necessity and the impossibility of political activism within proliferating art worlds, the structural logic of which artists can neither escape nor decisively engage.

3. As a pragmatics of social movements, ontologies of difference lead to splinter-interest coalitions that lose what Marx saw clearly as the power of the politically ascending class, the fact that its own self-interest is expressed in universal terms, so that it can claim with justification to act for the good of all humanity. (Affirming Marx's insight, we can nonetheless insist that

---

8   'Every age must strive anew to wrest tradition away from the conformism that is working to overpower it. The Messiah comes not only as the redeemer; he comes as the victor over the Antichrist. The only historian capable of fanning the spark of hope in the past is the one who is firmly convinced that *even the dead* will not be safe from the enemy if he is victorious. And the enemy has never ceased to be victorious' (Walter Benjamin, Thesis VI, 'On the Concept of History', *Selected Writings*, vol. 4, ed. Michael W. Jennings, trans. Edmund Jephcott [Cambridge, MA: Belknap Press of Harvard University Press, 2003], p. 391).

9   For this critique, see Candido Mendes, 'Difference and Dialectics of Reality', Academy of Latinity Reference Text for the Conference on 'Human Rights and their Possible Universality', Oslo, 2009 (Rio de Janeiro: Academy of Latinity, 2009).

no class owns this good as its exclusive, hereditary possession. Political virtue is not an inheritable property – not by liberal democrats, or the proletariat, or the descendants of slaves).

Without the moment of communism/universalism, both in the articulation of a political programme and in its inheritance by those who come afterward, the dominant strategy for superseding cultural particularity has been to go below collective politics to the individual, as understood by neo-liberalism. The individual subject, armed with abstract, universal rights and self-chosen identities, then confronts, as its ideological correlate, those multiple, retroactive forms of cultural populism that its self-understanding is complicit in constructing: fascist nationalism, fundamentalist dogmatism, racist xenophobia. Liberal theories of human rights based on difference suffer from this individualist articulation of the problem, and leave the door wide open for hegemonic actors to seize pragmatic, proprietary control of collective claims.

Even in the case of more moderate forms of cultural populism such as Third World nationalism, there is no direct path from anti-imperialism to human progress. When Ahmad criticizes the Bandung nations' protest against imperialism in terms of its historical pragmatics, he is right on target:

> The striking feature of the Three Worlds Theory as it passed through its many versions was that this theory, unlike all the great modern theories of social emancipation – for democratic rights, for socialist revolution, for the liberation of women; indeed, anti-colonial nationalism itself – arose not as a people's movement, in an oppositional space differentiated from and opposed to the constituted state structures, but, in all its major successive variants, as an ideology of already-constituted states, promulgated either collectively by several of them, or individually by one distinguishing itself from another . . . To the extent that it evoked the ideology of anti-colonial nationalism, its most striking feature was that the invocation came at a historical juncture and from particular countries when, and where, the revolutionary content of that anti-colonial ideology – namely, decolonization – had already been achieved.[10]

I want to argue on theoretico-pragmatic grounds, that is, as a principle for action in our own era, that there is *one* time, in which all partake, inside and out, present and past, in ways that blur these hypostasized boundaries

---

10   Ahmad, *In Theory*, p. 292.

irrevocably. As a corollary, against the left's eternal search for the enemy (is it capitalism? the capitalist class? imperialism? the global market? Western hegemony? cultural homogenization? Americanization? ecological devastation?), this claim challenges us to engage in a pragmatics of progress that is not based primarily on identifying an enemy Other. Note that my use of the term pragmatics has nothing to do with recent debates between Apel and Habermas that revolve around language theory (rhetoric, discursive consensus, the performativity of speech acts). Pragmatics here is closer to John Dewey's understanding, which in turn was indebted to the Hegelian-Marxist dialectic of theory and practice. It has to do with the practical implications of theory expressed within specific historical conjunctions.

2

The Hegelian dialectic of progress, the optimistic scenario of world history as inevitable transcendence through negation, was long ago stripped of legitimacy. In its wake, there has been an almost exclusive emphasis by the left on critical epistemology, the moment of negation, as if critique were all that is required of philosophy. There is another potentiality of the dialectic, however, one that has largely been overlooked by philosophers and politicians alike.

Let us recall that the Hegelian dialectic relies on a triad of meanings contained within the word *Aufhebung*. One is, indeed, negation, exemplified by algebraic mathematics: equivalent terms on both sides of an equation nullify each other; they cancel each other out (*sie heben einander auf*). A second meaning is the now-discredited transcendence of negation, the overriding synthesis, the 'supersession', that turns history's contradictions into progress as the (divinely guaranteed) cunning of Reason. But the verb *aufheben* has a third meaning as well. It is the German expression for 'to keep, to save', as in saving a material trace, a memento of the past. I would like for us to keep, to save, *this* meaning. It bears affinities with Walter Benjamin's idea of *rescuing* the past.

Of course, Marx paid even less attention to the conserving, rescuing gesture than did Hegel, whose dialectical logic was more scrupulous. Recall the famous passage at the beginning of Marx's *Eighteenth Brumaire of Louis Bonaparte*:

Hegel remarks somewhere that all great world-historic facts and personages appear, so to speak, twice. He forgot to add: the first time as tragedy, the second time as farce . . .

Men make their own history, but they do not make it as they please; they do not make it under self-selected circumstances, but under circumstances existing already, given and transmitted from the past. The tradition of all dead generations weighs like a nightmare [*Alptraum*] on the brains of the living. And just as they seem to be occupied with revolutionizing themselves and things, creating something that did not exist before, precisely in such epochs of revolutionary crisis they anxiously conjure up the spirits of the past to their service, borrowing from them names, battle slogans, and costumes in order to present this new scene in world history in time-honoured disguise and borrowed language. Thus Luther put on the mask of the Apostle Paul, the Revolution of 1789– 1814 draped itself alternately in the guise of the Roman Republic and the Roman Empire, and the Revolution of 1848 knew nothing better to do than to parody, now 1789, now the revolutionary tradition of 1793–95.[11]

History's persistence is for Marx the *Alp*, the mountain-high 'muck of the ages'[12] that weighs like a nightmare (*Alp-traum*) on the shoulders of the living. No room for melancholy here. The sooner this historical detritus is removed the better – and it *will* be removed, because the forces of history demand it. Marx's illustrative example is Cromwell citing the Biblical Habakkuk, before the revolutionaries turned to Locke's philosophy of bourgeois individualism and rights to property:

Similarly, at another stage of development a century earlier, Cromwell and the English people had borrowed from the Old Testament the speech, emotions, and illusions for their bourgeois revolution. When the real goal had been achieved and the bourgeois transformation of English society had been accomplished, Locke supplanted Habakkuk. Thus the awakening of the dead in those revolutions served the purpose of glorifying the new struggles, not of parodying the old; of magnifying the given task in the imagination, not recoiling from its solution in reality; of finding once more the spirit of revolution, not making its ghost walk again.[13]

One finds in Walter Benjamin's theory what looks like a similar observation, and yet the difference is crucial. Central to Benjamin's *Arcades Project* is the insight that new technologies, when they appear, mimic old

11   Karl Marx, *The Eighteenth Brumaire of Louis Bonaparte* (Moscow: Progress, 1937), p. 10.
12   Karl Marx and Frederick Engels, *The German Ideology* (London: Lawrence and Wishart, 1970), p. 95.
13   Marx, *The Eighteenth Brumaire of Louis Bonaparte*, pp. 11–12.

forms (the first electric light bulbs were shaped like gas flames; locomotive wheels were designed to mimic horses' hooves[14]). But developing the potentialities of the new in Benjamin's examples rests squarely on human imagination, an act of freedom that attends to the utopian possibilities latent within the technically transformed, material world. Because there is no dynamic of history that pushes irresistibly toward the socialist goal, the danger of an atavistic repetition of domination and *un*freedom is real: while property-slavery is negated and abolished, wage-slavery becomes entrenched; the socialization of production that supersedes capitalism leads to an intensification of state repression; the liquidation of bourgeois art is superseded disastrously by the political aesthetics of fascism.

Education of the imagination – a materialist pedagogy – therefore takes centre stage. Everything depends on it. But what precisely does this entail? And here is the surprise. Rather than shedding the past 'muck of the ages' as quickly as possible, relegating it to the dustbin of history, the charge of a *materialist* education is to *rescue* the past – *Aufhebung* in the unpopular, overlooked sense that I spoke of above. Nothing shows this surprising insistence in Benjamin's thought so obtrusively as his insertion of theology, wizened and deformed, directly into the prefatory thesis of his historical, materialist manifesto, 'On the Concept of History'.[15] The salvation of the socialist project is one with the rescue of theology for Benjamin, who has become the patron saint for a generation of leftists.

3

'After the death of God . . .' With these words a leading French intellectual began his contribution to a conference in Alexandria several years ago. A mere relative clause, a nod by the speaker towards what for him was Nietzsche's definitive act of secularization, clearing the ground for any discussion of relevance in the present, was for the people in the city and the region precisely a dismissal of radical, political possibility. Are we to understand this miscommunication as simply one of insensitivity to the Other, a presumed, Eurocentric universality when multi-culturality is called for? I think not. This critique, while it may salve the consciences of morally ardent leftists, does nothing to foster objective understanding of the real political situation. Let me take you to another location. It will demand a rescue of the past.

---

14   See Susan Buck-Morss, *The Dialectics of Seeing: Walter Benjamin and the Arcades Project* (Cambridge, MA: MIT Press, 1989), Chapter 5, esp. pp. 110–24.
15   Benjamin, Thesis I, 'On the Concept of History', *Selected Writings*, vol. 4, p. 389.

The place is, still, the Middle East; the time is 1964. In April of that year Malcolm X made the Hajj to Mecca, an event that signalled his transformed understanding of politics, no longer a strategy of Black Nationalism and separatism, but one of transcending race through the universality of Islam. That same year Sayyid Qutb's small book *Milestones* (*Ma'alim fi al-Tariq*) appeared, a call to action by a lay writer, in opposition to both the religious and the government establishment, to recreate the Muslim world on strictly Qur'anic grounds. The book rescued for Islam the substance of Marx's critique of socio-economic injustice, and argued – in Qur'anic terms that echoed the contemporaneous politics of liberation theology among Catholics – that obedience to God superseded the sovereign claim of any earthly power. It was the year, too, that the leftist intellectual Ali Shari'ati returned to Iran after exile in France, where he had corresponded with, and contributed to the Iranian translation of works by the Martinique-born Marxist psychoanalyst, Frantz Fanon, whose philosophy of liberation was foundational for post-colonial theory.[16] Arrested for a brief time by Shah Mohammad Reza Pahlavi, Shari'ati began his famous university lectures in Iran (including 'Fatima Is Fatima'[17]) articulating a truly *leftist* Islamic political position, drawing eclectically, *syncretically* (as opposed to Hegelian synthetics) on Marxist, Islamist, feminist, anti-imperialist and existentialist theoretical insights.[18] Two years later, the Sudanese Muslim, Mahmoud Taha, published *The Second Message of Islam*, a reading of the Qur'an that interpreted the Meccan revelations to the Prophet as universal in their truth, in contrast to the socio-historical specificity of the Medina revelations that, he argued, reflected the particular needs for pragmatic governance, given the customs and consciousness of the times: the Meccan revelations express radical racial and sexual equality.

Malcolm X was assassinated in the United States in 1965 (the plot involved the US Nation of Islam or the FBI, or both[19]). In 1966 Sayyid

---

16 Fanon died of leukaemia in 1961.

17 For excerpts, see www.shia.org/fatima.html

18 See the new biography by Ali Rahnema, *An Islamic Utopian: A Political Biography of Ali Shari'ati* (London: I. B.Tauris, 2009).

19 In the 1970s, the public learned about COINTELPRO and other secret FBI programmes directed towards infiltrating and disrupting civil rights organizations during the 1950s and 1960s. John Ali, national secretary of the Nation of Islam, was identified as an FBI undercover agent. Malcolm X had confided in a reporter that Ali exacerbated tensions between him and Elijah Muhammad. He considered Ali his 'archenemy' within the Nation of Islam leadership. According to the Wikipedia entry for Malcolm X, on 20 February 1965, the night before the assassination, Ali met with Talmadge Hayer, one of the men convicted of killing Malcolm X.

Qutb – former functionary in the Egyptian ministry of education, who became the intellectual inspiration for the Muslim Brotherhood (founded by Hassan al-Banna in 1928), and who spent years in Nasser's prisons, where he was tortured – was executed for alleged conspiracy against the Egyptian government. Ali Shari'ati died suddenly in Southampton, England, in 1978, just months before the outbreak of the Iranian Revolution (SAVAK, the Shah's secret police, remain the suspect). In 1983 Mahmoud Taha was executed for his views by the Sudanese dictator Numeri, who was backed at the time by the Sudanese chapter of the Muslim Brotherhood.[20]

All of these historical actors were part of the 1960s generation – a *global* generation, and this is the point. When biographically lived time crosses collective time – this historical conjuncture makes a generation. We are born twice, the first time into a culturally specific world of particulars: ancestral names, class backgrounds, family circumstances, religious traditions and educational possibilities. But the second birth is into the universal temporal dimension of history, and this second temporal baptism bestows upon us what Benjamin called a *'weak* messianic power'.[21]

The conjuncture of the personal and the political that makes a generation is a shared moment of lived time, the materialization of a transitory field of action. Why is a generation's messianic power characterized as 'weak'? A materialist-Marxist reading would interpret this as an acknowledgement of the limits of subjectivity given the priority of objective historical forces, and also the precariousness of manifesting such power given everything ideological that is stacked against its clarity of expression. This latter obstacle applies not only to the ideological force of the ruling class, but also to the existing ideologies of opposition. (Who on the streets of Paris, Berkeley, Athens, Mexico City, or Tokyo in the 1960s was aware of Qutb and Shari'ati? Who on the streets of Cairo or Tehran expressed solidarity with Taha or Malcolm X?) At the same time, objective crisis is not sufficient to propel a new consciousness adequate to the moment. (Benjamin's own generation, as he in 1940 was all too aware, failed to transform the crisis of global depression into a socialist future through a radical redemption of tradition.)

There is a blindness to institutionalized education that passes down the authority of tradition, a mental timidity, born of privilege or just plain laziness, that cloaks itself in the heavy bombast of cultural heritage and

20   The Muslim Brotherhood later recanted this decision.
21   Benjamin, Thesis II, 'On the Concept of History', *Selected Writings*, vol. 4, p. 390.

historic preservation. It generates enormous resistance to trespassing conceptual boundaries or exceeding the limits of present imagination, rewarding instead the virtues of scholastic diligence, disciplinary professionalism and elitist erudition, all escape routes from the pragmatic necessity of confronting the new. Indeed, extreme discomfort is caused by the truly new, the truly 'contemporary', that which Nietzsche called the 'untimely' – those aspects of the present moment that simply do not fit our established traditions or modes of understanding. At the same time, the contemporary cannot be understood *without* the past, hence the political centrality of a historical, materialist education that constructs new genealogies, breaking with traditions by passing through them.

It is at this point that the issue of universality becomes concrete. We – all of us alive today – who may have nothing more nor less in common than sharing *this* time, share as a consequence precisely the *untimeliness of the present* – the truly new, that none of our knowledge traditions has anticipated. The attempt, nonetheless, to seize the contemporary and stuff it back into the Procrustean bed of tradition, destroying precisely its global newness, is a moment of political danger. *This threat entails not merely a farcical repetition of past history, but an annihilation of future history's potential.* It opens the door to a reactive return to the past via trans-historical assertions of identities and continuities, whereby the new is flattened into that which has always been, reifying our individual identities within eternally fixed collectives, that are remembered as perpetually at war with each other. Political judgements are correspondingly ossified, based on fictive, ontological constants: there are determinately good collectives, but others are by definition evil; there are true beliefs while others are heretical; there are actors who are perennially *à propos* and others generically, if not genetically, behind the times.

A generation's messianic power demands the historical convergence of two ruptures. The first, albeit man-made, is objective. It is the moment of economic, military or ecological crisis, the 'shock and awe' that endangers the continuity of biographically lived time, the history of the individual.[22] The second rupture concerns the hidden potentialities of the present, the untimeliness of our time that demands in response a rupture in collective imagination, a transforming rescue of tradition that is the antithesis of reactive return.

---

22   See Naomi Klein, *The Shock Doctrine: The Rise of Disaster Capitalism* (New York: Metropolitan Books, 2007).

4

How does this set the terms for a historical, materialist pedagogy? Consider a recent theoretical discussion: Alain Badiou has provided an analysis of the historical moment of 'rupture' in terms of the 'event', encouraging us to return to the past and rescue it anew. Moreover, this is a rescue of theology in the literal sense. His prototype of the transforming event is the conversion of St Paul. And, as a Marxist, materialist and atheist, he insists on the totally secular character of this rescue, that is to be made fruitful for revolutionary politics today. Has not Badiou's Paul, then, fulfilled all of our criteria for a historical, materialist pedagogy, a transformation of intellectual imagination, one that already bears a temporal label as 'post-secular'? Has it not led to new genealogies of Western thought, expressed in a general discussion regarding the historical and political phenomenology of St Paul's event (amongst Žižek, Agamben and others)?

Badiou is modern, *au courant*, but he is not contemporary, not *against* the current. By returning to the Western tradition, *yet again* 'putting on the mask of St Paul' (Marx!) in order to speak politically of the rupturing power of the event, the pragmatics of his action reinforces that tradition and obliterates change, weakening the messianic, political power of the present that he intends to affirm.

Consider now the pragmatics of Sayyid Qutb. I am not interested in Qutb the man, his prudery, his repressed eroticism, his anti-American distaste for Colorado church socials or the 'noisy' jazz of 'Negroes' that 'whets their sexual desires'.[23] Political pragmatics cannot be judged *ad hominem*, that is, by the character of the actors (significant only in the dimension of biographical time), but, rather, by the messianic power of their intervention. What Qutb accomplished, in *Milestones* specifically, was the mobilization of tradition for politically radical engagement – not only against US *and* USSR imperialism, but also against the Islamic religious establishment that had made its peace with Egypt's dictatorial status quo.

In terms of historical pragmatics, the radical universality of Qutb's act lies not in his revival of Shari'a, but in his rescue of the revolutionary core of theology. Relentlessly criticizing the 'transfer to man [of] one of the greatest attributes of God, namely sovereignty', the work of Qutb, a Sunni, connects laterally in time with Latin American liberation theology,

---

23   See the Wikipedia entry for Qutb. This is indicative of the standard Western description.

as well as with the Christian-based civil rights movement in the United States. The left-interpretation of the Islamic revival by Shari'ati, a Shi'ite, brings him fully into this politically powerful constellation of thinkers who, in Qutb's words, consider religion not merely a belief, but a political practice, 'a declaration of the freedom of man from the servitude to other men'.[24]

Rescue here takes on concrete form. If we in the so-called West stick to our Western stories, content to criticize our critical critics, or to resurrect our own dusty thinkers of the past for a post-secular present defanged of religion's revolutionary power; if we do *not* rescue the progressive moments in present-day religious writers – Qutb, Shari'ati, and so many others – whose political actions we have neglected even to see, but who belong objectively to *our* time and who are, in the uncomfortable sense, our *contemporaries*, if we continue to ignore their highly influential work, abandoning them on the field of political imagination, then we allow their legacy to be taken over by those all too eager to appropriate it for their own hegemonic projects. A relevant anecdote: Nathan Coombs writes, 'When *Culture Wars* approached me to review a release from Verso's Radical Thinkers series, I responded "great, give me Ali Shari'ati". But Shari'ati was not in the collection.'[25]

It is easy to misunderstand my point here. I am not saying that we need to affirm everything in Qutb's or Shari'ati's writings, adhering to some notion of revolutionary solidarity with any and all who criticize the present order, nor am I advocating a Foucauldian glorification of the Iranian Revolution itself. I am arguing something more radical. It is that the writings of these deeply reflective intellectuals need to be engaged because they are our contemporaries, and only with the help of their think-ing are we able to think anew, strengthening the '*weak* messianic power' of our generation. (It needs to be noted that Shari'ati, like so many Islamic intellectuals, 'knows Western philosophy inside out'.[26]) Yes, we need to take the radical core of religion seriously, because in our time revolu-tionary power depends on its rescue and reinvention, and not on some

---

24   Sayyid Qutb's book *Milestones* can be downloaded in English translation at www.scribd.com. The quotations here are from that download, pp. 9 and 58.
25   See Nathan Coombs' review of Rahnema's biography of Shari'ati (above, note 18) for *Culture Wars*, 'Ali Shari'ati: Between Marx and the Infinite', available at www.culturewars.org.uk (posted May 2008).
26   'Nothing in his work suggests a return to the good old days, but rather leans towards existential concerns about the role of the intellectual and the necessity of decisive action, echoing aspects of Kierkegaard, Fanon, Husserl and Sartre' (ibid.).

facile assertion that 'we' have now progressed beyond religion, when the vast majority of the world's population is excluded in that statement.[27] At the same time, our rescue saves Shari'ati from appropriation by Iranian reactionaries as a tool of the ruling class – it is Benjamin's work that we do. Coombs writes: 'Thus it is not just that here in the complacent, naïve West we don't have the gumption to truly know Shari'ati, but that even in his native Iran, the true character of his work remains veiled.'[28] Our political responsibility, then, extends far beyond the rescue of the particular intellectual traditions into which we happen to have been born.

Such theoretical pragmatics implies a different criterion of political judgement. Rescue is tentative, decentralized, eclectic and often not theoretically coherent. It is syncretic rather than synthetic. Adopting a *radical* neutrality, dedicated to widening the field between enemy sides, a space where one is free to be neither 'with us' nor 'against us', we affirm fragments of incompatible discourses, judged by their pragmatic truth. Our task is to open up a theoretical terrain wherein Afghan women can demonstrate openly against Islamist laws that would fetter their autonomy, *without* this action being sucked into the ruling hegemony of the West. We will not succeed if we continue to read only Western writers, or only writers from the non-West who enter into our debates on our terms. It will not happen if we remain within the comfort zone of any civilization into which we happen to have been born. Communism for our time demands this re-articulation, this rescue of the left, but such a time is only slowly forthcoming.

---

27   'It would be all too easy to strike at Shari'ati with the same stratagem as the aforementioned writers [Badiou, Eagleton, Žižek, Agamben], i.e., to find within his philosophy the radical break and attempt to shake off the religious baggage. But alas the Idea of Shari'ati will never buckle to such a convenient formula. Religion is inscribed deep within his thought, is what made his writings ascend to public prominence' (ibid.). Badiou speaks of 'Islamism' as an example of his theory of 'the obscure subject' – 'formally fascistic' and 'nihilistic' – in *Logiques des mondes* (Paris: Seuil, 2006), pp. 67–8. He has, however, qualified that critique in a 2004 interview, doubting that there is any political value in the term 'political Islamism', whereas 'political Islam' he calls 'absolutely contemporary' (Alain Badiou, 'Las democracias están en guerra contra los pobres', *Revista N*, 23 October 2004; available at www.clarin.com). See also Alberto Toscano, 'The Bourgeois and the Islamist, or, The Other Subjects of Politics', in Paul Ashton, A. J. Bartlett and Justin Clemens (eds), *The Praxis of Alain Badiou* (Melbourne: re.press, 2006), pp. 354–65.

28   Coombs, 'Ali Shari'ati: Between Marx and the Infinite'.

5 Adikia: On Communism and Rights

Costas Douzinas

1

Back in the 1980s and 1990s, Marxist intellectuals, shaken by the Gulag revelations and the collapse of the communist states, started welcoming human rights. Claude Lefort, Jean-François Lyotard, Étienne Balibar and Jacques Rancière, amongst others, participated in this move.[1] It coincided with the 'end of history' bragging of liberal capitalists and revisionist histories of the French Revolution, which emphasized its failures, terror and totalitarianism. It was a time of defeat and demoralization for the left. All that had been solid in radical thinking started melting into air.

This period of defeat, introspection and penance came to an end with the recent financial and economic crisis. The return of radical theory and politics revived the suspicion towards the facile moralism and humanitarianism of liberal democracy and postmodern culture's abandonment of universalism. In his *Ethics*, Alain Badiou dismissed the humanism of rights;[2] Slavoj Žižek, after some wavering, questioned the emancipatory potential of human rights;[3] while Michael Hardt and Antonio Negri see human rights as an indispensable tool of Empire.[4] The rejection of the earlier rights revisionism is almost complete.

Yet, this rejection is somewhat problematic. Universalism is the rallying cry of liberal humanitarians. The defence of the *sans-papiers*, a major

1 Claude Lefort, *The Political Forms of Modern Society* (Cambridge: Polity, 1986); Étienne Balibar, 'Citizen Subject', in E. Cadava, P. Connor and J. L. Nancy (eds), *Who Comes after the Subject?* (New York: Routledge, 1991); 'The Rights of the Man and the Rights of the Citizen', in *Masses, Classes, Ideas: Studies on Politics and Philosophy before and after Marx*, trans. J. Swanson (New York: Routledge, 1994); Jean-François Lyotard, 'The Other's Rights', in Stephen Shute and Susan Hurley (eds), *On Human Rights* (New York: Basic Books, 1993); Jacques Rancière, 'Who is the Subject of the Rights of Man?', in Ian Balfour and Eduardo Cadava, *And Justice for All?*, *South Atlantic Quarterly* 103, 2/3 (2004): 297.
2 Alain Badiou, *Ethics*, trans. Peter Hallward (London and New York: Verso, 2001).
3 Slavoj Žižek, *The Ticklish Subject* (London and New York: Verso, 1999), pp. 215–28; *The Fragile Absolute* (London and New York: Verso, 1990), pp. 54–69, 107–11.
4 Michael Hardt and Antonio Negri, *Empire* (Cambridge, MA: Harvard University Press, 2000), pp. 393–414.

campaign of Badiou's *Organisation Politique*, cannot avoid some version of rights-talk. Hardt and Negri's recipe for turning the claims of Empire into the expression of the radical multitude takes the form of social rights. Jacques Rancière finds in human rights a good example of the radical politics he espouses. An embarrassed flirtation between the left and rights has been renewed in a direction which combines the defence of universalism with the rejection of human rights ideology.[5] This is the time to revisit rights history and theory in the context of late capitalism. If communist practice was a denial of liberal rights, can the philosophical idea of communism save (human) rights?

2

The history of human rights has been characterized by a conflict between liberal celebration and rejection by Marxism and communitarianism. Human rights are Janus-like, they have only paradoxes to offer. They can emancipate and dominate, protect and control.[6] This ambiguous attitude permeated the radical theory of rights until recently, with the negative side more pronounced.

Marx's writings on rights formed part of his wider critique of capitalism. In feudalism, political power, economic wealth and social status coincided. The political dominance of the rising bourgeoisie, on the other hand, could be ensured precisely through the apparent loss of direct political power. The rights of man removed politics from society and ended the identification of economic dominance with political leadership. Politics became confined to the separate domain of the state. At the same time, property and religion, the main safeguards of class dominance, were turned into private institutions located in civil society and protected from state intervention through the operation of natural rights. This 'demotion' to the private realm made property more effective, and guaranteed its continued dominance. In this dialectical formulation, the main aim of natural rights was to remove politics from society and de-politicize the economy. After the separation, the state is presented as (politically) dominant, while real (economic) power lies in capitalist society. The bourgeois abandonment of the direct political power of feudal lords and kings was the precondition for the ascendancy of bourgeois society and the triumph of its capitalist principles.

---

5   Costas Douzinas, *Human Rights and Empire* (New York: Routledge, 2007), chapters 1 and 12.
6   Costas Douzinas, *The End of Human Rights* (Oxford: Hart, 2000).

In this bourgeois hall of mirrors, natural rights support selfishness and private profit. Politics and the state, on the other hand, replace religion and the church, becoming a terrestrial quasi-heaven in which social divisions are temporarily forgotten as the citizens participate in limited formal democracy. The liberal subject lives a double life: a daily life of strife in pursuit of personal economic interest and a second life, which, like a metaphorical Sabbath, is devoted to political activity and the 'common good'. In reality, a clear hierarchy subordinates the political rights of the ethereal citizen to the concrete interests of the capitalist presented in the form of natural rights.

Marx's attack on natural rights inaugurated the various strands of 'ideology critique'. First, equality and liberty are ideological fictions emanating from the state and sustaining a society of inequality, oppression and exploitation. While natural rights (and today human rights) are hailed as symbols of universal humanity, they were at the same time powerful weapons in the hands of the particular (bourgeoisie). When glossed in the rights vocabulary, ideologies, class interests and egotistical concerns come to appear natural, eternal, for the public good.

Second, rights turn real people into abstract ciphers. The abstract man of the declarations has no history or tradition, gender or sexuality, colour or ethnicity, those elements that make people real. All content is sacrificed at the altar of abstract humanity. This gesture of universalization conceals, however, their real subject: a human-all-too-human, wealthy, white, heterosexual, male bourgeois standing in for universal humanity who combines the dignity of humanity with the privileges of the elite. The emancipation of universal man subjects real people to a very concrete rule: 'the rights of man as distinct from the rights of the citizen are nothing but the rights of the member of bourgeois society, i.e. egotistic man, man separated from other men and the community'.[7]

A related argument emphasizes the statism of rights. Effective rights follow national belonging. While proclaimed on behalf of universal humanity beyond local or historical factors, only national citizens get their full protection. The gap between universal man and national citizen is populated by millions of refugees, migrants, stateless, moving and nomadic people, the inhabitants of camps and internment centres, the *homines sacri* who belong to 'humanity' but have few if any rights because they do not enjoy state protection.

---

7   Karl Marx, 'On the Jewish Question', in *Early Texts* (Oxford: Blackwell, 1971), p. 102.

Third, formal equality (the legal entitlement to have property) treats unequals equally as a matter of right and fairness. This turns equality into an ideological construct; it also promotes material inequality, poverty and destitution and undermines close human relationships.

> Right by its very nature can consist only in the application of an equal standard; but unequal individuals (and they would not be different individuals if they were not unequal) are measurable only by an equal point of view, are taken from one definite side only . . . One worker is married, another not; one has more children than another and so on and so forth . . . To avoid all these defects, right instead of being equal would have to be unequal.[8]

Finally, Marx's critique of specific rights was scathing. They proclaim negative freedom based on a society of isolated monads who see each other as threats. The right to ownership is nothing more than the protection of private property of the means of production. Freedom of opinion and expression is the spiritual equivalent of private property, a claim fully validated in the era of Murdoch, Turner and Gates. Anticipating the recent bio-political turn, Marx argues that the right to security is the only real right. It constructs artificial links between (fearful) individuals and the state and promotes the ultimate social value, law and order. Policing, the 'supreme concept of bourgeois society, the insurance for [bourgeois] egoism',[9] undertakes to keep social peace and public order in a conflictual society.

Marx however did not dismiss rights out of hand. Commenting on the 1848 Revolution, he spoke of a different right: 'The right to work is, in the bourgeois sense, nonsense, a wretched, pious wish. But behind the right to work stands power over capital. The appropriation of the means of production, their subjection to the associated working class. That is, the abolition of wage labour, capital and the mutual relationship.'[10]

The communist revolution will realize the universal promise of rights by negating moralistic form and idealist content. Freedom will stop being negative and defensive and will become a positive power of each in union with others. Equality will no longer mean the abstract comparison of unequal individuals but catholic and full participation in a strong commu-

---

8   Karl Marx, 'Critique of the Gotha Programme', in *Selected Writings*, ed. David McLellan (Oxford: Oxford University Press, 1977), p. 569.
9   Marx, 'On the Jewish Question', p. 104.
10   Karl Marx, 'The Class Struggle in France: 1848 to 1850', *Selected Writings*, p. 88.

nity. Property will cease being the limitation of each to a portion of wealth to the exclusion of all others and will become common. Real freedom and equality look to the concrete person in community, abandon the formal definitions of social distribution, and inscribe on their banners the principle 'from each according to his ability, to each according to his needs'. For this to happen the political revolution symbolized by the rights of man must be superseded by a social revolution which will lead to the emancipation of humanity.

3

The Marxist philosopher who most emphasized the paradoxical action of rights was Ernst Bloch.[11] Bloch retains the main elements of Marx's critique of rights but discovers in the tradition of natural law the historically variable but eternal human traits of resisting domination and oppression and of imagining and fighting for a society in which 'man will walk upright'. There can be no real foundation of human rights without an end to exploitation and no real end to exploitation without respect for rights.

Bloch's criticisms of the illusions of 'bourgeois natural law' are devastating. But human rights hail also from the tradition of critique of power, convention and law and have developed in two directions. Initially, rights were associated with *dominium*, possession and property, the legal dominance over things and people, and were invented in order to protect creditors from debtors.[12] Human rights emerged from this early right to property but were 'adopted in a quite different way by the exploited and oppressed, the humiliated and degraded. It is precisely this that appears in its incomparable second sense as the subjective catchword of the revolutionary struggle and actively as the subjective factor of this struggle.'[13] Bloch concludes that a historically enduring sense of resistance and rebellion shows the human 'intention of freeing themselves from oppression and installing human dignity, at least since the time of the Greeks. But

---

11   Bloch's combination of utopianism, interest in natural law and qualified support for the communist states meant that he did not feature in the pantheon of Western Marxists, despite his affinity with Walter Benjamin and the Frankfurt School. See Vincent Geoghegan, *Ernst Bloch* (London: Routledge, 1996), and J. O. Daniel and T. Moylan (eds), *Not Yet: Reconsidering Ernst Bloch* (London: Verso, 1997).

12   See Richard Tuck, *Natural Rights Theories* (Cambridge: Cambridge University Press, 1979), Chapter 1.

13   Ernst Bloch, *Natural Law and Human Dignity*, trans. Dennis Schmidt (Cambridge, MA: MIT Press, 1987), p. 217.

only this will is immutable, and not . . . "man" and his so-called eternal right.'[14]

Bloch's *Natural Law and Human Dignity* is the most advanced Marxist reading of the history and philosophy of human rights. Influenced by German idealism and Marx's early writings, and penned at the height of the Cold War, it adopts an evolutionary philosophy of history and prophesies the realization of the *humanum* in communism. Radical human rights condemn bourgeois legality while at the same time realizing their kernel, the principle of hope of (socialist) humanism.

This type of Marxist historicism and humanism came under devastating attack from Althusserian and poststructuralist philosophy. Yet Bloch's insistence on the will to resist and rebel, freed from any humanist idealism, can help resituate the radical potential of normativity. If progress is no longer guaranteed by historical necessity and the revolutionary wager has been firmly placed on the long odds of the (coming) event, how can values and norms prepare the epiphany and the fidelity necessary for its realization? If radical change is not the linear unfolding of the human spirit, but a rare and unpredictable instance of eternal return, how does the event link with moral imperatives and psychological motivations? As Peter Hallward puts it, 'isn't there a danger that by disregarding issues of motivation and resolve at play in any subjective decision, the militants of truth will preach only to the converted?'[15] Is there a synchronic constant beyond historicism and finitude that moves people to answer the call of Badiou's 'void' and change the situation?

Radical philosophy tends to neglect such questions as secondary or 'superstructural'. Yet Antigone's defiance, Paul's conversion and Lenin's resoluteness did not emerge *ex nihilo*. The militants are partly prepared and supported by norms and beliefs pre-existing the dramatic act and leading to their abiding fidelity. Following Badiou's terminology, we can call them the normative pull of the void or, with Žižek, the normativity of the real. Where does this pull come from? What prepares the militant subjects? As rights are becoming the dominant language of politics, with all the problems this entails, we need perhaps a genealogy of radical normativity.

---

14   Ibid., p. 191.
15   Peter Hallward, 'Introduction', in Hallward (ed.), *Think Again: Alain Badiou and the Future of Philosophy* (London: Continuum, 2004), p. 17.

4

The Anaximander fragment, the oldest extant Greek text, reads: 'but where things have their origin, there too their passing away occurs according to necessity; for they are judged and make reparation (*didonai diken*) to one another for their *adikia* (disjointure, dislocation, injustice) according to the ordinance of time'.[16] Heidegger uses the fragment to confirm his fundamental ontology. The proper presence of beings is 'lingering awhile'. When they present themselves, they cannot be out of joint (*adikia*); on the contrary, they are joined with others (Heidegger translates *dike* as joint or jointure). But Being withdraws as it reveals itself in beings, conceals itself and keeps to itself. In this process of unconcealment/concealment, beings are cast adrift in errancy, and 'history unfolds . . . Without errancy there would be no connection from destiny to destiny: there would be no history.'[17] *Adikia* is the disorder of Being, its concealment accompanying its unconcealment or lingering.

Derrida returns to Heidegger's reading in *Specters of Marx*, agreeing with the ontological direction. Derrida objects, however, to the one-dimensional interpretation of *dike* and *adikia*, which emphasize pacific jointure and care. For Derrida, the centrality of *adikia* must be reinstated. There is disjuncture and dissension in Being, a dislocation that animates the relationship with the other than being, with the other as other and with death.[18]

Derrida's return to Being as dissension can help us develop an ontological thinking of *dike* as the response to enduring disorder and conflict (*adikia*). Following this correction, the fragment can be paraphrased as

16   This translation combines elements from a number of translations emphasizing both the ontological and normative character of the fragment with its abundance of terms such as *dike*, *adikia* and *tisis* (reparation). Nietzsche, in his early *Philosophy in the Tragic Age of the Greeks*, translates: 'Whence things have their origin, they must also pass away according to necessity; for they must pay the penalty and be judged for their injustice according to the ordinance of time.' Hermann Diels translates: 'but where things have their origin, there too their passing away occurs according to necessity; for they pay recompense and penalty to one another for their recklessness, according to firmly established time' (*Fragment of Presocratics*, quoted in Heidegger, *Early Greek Thinking* [New York: Harper Row, 1984], p. 14). Finally, J. M. Robinson translates the fragment as 'Into those things from which existing things have their coming into being, their passing away too, takes place according to what must be; for they make reparation to one another for their injustice according to the ordinance of time' (*An Introduction to Early Greek Philosophy* [Boston: Houghton Mifflin, 1968], 34). Martin Heidegger, in 'The Anaximander Fragment', in *Early Greek Thinking*, trans. D. F. Krell and F. Capuzzi (New York: Harper and Row, 1975), examines the various (mis)translations of the fragment.
17   Heidegger, 'The Anaximander Fragment', p. 41.
18   Jacques Derrida, *Specters of Marx: The State of Debt, the Work of Mourning and the New International* (New York: Routledge, 1994), pp. 23–9.

follows: 'An archaic *aдikia,* dissension or conflict, animates the unconcealment of Being. It endures in human history which is the unfolding (*tiлiл*)
of *aдikia's* overcoming (*дike*).' What creates this dislocation or injustice?
How is the reparation calculated and paid? [19]

An early answer is given by Sophocles in the *Oдe on Man,* the superb
choral song from *Antigone*:

polla ta дeina kouдen anthropou дeinoteron pelei (332).

Numberless wonders (*дeina*), terrible wonders walk the world
but none more wonderful and terrible (*дeinoteron*) than man.

Heidegger's reading of the song places power, violence and conflict at
the centre of history. *Deinon,* the key word, has two meanings: first, it is
man's violent and creative power, evident in *techne* (knowledge, art and
law). Secondly, *дike* is an overpowering power, the order and structure
into which humanity is thrown and has to struggle with. *Techne* confronts
дike and violently tears asunder the order of Being, using violent poie-
sis against *дike's* overpowering dispensation. In this confrontation, man
stops being at home and both home and the alien are disclosed. Humanity
opens paths and sets boundaries, introduces laws and institutions, masters
earth and sea.[20] *Techne* and *logoл* make manifest the manifold of beings and
humanity's own historical becoming.

But *дike,* the overpowering order, can never be fully overcome. It tosses
pantoporoл man (all-resourceful and everywhere-going) back to *aporoл* (without passage and resource). Catastrophe is humanity's inescapable condition
caught up as it is in the conflict between power and overpowering, between
the violence of knowledge, art and deed and the order of the world. Abiding
disaster lurks behind every achievement as its precondition. The fragment
calls it *aдikia,* dislocation, disjointure or injustice. Humanity rises on the
breach opened by the exercise of overwhelming force on primordial *дike.*[21]

Aдikia is the cause and effect of *дike.* There is an 'aboriginal injustice in

---

19   See Jean-François Lyotard, *Heiдegger anд the 'Jewл',* trans. A. Michel and A. Roberts
(Minneapolis: University of Minnesota Press, 1990); Stephen Ross, *Injuлtice anд Reлtitution: The
Orдinance of Time* (New York: State University of New York Press, 1993), p. 4. See also a superb
exegesis of Heidegger's text in Jacques de Ville, 'Rethinking of the Notion of a "Higher Law":
Heidegger and Derrida on the Anaximander Fragment', *Law anд Critique* 20 (2009): 59–78.
20   Heidegger discusses the *Oдe on Man* in *Introдuction to Metaphyлicл,* trans. R. Mannheim (New
York: Doubleday Anchor, 1961), pp. 155 ff.
21   Ibid., p. 163.

which we share, to which we belong. Older than time, than measure and law, it owns no measure of justice of equality or inequality.'[22] The sense of injustice, which prepares the militants of revolution against the dominant order, is history's judgement and reparation for the original and enduring *aδikia*. This dislocation is in excess of any possible restitution and opens history 'according to the ordinance of time'. *Aδikia* is both the unending struggle between *techne* and *δike* and the limit between them, what keeps freedom and necessity apart.

The struggle between *techne* as thinking and *δike* as *δoxa* led to the birth of philosophy and epistemic knowledge. At the same time, the *techne/δike* antagonism motivates militant subjects. Such is the conflict between Creon's stubbornness (Hegel greatly respected his achievement and predicament) and Antigone's defiance or *ate*:

> Nor did that (*δike*), dwelling with the gods
> beneath the earth, ordain such laws (*nomous*) for men.
> Nor did I think your edicts had such force
> that you a mere man, could override
> the great unwritten and certain laws of the gods
> (*agrapta kasphale theon nomima*) (*Antigone*, lines 448–53).

Aδikia endures as the world-making struggle between *techne* and *δike*. It has political, theoretical and subjective facets. Its political form is the epoch-ally specific confrontation of human action with the order of the world. Its philosophical form explores the epochal forms of *aδikia*, of order, freedom and their entanglement. Such was Plato's quest for a theory of justice against the *δoxa* of his time. Similarly, Marx's identification of class struggle and invention of communism against triumphant capitalism were theoretical responses to the *aδikia* or disorder of capitalism.

Finally, each type of *aδikia* creates its own subjectivity by inducing subjects who resist and radically transform it. Antigone as the champion of *δike*, Prometheus of *techne*, give names to rebellious subjectivity. This subjective response results from the epochal instantiation of *aδikia*. When the *kairos* gets out of joint, an affective and/or rational sense of dislocation incites subjects of resistance and revolution. Resistance and its militants therefore take two interlinked forms: theoretical exploration of the ruling dislocation and political action to resist or redress it. The dissidents and

---

22   Stephen Ross, *Injustice and Restitution* (New York: SUNY Press, 1993), p. 10.

revolutionaries, from Prometheus to Michael Kolhaas and Che Guevara, answer the sense of disorder *aδikia* begets. History moves in this combination of politics, theory and radical subjectivity.

We can now understand why the theory of justice is the oldest failure of human thought. Since Homer, the Bible and Plato, the best minds and fieriest hearts have tried to define justice or imagine the conditions of a just society. They have failed; indeed the successive and endless 'theories of justice' are a serial recognition of this miserable failure. Justice and injustice are not theoretico-political predicates but subjective motivations. *Aδikia*'s endurance generates the common feeling that we are surrounded by injustice without knowing where justice lies. This is the paradox of justice: while the principle has been clouded in uncertainty and controversy, injustice has always been felt with clarity, conviction and a sense of urgency. We know injustice when we come across it, its truth is felt. Every time, however, a theory of justice is put into practice, it soon degenerates into another instance of injustice. Justice applied leads to (feelings of) injustice. Life starts with injustice and rebels against it. Thinking follows.

The dialectic between justice and injustice does not lead to their synthesis. Injustice is not the opposite of justice; the unjust is not the contrary of the just; suffering injustice is not the logical opposite of doing injustice.[23] *Aδikia* is both the gap between justice and injustice and the endless but impossible attempt to bridge it. It is what the symbolic order tries to suppress and the prolific theories of justice (the imaginary) to legitimize, failing each time. In this sense, the Real is a name for *aδikia*, the constituting dislocation of the social bond. As Jean-François Lyotard put it, a residue, a 'nonlinked thing'[24] or faultline beyond control, founds every community and law. It is analogous to an 'unconscious affect', encountered in the 'sharp and vague feeling that the civilians are not civilized and that something is ill-disposed towards civility' which 'betrays the recurrence of the shameful sickness within what passes for health and betrays the "presence" of the unmanageable'.[25]

This unmanageable *aδikia* has been called successively the unbridgeable

---

23   'That is what is unjust. Not the opposite of the just, but that which prohibits that the question of the just and the unjust be, and remain, raised' (Jean-François Lyotard, *Just Gaming*, trans. W. Godzich [Manchester: Manchester University Press, 1985], pp. 66–7). Derrida's 'indeconstructibility', 'incalculability' and unconditionality of justice lead to the same conclusion. Justice is always to come, but we do not know its nature and cannot theorize it besides proclaiming its radical otherness.
24   Jean-François Lyotard, 'A l'Insu (Unbeknownst)', in Miami Theory Collective (ed.), *Community at Loose Ends* (Minneapolis: Minnesota University Press, 1991), pp. 42–8, 46.
25   Ibid., pp. 44, 43.

gap between God and world, class struggle, self–other division, friend/enemy antagonism or the death drive. In all these nominations, 'the kernel of the real encircled by failed attempts to symbolize-totalize it is radically non-historical: history itself is nothing but a succession of failed attempts to grasp, conceive, specify this strange kernel'.[26] Its earliest generic name was *aδikia*.

5

The idea of communism is a response to capitalism, the modern form of *aδikia*. Do norms and maxims play a role in preparing radical change and its militant subjects? Let us pursue this question in relation to perhaps the greatest modern normative maxim: 'All men are born and remain free and equal in rights', pronounces the French Declaration of the Rights of Man and Citizen, radically transforming the political and legal universe.

The juridico-political maxim of the classical world was *suum cuique tribuere*, give everyone his due. It was both a moral and a legal principle. The Greek *δikaion* or the Roman *jus* was the morally correct and legally right answer to a social dispute. In the pre-modern hierarchical order, social status determined what was due to each, what duties masters had towards slaves, husbands to wives, Greeks to barbarians. Right and wrong revolved around the *suum*, what is properly owed to each according to his given place in the social order. Backed by a teleology of natural ends, social standing assigned roles, tasks and duties.

Classical *δike* was transformed by Christianity. The first challenge was the idea of universal spiritual equality exemplified in St Paul's statement that 'there is no longer Jew or Greek, there is no longer slave or free, there is no longer male or female; for all of you are one in Jesus Christ' (Galatians 3:28). In the fourteenth century, the Franciscan nominalists Duns Scotus and William of Ockham prepared the second attack when they argued that the historical incarnation of Christ made individuality the supreme expression of creation. Its knowledge takes precedence over that of universal forms. Abstract concepts owe their existence to linguistic practices and have no ontological weight or empirical value. For William, God has given individuals control over their lives and bodies similar to that of *δominium* or property.[27] For Duns Scotus, God's will has priority over his reason; the good exists because the omnipotent ordained it and not on account of some other independent quality.

---

26   Slavoj Žižek, *For They Know Not What They Do* (London and New York: Verso, 2008), p. 101.

27   Michel Villey, *Le δroit et les δroits de l'homme* (Paris: PUF, 1983), pp. 118–25.

The normative innovation of the French Declaration was to bring together the classical maxim of due deserts and the Christian command of universal equality. It disengaged the *suum* from social status and gave it, rhetorically at least, to 'all men'. The pre-modern (moral and legal) *jus*/right, determined by natural reason in a fixed ontological universe, turned into a set of individual rights belonging to all.

The confrontation between hierarchical teleology and individualist ontology was resolved through revolution. Revolution was not just radical socio-political change. It became a normative principle, the modern expression of *techne*. The 'right to resistance to oppression', a key political maxim of the French Declaration, became the highest form of freedom. The rights of man emerged through revolution; resistance sustains their vitality. The declaration, 'an act of war against tyrants', proclaimed revolution as modernity's *techne* and the right to revolution as freedom's due.[28] The constitutionalization of the right to revolution was as radical a normative innovation as was the proclamation of universal equality.

German idealism commended the revolution for incarnating freedom into history but rejected the Declaration's revolutionary right. Once constituent power had been constituted, the right to revolution retired. Immanuel Kant typically went to great lengths to dismiss a right to revolution as a contradiction in terms. The law cannot tolerate its own overthrow:

> Revolution under an already existing constitution means the destruction of all relationships governed by civil right, and thus of right altogether. And this is not a change but a dissolution of the civil constitution; and a *palingenesis*, for it would require a new social contract on which the previous one (which is now dissolved) could have no influence.[29]

Kant's ethico-political dislike of the right to revolution was adopted by the victorious revolutionaries and later by the human rights movement. The 1793 Declaration started weakening the revolutionary right by making it supplementary to the guaranteed rights. Only their violation (and no other injustice) could justify resistance, indicating that rights had started their long mutation from revolutionary maxims into legitimation myths.

The first epigrammatic article of the Universal Declaration of Human

---

28   Norberto Bobbio, *The Age of Rights* (Cambridge: Polity, 1996), p. 88, quoting Mirabeau.
29   Immanuel Kant, *The Metaphysics of Morals* (Cambridge: Cambridge University Press; second edition, 1996), p. 162. See also Stathis Kouvelakis, *Philosophy and Revolution* (London and New York: Verso, 2008).

Rights (1948) repeats the French statement of equal freedom. Yet no right to resistance is found in the much longer epigonal recitation. On the contrary, the preamble states that these rights are given in order to prevent revolution, and article 30 prohibits radical challenges to the political and legal system. Articles 15, 16 and 17 of the European Convention of Human Rights repeat and augment this self-serving conservatism, by allowing states to declare a state of emergency and derogate rights, outlawing attacks on the juridico-political established order and prohibiting political activities by foreigners. These provisions of human rights treaties and the associated criminal laws had dire consequences. Despite the liberal rhetoric, communist and radical parties and groups were banned in Germany, Greece, Britain and the United States, amongst others, their members sent into exile, prison or camps. The reversal of priorities between the right to revolution and substantive rights was complete.

For Kant and the legal mentality, the revolutionary event leads to a *palin-genesis*, a re-birth of nation, community or class. This is the eventuality constitutions and treaties morally reject and formally negate. As a result, the order initiated by revolution leads each time to the repudiation of its founding principle. The rights of man started as normative marks of revolutionary change. Positive human rights, their descendants, have become defence mechanisms against the possibility of resistance and revolution. The removal of the right to revolution was an attempt to foreclose radical change by making rights into an insurance policy for the established order. In this sense, the order of the world is but a species of its dislocation. This unending confrontation brings back resistance and revolution through the sense of injustice *adikia* begets. The consecrated right to revolution, the foundation and guarantor of the ongoing struggle between *techne* and *dike*, cannot be wished away. Permanent revolution is the modern condition in science and art. In politics, it has turned into a ghostly normativity, the 'right to the event' one could call it, which eternally returns as perhaps the most important moral command of modernity.

6

In the post-1989 world, rights have expanded and touch almost every part of daily existence. Democracy is presented as the exercise of a series of rights; policy priorities and decisions take the form of extensions or expansions of rights; criminal law protects the rights of victims, commercial law the rights of customers, public law upholds the rights of citizens.

Rights become negative protections against state power of all kinds – from taxation and the provision of health care to immigration policy and slum clearance; and positive projections of individual will – we all have a human right to properly functioning kitchen gadgets, a British minister recently intoned. Every individual desire and want can be dressed in the language of rights: for the affluent middle class, rights are the public and legal recognition of an unlimited and insatiable desire. In a society of free choice, it is forbidden to forbid.[30]

These developments mean that rights have become both the site and the stake of politics. Marx argued in the nineteenth century that the rights to property and religious freedom removed them from state intervention, de-politicizing and offering them the strongest protection possible. What is the effect of the contemporary proliferation of rights-talk and its colonization of major aspects of life? Adjusting Marx's pioneering work, one could claim that rights attempt to legalize social struggle: they individualize political claims, turning them into technical disputes and removing the possibility of radical change, in other words, rights de-politicize politics. In this sense, human rights operate on a dual register: they conceal and affirm the dominant structure but they can also highlight inequality and oppression. Can they help challenge oppression?

This double operation recalls the distinction between politics (*la politique*) and the political (*le politique*) and its influential recent use by Jacques Rancière.[31] Rancière defines normal politics (or 'policing') as the process of argumentation and negotiation amongst the various parts of the social whole.[32] It aims at (re)distributing benefits, rewards and positions without challenging the overall balance. Against this routine policing, politics proper is a form of disruption of the established social order. Badiou similarly defines politics as 'collective action, organized by certain principles, that aims to unfold the consequences of a new possibility which is currently repressed by the dominant order'.[33] Politics proper erupts only when an excluded group or class, the 'part of no part', demands to be included and must change the rules of inclusion and the established equilibrium. This kind of antagonism or 'dissensus' 'is not a conflict of interests, opinions or values; it is a division put in the "common sense": a

---

30   See Douzinas, *The End of Human Rights*, chapters 10 and 11.

31   See Chantal Mouffe, *On the Political* (London: Routledge, 2005), pp. 8–9.

32   Jacques Rancière, *Disagreement*, trans. Julie Rose (Minneapolis: University of Minnesota Press, 1998); *On the Shores of Politics*, trans. Liz Heron (London and New York: Verso, 1995); 'Who is the Subject of the Rights of Man?', *South Atlantic Quarterly* 103, 2/3 (2004): 297.

33   Alain Badiou, 'The Communist Hypothesis', *New Left Review* 49 (2008), p. 31.

dispute about what is given, about the frame within which we see some-thing as given'.[34] A new political subject is constituted, in excess of the hierarchized and visible list of groups, places and functions in society.[35] The inclusion of the invisible part overthrows the rules of the game and interrupts the natural order of domination. This is the political's operation *par excellence* and reminds one of Alain Badiou's event.

Based on this analysis, Rancière argues, *contra* Arendt and Agamben, that rights do not belong exclusively to subjects or citizens. Those with-out rights can equally invoke them. Human rights move back and forth between abstract statements of principle and denial in practice. This disso-nance allows the excluded to put the statements of principle to the test. Freedom and equality are not qualities people have; they are political predi-cates, the meaning and scope of which is the object of political struggles.

Rancière's attempt to save human rights for radical politics is ingen-ious but problematic. Rights have become the main stake and tool in the routine 'politics of consensus' Rancière denounces. The evolution of rights from inscriptions of constituent power to central expressions of the established juridico-political order has all but removed their radical edge. They stabilize intersubjective relations by giving minimum recognition to multiple identities; they codify the liberal ideology of limited freedom and formal equality; they express and promote individual desires, turn-ing them into the litmus test of freedom (of choice). Most rights claims reinforce the established social order. First, they accept the established balance and aim to admit peripherally new claims or claimants. Second, they turn law into the gatekeeper and protector of the social order, trans-forming the political claim into a demand for admission to the law. Law transforms social and political conflict into a set of technical problems regulated by rules and hands them over to rule experts. In this sense, rights express and promote established political arrangements and socio-economic distributions and belong to the domain of police. The rights claimant is the opposite of Rancière's political subject whose task is to transform radically the overall balance.

Successful human rights struggles marginally re-arrange social hierar-chies and mildly re-distribute the social product. Right-claims bring to the surface the exclusion, domination and exploitation and the inescapable

---

34   Rancière, 'Who Is the Subject of the Rights of Man?', p. 304.
35   For the obvious links and some differences between Badiou's and Rancière's theory of politics, see Alain Badiou, *Metapolitics* (London and New York: Verso, 2005), Chapters 7 and 8, and Rancière in the present volume.

strife that permeate social life. But at the same time, they conceal the deep roots of strife and domination by framing struggle and resistance in the terms of legal and individual remedies which, if successful, lead to small improvements and marginal re-arrangements of the social edifice. Rancière seems to agree that 'these liberties each person has are the liberties, that is the domination, of those who possess the immanent powers of society. It is the empire of the law of the accumulation of wealth.'[36] Human rights promote 'choice' against freedom, conformism versus imagination. Children are given rights against their parents; patients, students and welfare recipients are termed 'customers' and are offered consumer rights and fake 'choices'. In Western capitalist societies, freedom and choice have become the mantras of politics. Rights have become rewards for accepting the dominant order, but they are of little use to those who challenge it.

Rancière's 'excessive' subjects, who stand for the universal from a position of exclusion, have been replaced by identity and social groups seeking recognition and limited re-distribution. The excluded have no access to rights, which are foreclosed by political, legal and military means. Economic migrants, refugees, prisoners in the war on terror, torture victims, inhabitants of African camps, these 'one-use humans' attest to the 'inhuman' in the midst of humanity. They are the indispensable precondition and proof of the impossibility of human rights. The law not only cannot understand the 'surplus subject', its operation prevents its emergence. At that point we send those abroad 'medicines and clothes, to people deprived of medicine, clothes and rights'.[37] As Wendy Brown put it, rights not only 'mask by depoliticizing the social power of institutions such as private property or the family, they organize mass populations for exploitation and regulation'.[38] The dark side of rights leads to the inexorable rise in the surveillance, classification and control of individuals and populations.

7

The French Declaration created a dual normative legacy. First, 'people are born free and equal'; second, there is a (moral and legal) right to resistance and revolution. The equality maxim can be interpreted in three ways. Jeremy Bentham, following Edmund Burke, insisted that read as constative the Declaration is hopelessly misleading, a false and illegitimate

---

36   Jacques Rancière, *Hatred of Democracy* (London and New York: Verso, 2006), p. 57.
37   Rancière, 'Who Is the Subject of the Rights of Man?', p. 307.
38   Wendy Brown, *States of Injury* (Princeton: Princeton University Press, 1995), p. 99.

passage from a false *is* to an invalid *ought*. The human child is not born free but weak, vulnerable, utterly dependent on others for survival. Similarly, the infant is not born equal but inferior, pathetic, subjected to others. Natality throws us into a world not of our choosing. The accidents of class, race, gender and so on, inscribe us into hierarchies, conditions and determinations. *Dike* determines being.

Liberal legal philosophy interprets the statement as a regulative idea with limited illocutionary force. Men are not born free and equal, but ought to become so. The state of un-freedom and inequality necessitates the intervention of political and legal institutions. Yet 'even where it is recognized, the equality of "men" and of "citizens" only concerns their relation to the constituted juridico-political sphere'.[39] Liberal orthodoxy uses institutional (legal, political, military) means to spread limited freedom and formal equality. This is the basis of 'equality' legislation with its marginal effects as well as of the war on Iraq. The critique of ideology compellingly shows why the normative reading was doomed to fail. *Techne* acts as *dike*'s palliative.

Communism reads equality in conjunction with the right to resistance and revolution. The French and the Russians placed the idea of equality on the world stage through their self-authorizing revolutions. The *techne* of revolution confronted the pre-modern *dike* of world. But legal equality has reproduced the gap between rich and poor. Equality of opportunities means that outcomes on the output side will closely follow the differential inputs. Inequality created in the name of equality is an extreme symptom of contemporary *adikia*; it fuels the sense of injustice, revives the dormant right to resistance and ferments the *techne* of rebellion. Communism's normative call, which educates militants, results from the failure of the promise of equality. It turns equality from a conditioned norm into Badiou's unconditional axiom: people *are* free and equal; equality is not an objective or an effect but the premise of action.[40] Whatever denies this simple truth creates a right and duty of resistance. Late modern *adikia* pits the performative of axiomatic equality against its pale regulative version. 'The subject is only partially the subject inspired by the event . . . social agents share, at the lever of a situation, values, ideas, beliefs, etc. that the truth . . . does not put entirely into question.'[41] Axiomatic equality motivates militant subjects in late modernity.

---

39   Rancière, *Hatred of Democracy*, p. 57.
40   Badiou, *Metapolitics*, chapters 6, 7 and 8.
41   Ernesto Laclau, 'An Ethics of Militant Engagement', in Peter Hallwood (ed), *Think Again*, pp. 134, 135.

The law rejects and deletes the right to resistance and revolution. Yet, it keeps coming back like the repressed. Most modern states were founded against the protocols of constitutional legality. They are the result of revolution, victory or defeat in war, colonial occupation or liberation. Revolutionary violence suspends law and constitution and justifies itself by claiming to be founding a new state, a better constitution and a just law to replace a corrupt or immoral system. It appeals to a right to revolution which, while uncodified, accompanies like a ghostly shadow every established order. At the point of its occurrence, the uprising is condemned as illegal, brutal, evil. But when it succeeds, it is retrospectively legitimized as a social *palingenesis* and as an expression of the eternally returning right to rebel against injustice.

The founding violence is re-enacted in distorted forms in the great pageants celebrating nation, state or regime; or, is repressed in acts of enforcement of the new law and interpretation of the new constitution. The French Revolution was retrospectively legitimized by its *Déclaration des droits de l'homme*, the American by the Declaration of Independence and the Bill of Rights. These documents carry the constituent violence of their foundations, even though they have concealed it under the constituted representations and interpretations. Behind every legislative and executive act of the state lies a 'right to law' based on the constituent force that inaugurated the legal system. Similarly, law's reluctant acceptance of a limited right to protest and strike acknowledges that the right to revolution cannot be eliminated even if it is written out of the constitution.

Public disorder and insurrections are subjective responses to the *adikia* of law, and symptoms of its repressed foundations. They are routinely condemned by the ruling order as undemocratic. This happened recently during the 1984 British miners' strike, the anti-globalization demonstrations, and the Greek campaigns against the neo-liberal reforms. Yet history is full of insurrections and riots which, condemned as they were at the time, changed constitutions, laws and governments. Protests mostly challenge Benjamin's conserving violence of law, breaking public order regulations in order to highlight greater injustices. As long as the protesters ask for this or that reform, this or that concession, however important, the state can accommodate it. What the state fears is the fundamental challenge to its power by a force that can transform the relations of law and present itself as having a right to law. This 'right to law', based on the retrospective legitimation of origins, supports state action; by the same token, it remains vulnerable and subject to challenge since it exposes the violent foundations of the state and the repressed and ghostly right to revolution. This right is the impossible and forbidden kernel of law, the real that sustains normal legality and rights. It always returns like the repressed.

The same applies to the axiom of equality. The formal equality of rights has consistently supported inequality; axiomatic or arithmetic equality (each counts as one in all relevant groups) is the impossible boundary of rights culture.[42] As Badiou put it, 'anyone who lives and works here, belongs here'.[43] It means that health care is due to everyone who needs it, irrespective of means; that rights to residence and work belong to all who find themselves in a part of the world irrespective of nationality; that political activities can be freely engaged in by all, irrespective of citizenship and against the explicit prohibitions of human rights law.[44]

Paraphrasing Badiou, we can conclude that rights are about recognition and distribution amongst individuals and communities; except that there is a right to revolution. The right to resistance/revolution against whatever denies the axiom of equality forms the normative maxim of the communist idea. The combination of equality and resistance projects a generic humanity opposed both to universal individualism and communitarian closure. Universalists claim that cultural values and moral norms should pass a test of universal applicability and logical consistency, and often conclude that if there is one moral truth but many errors, it is incumbent upon their agents to impose it on others. Communitarians start from the obvious observation that values are context-bound and try to impose them on those who disagree with the oppressiveness of tradition. Both are versions of humanism which, having decided what counts as human, follows it with a stubborn disregard and finds everything that resists them expendable.

The individualism of universal principles forgets that every person is a world and comes into existence in common with others, that we are all in community. Being in common is an integral part of being oneself: a self is exposed to the other, it is posed in exteriority, the other is part of the intimacy of a self. Being in community with others is the opposite of common being or of belonging to an essential community. Most communitarians, on the other hand, define community through the commonality of tradition, history and culture, the various past crystallizations whose

---

42   Badiou, 'Truths and Justice', in *Metapolitics*, pp. 96–106.

43   Quoted in Jason Barker, 'Translator's Introduction', Badiou, *Metapolitics*, p. xv.

44   Art. 19 of the ECHR bans foreigners from exercising political rights.

inescapable weight determines present possibilities. The essence of the communitarian community is often to compel or 'allow' people to find their 'essence', common 'humanity' now being defined as the spirit of the nation or of the people or the leader. We have to follow traditional values and exclude what is alien and other.

From the communist perspective, humanity has no foundation and no ends, it is the definition of groundlessness. Its metaphysical function lies not in a philosophical essence but in its non-essence, the incessant surprising of the human condition and its exposure to the event that radically changes the world. Revolution and equality are brought together by the eternal dialectic of *adikia*, the confrontation of *techne* and *dike*. Alain Badiou in this volume argues that the idea of communism helps us prepare ourselves, our family and friends for the surprise of the event, for new possibilities out of the impossible. Yet no idea of communism and no theory of justice can achieve this without the warm grip of injustice. Outrage at injustice and the decision to confront it can only develop against the claims to order (*dike*), which today include rights and (formal) equality. Revolutionary equality is both the rejection and the sublation of rights culture.

The neo-liberal state combines the functions of capitalist enterprise and muscleman for the market. The *adikia* hypothesis and the communist response, with its centrality of the enduring struggle between *techne* and *dike*, cannot wait for the withering away of state and law. Communism cannot survive if it abandons its opposition to the capitalist state. But generic communism exists also in the here and now, when militants resist in Latin *favelas*, French *banlieues* or the Athens streets, proclaiming the equal singularity of all against the unequal differences sanctioned by the state. Its action revives the right to dissent and rebellion as the highest form of freedom. In the process, rights change from individual entitlements and possessions to a new conception of 'being in the right' or 'right-ing being':[45] giving equally to each what is due to all. It may be that only the idea of communism can save rights.

---

45   Douzinas, *The End of Human Rights*, pp. 209–16.

6   Communism: Lear or Gonzalo?

Terry Eagleton

Everyone knows who Lear is, but what of Gonzalo? Gonzalo is the courtier who in Shakespeare's last play *The Tempest* articulates a moving, beautiful vision of communism, only to be mocked for his pains by the hardboiled young cynics around him:

> . . . no kind of traffic
> Would I admit
> No name of magistrate . . .
> No occupation, all men idle, all,
> No sovereignty . . .
> All things in common Nature should produce
> Without sweat or endeavour . . . and should bring forth,
> Of its own kind, all foison, all abundance,
> To feed my innocent people.

It is a traditional enough vision of utopia: Arcadia, the Land of Cockayne, spontaneity, profligacy, fertility, superabundance, inexhaustible treasure, the blessed transcendence of labour, a bounteous plenitude unpunctured by desire. No desire, no enterprise, just an endless imaginary sucking at the great dug of a lavishly all-providing Nature. As with the Christian notion of the inexhaustible fertility of the Godhead, desire in the sense of a Faustian striving – desire as negativity, as the dynamic of a history of scarcity – gives way not to stasis, but to an infinite exploration of these unfathomable depths. Infinity in the sense of an endless linear process yields ground to infinity in the sense of this plenitude's endless self-exploration and self-delight.

The Marxist idea of communism involves the development of the productive forces, free from the stymieing and blockages of pre-history or class society, to the point where they can give birth to a surplus sufficient for the abolition of labour and the fulfilment of the needs of everyone. If this hasn't come about yet, it is among other reasons because the only historical mode of production capable of generating such a surplus – capitalism – is by a supreme irony the one which deploys it to create scarcity. The point of communism, conceived in this classical way, is not only to escape scarcity but to forget the very possibility of it. One thinks of those American heiresses in Henry James who are so fabulously rich that they don't need to think about money at all, in fact hardly have a clue what it is, as opposed to the bourgeois vulgarians who can think about nothing else. (Though George Eliot shrewdly perceived that a disdainful ignorance of money is also a kind of vulgarity.) The full-blown Marxist notion of communism is simply this situation on a collective scale. If human energies are to become an end in themselves, a great deal of purely instrumental infrastructure must first be in place. If you are to be free to turn your thoughts to higher, purer things, you need to be excessively well-heeled. To be free demands leisure, which in turn requires material resources – and if everyone is to be free, material resources beyond the wildest dreams of the most avaricious banker. In classical Marxist terms, the material base needs to be developed to the point where it can simply negate its brutally obtrusive presence and drop clean out of consciousness, like a valet who caters to your every need while remaining discreetly invisible. In this vision of the future, the material infrastructure becomes a trampoline whose point is to bounce you beyond itself. At a certain point of superabundance, the material transcends itself.

The dialectical Marxist twist is that only materiality will release you from the dull compulsion of the material. Freedom does not mean being free of determinations, but being determined in such a way as to sit transformatively loose to one's determinants; and communism, which would allow you do precisely this in material terms, is in this sense the acme of human freedom. That only the material will emancipate you from the material: this, surely, is the true riposte to the various varieties of idealism, not the claim that we must at all costs stay tenaciously loyal to how things are, or respect the density and objectivity of the material world. (So-called objective idealism is easily able to do the latter.) Just as you have to insist on the reality of social class in order to get rid of it, or as a revolutionary nationalist affirm the uniqueness of the nation so that it can eventually take its place in the community of nations, so the point of insisting on the material infrastructure in the Marxist manner is to arrive at the point where you no longer need to do so. You can then speak of something more interesting for a change, like the image of the angel in the poetry of Rilke or whether Prince Charles's ears might cause him to lift briefly off the ground on a particularly windy day. This, one might claim, is the comic dialectic of Marxism, its own peculiar brand of self-deconstruction. Socialists are in temporary, not full-time employment. Socialism is a self-abolishing project. This is one reason why being a socialist is nothing like being a Jew or a Muslim. Marxism itself belongs to the epoch of pre-history. In a communist society, its role is to wither away as soon as it decently can. What it will give way to is history proper, about which we know nothing.

In a related paradox, communism is at once the fruit of intensive productivity and its implacable antagonist. It is, so to speak, productivity turned against itself. One question that therefore arises is how long it would take us to unlearn the ingrained habits of pathological productivity, which after a while acquires a well-nigh unstoppable momentum of its own. Do we have enough time – will an already crippled and wounded Nature yield us enough time – for this massive re-education of the senses, the body, the psyche, the dispositions, of desire itself? How can this productivity undo its own enabling conditions? How can one draw upon an abundance of productive forces while at the same time spurning the cultural habits involved in their development? Isn't communism demanding of us the impossible? Does it not resemble the twisted Cold War logic of stockpiling as many nuclear weapons as possible in the hope that we can then forget about warfare altogether (since it becomes too dreadful to contemplate) and instead enjoy a perpetual peace?

Shakespeare provides us in *The Tempest* with an imaginary resolution of this contradiction by re-locating ceaseless productivity on the side of Nature rather than of humanity, thus ensuring an abundance of production along with a minimum of sweated labour. In Shakespeare's view, compulsive, unceasing, self-creating agency is very close to evil, in its incapacity to be open to the sensuous needs of others. The demonic lacks a body. It is the corporeal it finds most scandalous. Evil is virulently anti-material, unable to suffer and sympathize with the pain of others. A lot of Shakespearian villains are of this kind. Gonzalo, however, bends the stick alarmingly far in the opposite direction. Communism in his view is all about being deliciously indolent, though the play itself is none too convinced of this idleness. This is why, just before the courtier's great speech, Francisco describes the act of swimming in these terms:

> Sir, he may live;
> I saw him beat the surges under him,
> And ride upon their backs.

Here both Nature (the ocean) and humanity (the swimmer) are passive and active at the same time. To swim is to shape Nature in a way which allows it simultaneously to sustain you. It is a dialectical affair, whereas Gonzalo's ideal commonwealth is not. There is a similar, supremely delightful fantasy of an all-bounteous Nature in Andrew Marvell's great poem 'The Garden':

> What wondrous life is this I lead!
> Ripe apples drop about my head.
> The luscious clusters of the vine
> Upon my mouth do crush their wine.
> The nectarine and curious peach
> Into my hands themselves do reach;
> Stumbling on melons, as I pass,
> Insnared with flowers, I fall on grass.

In a pleasant irony, the speaker's only active expenditure of energy is to fall over.

There is a sense, then, in which the true harbinger of communism is not the proletarian but the patrician, as Oscar Wilde, a man who believed devoutly in communism in between dinner parties, was ironically aware. What better image of the indolent future than the dandy and aristocrat? Wilde thus had a wonderful political rationalization for his extravagantly privileged existence: just lie around all day in loose crimson garments reading Plato and sipping brandy and be your own communist society. In what Marx calls pre-history, being idle means that you die; in post-history, it becomes the finest way to live. This is why Wilde is both a convinced socialist and an unabashed aesthete, since he finds in the work of art the paradigm of the profoundly creative uselessness of communism. The work of art, in its ludic, pointless, gratuitous, self-grounding, auto-telic, self-determining way, offers us a foretaste of how men and women might themselves exist under transformed political conditions. Where art was, there shall humanity be.

In Marx's view, however, communism would by no means look anything like a classical work of art. Classical artworks seek a fine balance of form and content, whereas in a socialist society, as Marx puts it in the *Eighteenth Brumaire of Louis Bonaparte*, the content, in his cryptic phrase, 'goes beyond the phrase' – or, one might say, the form. He means, however, that socialism transcends the political and economic forms of the present, not that (like communism) it presents us with a crisis of representation. The capitalist social order is like a shoddy work of art, at once too abstract (the commodity form, the alienation of the state) and too myopically particular (bourgeois individualism, raw appetite). It is both an orgy of anarchic desire and the reign of a supremely bodiless reason. Socialism, like the classical or 'beautiful' work of art, strives to bring these dimensions into equipoise, but in doing so still works by *measure* – justice, equity, equality, to each according to his labour.

Communism, by contrast, is characterized for Marx not by the symmetry of the classical or beautiful artefact, but by the immeasurable excess of the sublime. It is this that he refers to in the *Brumaire* as the 'poetry of the future'. If one thinks of communism as involving the disappearance of the superstructure, as some Marxists do, this is among other things because superstructural forms simply won't be up to representing this unschematizable superabundance, which will consequently, so to speak, have to represent itself. The only relevant representational form would be what one might risk calling the form of its own content, not one external to it. As Marx writes in the *Grundrisse*: true wealth cannot be measured according to a pre-determined yardstick. In communism, the release of creative powers for their own sake is its own measure. Which is to say, not really a measure at all in the current sense of the term. For something to behave as its own measure echoes the absurd situation sketched by Ludwig Wittgenstein in his *Philosophical Investigations*, where a man exclaims 'But I know how tall I am!' and places his hand on top of his head. One thinks also of Antony's poker-faced description of a crocodile to the thick-skulled Lepidus in Shakespeare's *Antony and Cleopatra*: 'It is shap'd, sir, like itself, and it is as broad as it hath breadth; it is just so high as it is, and moves with its own organs . . .' This, so to speak, is the final refutation of exchange-value; the only problem, as Wittgenstein remarks, is that there is no more useless proposition than the identity of a thing with itself. It is not, one takes it, this kind of pointless self-referentiality that Marx has in mind. It is rather a transformation of the very idea of the commensurable, one which goes beyond the whole artificial (and bourgeois) notion of equality.

Communism is sublime because it is iconoclastic. It gives the slip to the image or icon, which is not true of socialism. That much we can extrapolate to some degree from certain powers, contradictions and possibilities in the present. Even so, we need to keep in mind the wise words of Raymond Williams in the Conclusion to *Culture and Society 1780–1950*: 'We have to ensure the means of life, and the means of community. But what will then, by these means, be lived, we cannot know or say.'[1] It would seem to follow, then, as someone once said, that of that of which we cannot speak it is better to remain silent. The only problem is that there are also urgent political reasons for not remaining silent. So let me quote St Augustine's *Confessions*, farcically substituting the word 'God' for the word 'communism': 'And what shall we say, O my Communism, my life, my holy, dear delight, or what can any one say when he speaketh of thee? And woe be to them that are silent in thy praise, even when they who speak most thereof may be accounted to be but dumb.'[2]

The 'good' sublimity of communism, as one might call it, can then be contrasted with the 'bad' sublimity of capitalism itself. Money for Marx is a kind of monstrous sublimity, an infinitely spawning signifier which engulfs all specific identities, a dissolution of determinate forms. So capitalism and communism share a common feature: they are both modes of sublimity. But whereas capitalism is sublimely unrepresentable because of its formlessness and disproportionateness, communism does indeed have a form. It is just that, like the 'law' of the artefact for Kant, this form is no more than what is created by the activity of its members, rather than a pre-determined structure into which they must be forced to fit. To this extent, one might claim, the solution to the problem of form and content is known as socialist democracy. The work of art, whose 'law' or overall form is nothing more than the concrete or practical interrelations of its individual particulars, utterly inseparable from this 'activity', is to this extent a place-holder for a political order that is yet to be realized.

Let me just add, without having time to develop the point, that the transition from socialism to communism has in this sense something in common with the Pauline transition from the realm of the Law to the domain of grace. Under the Law we are still bound to sin, just as socialism is still a matter of the state, class, political dominion (the dictatorship of the proletariat) and so on, and thus bound fast by its forms to the previous regime at the very moment it overturns it. Grace means among other things the acquired *habit* of virtue, as opposed to the idea of a series of

---

1   Raymond Williams, *Culture and Society, 1780–1950* (London: Columbia University Press, 1958), p. 355. .

2   St Augustine, *The Confessions of St Augustine* (London: Temple Press, 1907), p. 3.

strenuous Kantian or Protestant acts of will. In class society, for example, and even under socialism, cooperation or selflessness or solidarity
demands an effort, a conformity to a moral or political law; in a social
order of self-governing cooperatives, these qualities have been built into
social institutions themselves, so that we no longer need think about them
and simply act them out spontaneously as ingrained dispositions. This is
the political equivalent of what Aristotle knows as virtue.

Across this brave vision of superabundance, however, lies the minatory
shadow of Lear. *Lear* grasps the paradox that surplus, excess, is what is
natural to the kind of animals we are:

> O reason not the need! Our basest beggars
> Are in the poorest things superfluous.
> Allow not nature more than nature needs,
> Man's life is cheap as beast's.

What is supplementary to our natures is also built into them, and one
name for this dangerous supplement is culture. Unlike Gonzalo, however,
the play grasps the point that there are cruelly destructive forms of
surplus as well – as when culture, our creative surplus over Nature, fails
to ground itself in the finitude of Nature and the material body and, like
Lear himself, fantasizes that humanity is infinite. It is a fantasy that has
cropped up again in some left-wing theory in our own day. If Gonzalo's
generous-hearted vision may not be one for us, it is partly because we
know to our cost that Nature is a far from inexhaustible resource. His is
not a commonwealth in which the oil is likely to run out. So we have to
rethink that moving and beautiful image in a world increasingly niggardly
of its resources. And here the bleak world of *Lear* can be of some use.
For, as the play reminds us, communism was always in a sense about
finitude. It is about finitude in the sense that the self-development of
each is creatively constrained by the self-development of all. It is also
the case that although human needs cannot be pre-calculated, and are
not always mutually commensurable, they are not infinite either. What
is infinite about humanity is desire; and communism, as I have argued,
is about the conversion of desire in its 'linear', unstoppable sense, which
has a lordly way with material particulars, to an unending exploration
and enjoyment of the world for its own sake. What the transcendence of
material need accordingly frees us from is, paradoxically, the immaterial.
It is the immateriality of ceaseless acquisition which it seeks to rebuke.

The transcendence of the material thus returns us *to* the material, in the sense of freeing us from those wants and practices which prevent us from savouring the sheer material use-values of the world. Only through communism can we come to experience our bodies once again.

The vision of communism Lear himself articulates is thus very different from Gonzalo's – more modest, more chastened, more corporeal, based as it is on the sensitive, suffering, material body, the poor forked creature, in all its fragility and limitation. Like the young Marx of the *Economic and Philosophical Manuscripts*, Shakespeare argues his way up from an insistence on the mortal, material body to a communist ethics:

> Poor naked wretches, wheresoe'er you are,
> That bide the pelting of this pitiless storm,
> How shall your houseless heads and unfed sides,
> Your loop'd and window'd raggedness, defend you
> From seasons such as this? O I have ta'en
> Too little care of this! Take physic, pomp;
> Expose thyself to feel what wretches feel,
> That thou mayest shake the superflux to them.
> And show the heavens more just . . .
> Let the superfluous and lust-dieted man
> That slaves your ordinance, that does not see
> Because he does not feel, feel your power quickly;
> So distribution should undo excess,
> And each man have enough.

These words are wrenched on a storm-tossed heath from a mind at the end of its tether. As such, they spur us to ask, in suitably glum, apocalyptic mood, whether the species of communism we are most likely to find ourselves landed with might be, like Lear's, a catastrophic one – one born of tragic destitution rather than comic superfluity. Might it only be on the other side of some inconceivable disaster that men and women are forced by material circumstance into sharing and solidarity with one another? Not so much war communism, in short, as post-war communism? Socialism and barbarism, to be sure, are usually posed as opposites; but they may prove closer than we would wish. Such a regime might well be marked by a far greater equality and cooperativeness than we have now. But it would not be communism in the Marxist or Gonzalo sense, because it would involve neither positive nor negative freedom. There would be no negative freedom in the sense of emancipation from drudgery, and there would be no positive freedom in the sense of a superabundance of resources releasing us from the dull compulsion of the economic into mutually creative endeavour.

The idea of communism is an ancient one. It certainly runs back far beyond Gonzalo. Marxism is a relative latecomer on the scene. The originality of Marxism's conception of communism lies in its insistence on the material conditions it would require. This is an extraordinary move, since those who are entranced by remote dreams of justice and equality are usually the last thinkers to bother themselves with such quotidian matters. Like Macbeth in the scornful opinion of his wife, they desire the end but contemn the means. The problem is then how to be both a communist and a materialist. It is a question of accepting that freedom, justice, equality, cooperation and self-realization require certain enabling material conditions, while acknowledging at the same time that given our devastation of the planet, these material conditions are increasingly hard to come by. One must not lose one's grip on such political realism. But neither must one simply abandon the dream of Gonzalo as pre-environmentalist naivety.

7 'Communism of the Intellect, Communism of the Will'

Peter Hallward

Posing the question of communism in terms of its 'idea' has at least two initial virtues.[1]

In the first place, it helps to distinguish communism from its reduction purely and simply to anti-capitalism. Of course the critique of capitalism is the central concern of Marx's mature work, and remains an essential part of any account that might try to anticipate an eventual transition to a communist mode of production. Of course capitalism establishes and then intensifies some of the historical conditions within which it became possible, for the first time, to pursue the abolition of classes and inequalities in more than merely utopian terms. But to privilege the destruction of capitalism over the construction of communism is to concede too much to capitalism itself. In so far as communism is conceived only as a more or less 'inevitable' consequence of capitalism's self-destruction its formulation remains limited and compromised by the history it seeks to overcome: the more we insist that in order to think communism we must first wait for capitalism to create the conditions for its eventual self-destruction, the harder it becomes to distinguish anti-capitalist resistance from an effectively pro-capitalist enthusiasm for the full subsumption of all aspects of social life within a single, globally integrated machinery of production.

In the second place, emphasis on the idea of communism invites a certain amount of free or 'reckless' speculation, a reflection on communism as a project or possibility independent of the legacy of formerly existing communism. It rightly encourages us to dismiss as secondary the questions forever posed by the sceptical and the disillusioned, or those who want to inspect the full solution to a problem before they are willing to begin tackling the problem itself. How dare we talk about communism, they say, when we haven't come up with viable large-scale alternatives to

---

1 A considerably longer version of the second and third parts of this chapter first appeared under the title 'The Will of the People: Notes Towards a Dialectical Voluntarism', *Radical Philosophy* 155 (May–June 2009).

the market, when we haven't solved the problem of a centralized bureau-cratic state, when we haven't exorcized the ghosts of Stalin or Mao, etc. This sort of objection reminds me a little of the way otherwise 'progressive' people once talked about the end of slavery in the United States. Even a genuine democrat like Thomas Jefferson, along with virtually all his revolutionary contemporaries, balked at the question of emancipation or abolition because they could not yet imagine a practicable solution to the problem they had inherited and accepted: they could not imagine (apart from fantasies of back-to-Africa deportation) how racial reconciliation might proceed after abolition, given the legacy of brutality and resentment it had created. A similar lack of political imagination serves to preserve the still dominant sense that 'there is no alternative', and to keep communism, along with a few other ideas, firmly off the agenda.

We would do better, I think, to follow the example given by people like Robespierre, Toussaint L'Ouverture or John Brown: confronted with an indefensible institution like slavery, when the opportunity arose they resolved to work immediately and by all available means for its elimination. Che Guevara and Paulo Freire would do the same in the face of imperialism and oppression. Today Dr Paul Farmer and his 'Partners in Health', in Haiti, Chile and elsewhere, adopt a somewhat similar approach when confronted by indefensible inequalities in the global provision of health care.[2] In each case the basic logic is as simple as could be: an idea, like the idea of communism, or equality, or justice, commands that we should strive to realize it without compromises or delay, before the means of such realization have been recognized as feasible or legitimate, or even 'possible'. It is the deliberate striving towards realization itself that will convert the impossible into the possible, and explode the parameters of the feasible.

1

Marx himself was not tempted to write 'recipes for the cook-shops of the future',[3] and was famously reluctant to expand on the idea of communism. But, as is widely recognized, in Marx this idea evokes two distinct concerns. On the one hand reference to communism serves as a guid-

---

2   The Partners in Health website is www.pih.org; cf. Tracy Kidder, *Mountains Beyond Mountains: The Quest of Dr. Paul Farmer* (New York: Random House, 2004).

3   Karl Marx, *Capital I*, postface to the second edition, trans. Ben Fowkes (London: Penguin Classics, 1976), p. 98.

ing norm, the anticipation of a society organized in keeping with the old slogan, adapted from Babeuf and then Louis Blanc, 'from each according to his ability, to each according to his needs'.[4] Communism in this sense serves as a guiding principle for future development. 'In place of the old bourgeois society', as the *Manifesto* puts it, 'with its classes and class antagonisms, we shall have an association in which the free development of each is the condition for the free development of all.'[5] To work towards such an association is to strive to actualize that 'realm of freedom' which for Marx, as for Kant and Hegel before him, informs our most essential normative principle: the autonomous deployment of 'human energy as an end in itself'.[6] On the other hand, for the Marx who is relentlessly critical of merely 'utopian' forms of socialism, communism names an actual historical project. 'Communism is for us not a state of affairs which is to be established, an ideal to which reality [will] have to adjust itself. We call communism the real movement which abolishes the present state of things. The conditions of this movement result from the premises now in existence.'[7]

Debate over how best to understand the integration of these two concerns has divided partisans of the communist project from the beginning. A version of Kant's prescription of a rational principle independent of all merely empirical instantiation (an idea as 'regulative ideal') still stands at one pole of the argument; a version of Hegel's insistence on concrete, historical and institutional mediation (an idea as 'unity of concept and actuality') stands at the other. It's easy enough to recognize these two poles in the work of the two people who have sponsored this conference, Alain Badiou and Slavoj Žižek – and the comparison has often been made, not least by Žižek himself.

Badiou's refusal to compromise with the 'necessary movement of history' during the profoundly reactionary period that began in the mid 1970s has helped him to remain the most forceful and significant political thinker of

---

4   Marx, *Critique of the Gotha Programme* (Beijing: Foreign Languages Press, 1972), p. 17.
5   Karl Marx and Friedrich Engels, *Manifesto of the Communist Party* (Beijing: Foreign Languages Press, 1965), p. 59.
6   Marx, *Capital III* (Moscow: Progress, 1966), p. 820.
7   Or again, in the more emphatically Hegelian terms of the third 1844 manuscript: '*Communism* as the *positive* supersession of *private property* as *human self-estrangement*, and hence as the true *appropriation* of the *human* essence through and for man; it is the complete restoration of man to himself as a *social*, i.e., human, being – a restoration which has become conscious . . . Communism is the solution of the riddle of history and knows itself to be the solution' (Marx, *Economic and Social Manuscripts*, in Marx, *Early Writings*, trans. Rodney Livingstone and Gregor Benton [London: Penguin Books, 1975], p. 348).

his generation. He is perhaps the only great philosopher of his day who has never qualified his commitment to the revolutionary ideals of universal justice and equality. His philosophy also provides some resources for thinking the 'situated' character of a universal truth, for instance its localization in an 'evental site', or its incorporation in a 'body' shaped by regional norms of appearing or existence. Nevertheless, Badiou's insistence on the exceptional and autonomous status of an 'immortal truth' lends some force to Žižek's characterization of his philosophy as broadly Kantian in its orientation. Badiou's lifelong insistence on the primacy of formalization, on the subtraction of thought from its mediation through experience, history or relation, on the priority of Plato over Aristotle, on the generally 'thoughtless' configuration of the world in its mundane normality, etc., all indicate the more or less 'extra-worldly' bias of his conception of truth. For Badiou, a truth is not so much articulated with and through the world as it is excepted or subtracted from it, and for that very reason invested with an absolute and eternal capacity to change it.

This extra-worldly orientation continues to guide Badiou's recent reformulation of the 'communist hypothesis' itself. This reformulation assumes that 'our problem is neither that of the popular movement conceived as the vehicle of a new hypothesis', as during the 'classic' period of Marxist innovation in the mid-nineteenth century, 'nor that of the proletarian party conceived as leading it towards victory', as in a twentieth century marked by Lenin and Mao.[8] Rather than rework and strengthen central aspects of previous contributions to the communist project, Badiou seems willing to abandon them in favour of an axiomatic principle explicitly conceived as a sort of guiding norm or ideal, rather than as a concretely mediated imperative. 'It's a matter of a regulative Idea, to use Kant's terms, and not of a programme.'[9] Badiou is prepared to pay a high price to preserve this Idea in its regulative purity.

Marxism, the workers' movement, mass democracy, Leninism, the party of the proletariat, the socialist state – all these remarkable inventions of the twentieth century – are not really useful to us any more. At the theoretical level they certainly deserve further study and consideration; but at the level of practical politics they have become unworkable [*impraticables*].[10]

---

8   Alain Badiou, *De quoi Sarkozy est-il le nom? Circonstance, 4* (cf p. 53, n. 44, Paris: Lignes, 2007), p. 150.
9   Ibid., p. 132.
10   Ibid., p. 150.

Similar priorities may help to explain Badiou's relative lack of interest in recent political mobilizations in places like Bolivia, Ecuador and other Latin American countries, mobilizations that Badiou sometimes presents (on account of their apparent failure to 'advance' beyond Mao's conception of politics) as the political equivalent of mathematicians who, oblivious to the revolutionary developments of the nineteenth century, continue to remain faithful to the old Euclidean form of geometry.

Žižek, by contrast, sometimes courts the opposite danger. He experiments with the different ways in which thought and action might converge if not identify with the 'real movement that abolishes the existing state of things'. After Hegel, he conceives of freedom and truth primarily in terms of their concrete or material realization; in the process he tends to downplay autonomous and deliberate self-determination in favour of an 'extimate' process of extra-voluntary compulsion or 'drive'. The more Žižek valorizes the remorseless imperatives of unconscious drive, the more he deprives the prescription of radical political action of any clear and consistent criteria other than those of radicality itself. Depending on the situation, Žižek may urge us to withdraw and 'do *nothing*' (in moments when 'the truly violent act is doing nothing, a refusal to act'), or to embrace the impossible and thus 'do *everything*' (as illustrated by Stalin's 'revolution from above'), or again (on the model of Aristide or Chávez) to adopt the more pragmatic posture of someone who is at least prepared to 'do *something*', by accepting some of the compromises that accompany a readiness to take and retain state power.

As for Marx himself, the 'ideal' and the 'real' aspects of communism were held together by the process that works to abolish the capitalist regime of property, exploitation and inequality. 'The distinguishing feature of communism', says the *Manifesto*, 'is not the abolition of property generally, but the abolition of bourgeois property . . . [i.e.] property, in its present form, [which] is based on the antagonism of capital and wage labour' and the exploitation of the one by the other.[11] Though for Marx such abolition only becomes a viable project under the specific historical conditions of advanced capitalism, it remains first and foremost a *project* or task. What is most fundamental in Marx, it seems to me, is not the 'inevitable' or involuntary process whereby capitalism might seem to dig its own grave, but rather the way in which it prepares the ground upon which the determined diggers might appear. What is decisive is the

---

11   Marx and Engels, *Manifesto of the Communist Party*, p. 49.

deliberate process of this digging itself. 'The emancipation of the working classes', stipulates the well-known opening sentence of the rules Marx drafted for the First International, 'must be conquered by the working classes themselves.'[12]

The best way to describe Marx's project, then, is as an effort 'not only to make History but to get a grip on it, practically and theoretically'.[13] Even his most apparently anti-voluntarist work is geared first and foremost to showing 'how the will to change capitalism can develop into successful transformative (revolutionary) activity'.[14] In the early manuscripts this emphasis is explicit. The '*actual* act of creation of communism – the birth of its empirical existence – and, for its thinking consciousness, the *comprehended* and known movement of its *becoming*', just as the proletarian movement is 'the self-conscious, independent movement of the immense majority' of the people.[15] In his later critique of political economy, Marx anticipates that the concentration of capital and the intensification of exploitation and misery which accompanies it will lead not to the automatic collapse of capitalism but to a growth in the size, frequency and intensity of 'the revolt of the working-class'. It is this class which will have to carry out the deliberate work of 'expropriating the expropriators'.[16] Once victorious, this same class will preside over the establishment of a mode of production marked above all by the predominance of autonomy, mastery, purpose and freedom. The newly 'associated producers [will] regulate their interchange with nature rationally and bring it under their common control, instead of being ruled by it as by some blind power' – and thus enable affirmation of human creativity and 'energy [as] an end in itself'.[17] The free association of producers will displace capital as the 'pseudo-subject' of production and society. The Paris Commune of 1871 anticipates such an outcome in a limited and short-lived form, through the implementation of communist forms of association undertaken by 'working men who have taken the work of their emancipation into their own

---

12   Marx, 'Rules and Administrative Regulations of the International Workingmen's Association' (1867), in *Collected Works of Marx and Engels* (London: Lawrence and Wishart, 1975–2005), vol. XX, 441; cf. Hal Draper, 'The Two Souls of Socialism' New Politics, 5:1 (1966), pp. 57–84, and Draper, 'The Principle of Self-Emancipation in Marx and Engels', *Socialist Register*, 8 (1971), pp. 81–109.

13   Jean-Paul Sartre, *Search for a Method*, trans. Hazel Barnes (New York: Vintage, 1968), p. 89.

14   Ben Fine and Alfredo Saad-Filho, *Marx's Capital* (London: Pluto, 2003), pp. 11–12.

15   Marx, *Early Writings*, p. 348; Marx and Engels, *Manifesto of the Communist Party*, 45.

16   Marx, *Capital I*, p. 929; cf. Marx, *Civil War in France* (Beijing: Foreign Languages Press, 1977), pp. 75–6.

17   Marx, *Capital III*, Chapter 48; cf. Marx, *Grundrisse*, trans. Martin Nicolaus (London: Penguin, 1973), pp. 611, 705–6.

hands with a will'. In the process the Communards made, Marx notes, the 'impossible' possible.[18]

Understood in this sense, we might say that communism seeks to enable the conversion of work into will. Communism aims to complete the transition, via the struggle of collective self-emancipation, from a suffered necessity to autonomous self-determination. It is the deliberate effort, on a world-historical scale, to universalize the material conditions under which free voluntary action might prevail over involuntary labour or passivity. Or rather: communism is the project through which voluntary action seeks to universalize the conditions for voluntary action.

2

Only such a 'communism of the will', it seems to me, can integrate the two dimensions of its idea, the dimensions of principled ideal and material development, and thereby align a revolutionary theory with a revolutionary practice. In the process it will invent new ways for testing the truth expressed in the old cliché, 'where there's a will there's a way'. Or to adapt Antonio Machado's less prosaic phrase, taken up as a motto by Paulo Freire: a communist assumes that if 'there is no way, we make the way by walking it'.[19]

To say that we make the way by walking it is to resist the power of the historical, cultural or socio-economic terrain to determine our way. It is to insist that in an emancipatory political sequence what is 'determinant in the first instance' is a collective will to prescribe, through the terrain that confronts us, the course of our own history. It is to privilege, over the complexity of the terrain and the forms of knowledge and authority that govern behaviour 'adapted' to it, the purposeful will of the people to take and retain their place as the 'authors and actors of their own drama'.[20]

To say that we make our way by walking it is not to pretend, however,

---

18 'Yes, gentlemen, the Commune intended to abolish that class property which makes the labour of the many the wealth of the few. It aimed at the expropriation of the expropriators. It wanted to make individual property a truth by transforming the means of production, land and capital, now chiefly the means of enslaving and exploiting labour, into mere instruments of free and associated labour. But this is communism, "impossible" communism! . . . If co-operative production is not to remain a sham and a snare; if it is to supersede the capitalist system; if united co-operative societies are to regulate national production upon a common plan, thus taking it under their own control, and putting an end to the constant anarchy and periodical convulsions which are the fatality of capitalist production – what else, gentlemen, would it be but communism, "possible" communism?' (Marx, *Civil War in France*, pp. 75–6).

19 Antonio Machado, 'Proverbios y Cantares – XXIX' (1912), in *Selected Poems of Antonio Machado*, trans. Betty Jean Craige (Baton Rouge: Louisiana State University Press, 1978).

20 Marx, *The Poverty of Philosophy* (Beijing: Foreign Languages Press, 1966), p. 109.

that we invent the ground we traverse. It is not to suppose that a will creates itself and the conditions of its exercise abruptly or ex nihilo. It is not to assume that the real movement which abolishes the existing state of things proceeds through empty or indeterminate space. It is not to disregard the obstacles or opportunities that characterize a particular terrain, or to deny their ability to influence the forging of a way. Instead it is to remember, after Sartre, that obstacles appear as such in the light of a project to climb past them. It is to remember, after Marx, that we make our own history, without choosing the conditions of its making. It is to conceive of terrain and way through a dialectic which, connecting both objective and subjective forms of determination, is oriented by the primacy of the latter.

In a European context, the optimism characteristic of such an approach is still emphatic in Gramsci (who seeks 'to put the "will", which in the last analysis equals practical or political activity, at the base of philosophy'[21]) and in the early writings of Lukács (for whom 'decision', 'subjective will' and 'free action' have strategic precedence over the apparent 'facts' of a situation[22]). Comparable priorities also orient the political writings of a few more recent philosophers, like Beauvoir, Sartre and Badiou. Obvious differences aside, what these thinkers have in common is an emphasis on the practical primacy of self-determination and self-emancipation. However constrained your situation you are always free, as Sartre liked to say, 'to make something of what is made of you'.[23]

Overall, however, it is difficult to think of a canonical notion more roundly condemned, in recent 'Western' philosophy, than the notion of will, to say nothing of that general will so widely condemned as a precursor of tyranny and totalitarian terror. In philosophical circles voluntarism has become little more than a term of abuse, and an impressively versatile one at that: depending on the context, it can evoke idealism, obscurantism, vitalism, infantile leftism, fascism, petty-bourgeois narcissism, neocon aggression, folk-psychological delusion . . . Of all the faculties or capacities of that human subject who was displaced from the centre

---

21   Antonio Gramsci, 'Study of Philosophy', *Selections From the Prison Notebooks*, ed. and trans. Quintin Hoare and Geoffrey Nowell Smith (London: Lawrence and Wishart, 1971), p. 345; cf. Gramsci, 'The Modern Prince', in ibid., pp. 125–33, 171–2.

22   Georg Lukács, 'What is Orthodox Marxism?', in *Political Writings 1919–1929*, ed. Rodney Livingstone, trans. Michael McColgan (London: NLB, 1972), pp. 26–7; cf. Lukács, *History and Class Consciousness*, trans. Rodney Livingstone (London: Merlin Press, 1971), pp. 23, 145, 181.

23   Sartre, *Search for a Method*, p. 91; Sartre, 'Itinerary of a Thought', *New Left Review* 58 (November 1969: 45.

of post-Sartrean concerns, none was more firmly proscribed than its conscious volition. Structuralist and poststructuralist thinkers, by and large, relegated volition and intention to the domain of deluded, imaginary or humanist-ideological miscognition. Rather than explore the ways in which political determination might depend on a collective subject's self-determination, recent philosophy and cultural theory has tended to privilege various forms of either indetermination (the interstitial, the hybrid, the ambivalent, the simulated, the undecidable, the chaotic . . .) or hyper-determination ('infinite' ethical obligation, divine transcendence, unconscious drive, traumatic repression, machinic automation . . .). The allegedly obsolete notion of a *pueblo unido* has been displaced by a more differentiated and more deferential plurality of actors – flexible identities, negotiable histories, improvised organizations, dispersed networks, 'vital' multitudes, polyvalent assemblages, and so on.

Even the most cursory overview of recent European philosophy is enough to evoke its general tendency to distrust, suspend or overcome the will – a tendency anticipated, in an extreme form, by Schopenhauer. Consider a few names from a list that could be easily expanded. Nietzsche's whole project presumes that 'there is no such thing as will' in the usual (voluntary, deliberate, purposeful . . .) sense of the word.[24] Heidegger, over the course of his own lectures on Nietzsche, comes to condemn the will as a force of subjective domination and nihilist closure, before urging his readers 'willingly to renounce willing'.[25] Arendt finds, in the affirmation of a popular political will ('the most dangerous of modern concepts and misconceptions'), the temptation that turns modern revolutionaries into tyrants.[26] For Adorno, rational will is an aspect of that enlightenment pursuit of mastery and control which has left the earth 'radiant with triumphant calamity'. Althusser devalues the will as an aspect of ideology, in favour of the scientific analysis of historical processes that proceed without a subject. Negri and Virno associate a will of the people with authoritarian state power. After Nietzsche, Deleuze privileges transformative sequences that require the suspension, shattering or paralysis of voluntary action. After Heidegger, Derrida associates the will with self-presence and self-coincidence, an unredeemably futile effort to appropriate the inappropriable (the unpresentable, the equivocal, the undecidable, the differential, the deferred, the discordant, the

---

24 Friedrich Nietzsche, *The Will to Power*, ed. Walter Kaufmann (New York: Vintage, 1968), §488.

25 Martin Heidegger, *Discourse on Thinking* (New York: Harper and Row, 1969), p. 59.

26 Hannah Arendt, *On Revolution* (London: Penguin, 1990), p. 225.

transcendent, the other . . .). After these and several other philosophers, Agamben summarizes much recent European thinking on political will when he effectively equates it with fascism pure and simple. Even those thinkers who, against the grain of the times, have insisted on the primacy of self-determination and self-emancipation have tended to do so in ways that devalue political will. Take Foucault, Sartre and Badiou. Much of Foucault's work might be read as an extended analysis, after Canguilhem, of the ways in which people are 'de-voluntarized' by the 'permanent coercions' at work in disciplinary power, coercions designed to establish 'not the general will but automatic docility'.[27] Foucault never compromised on his affirmation of 'voluntary insubordination' in the face of newly stifling forms of government and power, and in crucial lectures from the early 1970s he demonstrated how the development of modern psychiatric and carceral power, in the immediate wake of the French Revolution, was designed first and foremost to 'over-power' and break the will of people who had the folly literally to 'take themselves for a king'.[28] Nevertheless, in his published work Foucault tends to see the will as complicit in forms of self-supervision, self-regulation and self-subjection. Sartre probably did more than any other philosopher of his generation to emphasize the ways in which an emancipatory project or group depends upon the determination of a 'concrete will', but his philosophy offers a problematic basis for any sort of voluntarism. He accepts as 'irreducible' the 'intention' and goals which orient an individual's fundamental project, but makes a sharp distinction between such intention and merely 'voluntary deliberation' or motivation. Since for Sartre the latter is always secondary and 'deceptive', the result is to render the primary intention opaque and beyond 'interpretation'.[29] Sartre's later work subsequently fails to conceive of a collective will in other than exceptionalist and ephemeral terms. Badiou's powerful revival of a militant theory of the subject is more easily reconciled with a voluntarist agenda (or at least with what he calls a *volonté impure*[30]), but suffers from some similar limitations. It's no accident that, like Agamben and Žižek, when Badiou looks to the Christian tradition

27   Michel Foucault, *Discipline and Punish*, trans. Alan Sheridan (New York: Pantheon Books, 1977), p. 169.
28   Foucault, 'What Is Critique?', in *The Politics of Truth*, ed. Sylvère Lotringer and Lysa Hochroth (New York: Semiotext(e), 1997), p. 32; Foucault, *Psychiatric Power*, trans. Graham Burchell (New York: Palgrave, 2006), pp. 11, 27–8, 339.
29   Sartre, *Being and Nothingness*, trans. Hazel Barnes (London: Routledge Classics, 2003), pp. 585–6, 472, 479.
30   Badiou, 'La Volonté: Cours d'agrégation', notes taken by François Nicolas, available at www. entretemps.asso.fr.

for a point of anticipation he turns not to Matthew (with his prescriptions of how to act in the world: spurn the rich, affirm the poor, 'sell all thou hast' . . .), or to liberation theology's 'preferential option for the poor', but to Paul (with his contempt for the weakness of human will and his valorization of the abrupt and infinite transcendence of grace).

Pending a more robust philosophical defence, contemporary critical theorists tend to dismiss the notion of will as a matter of delusion or deviation. But since it amounts to little more than a perverse appropriation of more fundamental forms of revolutionary determination, there is no reason to accept fascist exaltation of an 'awakening' or 'triumph of the will' as the last word on the subject. The true innovators in the modern development of a voluntarist philosophy are Rousseau, Kant and Hegel, and the general principles of such a philosophy are most easily recognized in the praxis of Rousseau's Jacobin followers.

Of course the gulf that separates Marxist from Jacobin conceptions of political action is obvious enough. In the movement from Rousseau to Marx, via Kant and Hegel, the category of a 'general will' expands from the anachronistic idealization of a small homogeneous community towards an anticipation of humanity as a whole. Kant's abstract universalization makes too sharp a distinction between determination of the will and its realization, between determination in its subjective and objective senses; Hegel goes too far in the other direction. I will assume here that the most fruitful way to begin thinking a dialectical voluntarism that might eventually draw on aspects of Kant, Hegel and Marx is to *start* with a return to Rousseau and the Jacobins, supplemented by reference to more recent interventions that might be described in roughly neo-Jacobin terms. Rousseau's conception of a general will remains the single most important contribution to the logic at work in the sort of 'dialectical voluntarism' that informs a communism of the will. Unlike Rousseau or Hegel, however, my concern here is not with a community conceived as a socially or ethically integrated unit, one that finds its natural horizon in the nation-state, so much as with the people who participate in the active willing of a general or generalizable will as such. Such a will is at work in the mobilization of any emancipatory collective force – a national liberation struggle, a movement for social justice, an empowering political or economic association, and so on – which strives to formulate, assert and sustain a fully common (and thus fully inclusive and egalitarian) interest.

3

On this basis we might briefly enumerate, along broadly neo-Jacobin or proto-communist lines, some of the characteristic features of emancipatory political will:

1. Political *will* commands, by definition, voluntary and autonomous action. Unlike involuntary or reflex-like responses, if it exists then will initiates action through free, rational deliberation. For Rousseau the fundamental 'principle of any action lies in the will of a free being; there is no higher or deeper source', and as Patrick Riley notes, according to Rousseau's conception of both politics and education, 'without will there is no freedom, no self-determination, no "moral causality"'.[31] Robespierre soon drew the most basic political implication when he realized that when people will or 'want to be free they will be'. Abbé Sieyès anticipated the point, on the eve of 1789: 'every man has an inherent right to deliberate and will for himself', and 'either one wills freely or one is forced to will, there cannot be any middle position'. Outside voluntary self-legislation 'there cannot be anything other than the empire of the strong over the weak and its odious consequences'.[32]

An intentional freedom is not reducible to the mere faculty of free choice or *liberum arbitrium*.[33] If we are to speak of the 'will of the people' we cannot restrict it (as Machiavelli and his followers do) to the passive expression of approval or consent.[34] It is the process of actively willing or choosing that renders a particular course of action preferable to another. 'Always engaged', argues Sartre, freedom never 'pre-exists its choice: we shall never apprehend ourselves except as a choice in the making'.[35] Augustine and then Duns Scotus already understood that 'our will would not be will unless it

---

31   Jean-Jacques Rousseau, *Émile, ou de l'éducation*, (Paris: Garnier, 1964), p. 340; Patrick Riley, 'Rousseau's General Will: Freedom of a Particular Kind', *Political Studies* 39 (1991): 59, citing Rousseau, *Première version du Contrat social*, in *Political Writings*, Charles Vaughan ed., (New York: Wiley, 1962), I, p. 499.

32   Maximilien Robespierre, *Œuvres complètes*, ed. Eugène Déprez et al. (Paris: Société des Études Robespierristes, 1910–1967), vol. 9, p. 310; Emmanuel Joseph Sieyès, *Views of the Executive Means Available to the Representatives of France in 1789*, *Political Writings*, ed. and trans. Michael Sonenscher (Indianapolis: Hackett, 2003), p. 10.

33   Cf. Arendt, 'Willing', in *The Life of the Mind* (New York: Harcourt, 1978), II, pp. 6–7.

34   Machiavelli, *Discourses*, trans. Harvey C. Mansfield and Nathan Tarcov (London: Penguin, 1983), 2:24, 3:5; cf. 1:16, 1:32; Machiavelli, *The Prince*, trans. George Bull (London: Penguin, 2004), Chapter 9.

35   Sartre, *Being and Nothingness*, p. 501.

were in our power'.[36] Descartes likewise recognized that 'voluntary and free
are the same thing', and finds in the 'indivisible' and immeasurable freedom
of the will our most fundamental resemblance to divinity.[37] Kant (followed
by Fichte) then radicalizes this voluntarist approach when he defines
the activity of willing as 'causality through reason' or 'causality through
freedom'.[38] For Kant, will achieves the practical liberation of reason from
the constraints of experience and objective knowledge, and it is the active
willing which determines what is possible and what is right, and makes it
so. As the French Revolution will confirm, it is as willing or practical beings
that 'people have the quality or power of being the *cause* and . . . *author*
of their own improvement'.[39] Those sceptical of political will, by contrast,
assume that apparently voluntary commitments mask a more profound
ignorance or devaluation of appetite (Hobbes), causality (Spinoza), context
(Montesquieu), habit (Hume), tradition (Burke), history (Tocqueville),
power (Nietzsche), the unconscious (Freud), convention (Wittgenstein),
writing (Derrida), desire (Deleuze), drive (Žižek) . . .

2. *Political* will, of course, involves collective action and direct participation.
A democratic political will depends on the power and practice of inclusive
assembly, the power to sustain a common commitment. The assertion of
what Rousseau calls a general will is a matter of collective volition at every
stage of its development. The inaugural 'association is the most voluntary
act in the world', and to remain an active participant of the association 'is to
will what is in the common or general interest'. In so far (and only in so far)
as they pursue this interest, each person 'puts his person and all his power
in common under the supreme control of the general will'.[40] Defined in this
way, 'the general will is always on the side most favourable to the public

36   Saint Augustine, *On Free Choice of the Will*, trans. Thomas Williams (Indianapolis: Hackett,
1993), pp. 76–7; cf. Duns Scotus, 'The Existence of God', in *Philosophical Writings*, trans. Allan Wolter
(Indianapolis: Hackett, 1987), pp. 54–6.
37   René Descartes, Letter to Père Mesland, 9 February 1645, in John Cottingham et al. (eds),
Philosophical Writings of Descartes (Cambridge: Cambridge University Press, 1984), vol. 3, p. 246;
Descartes, *Meditations IV*, ibid., vol. 2, pp. 39–40; *Principles of Philosophy*, ibid. vol. 1, §35, §37.
38   Immanuel Kant, *Groundwork of the Metaphysics of Morals*, in his *Practical Philosophy*, ed. and
trans. Mary McGregor (Cambridge: Cambridge University Press, 1996; references to Kant use the
standard German pagination), pp. 4:461, 4:446. In his 1930 lectures on Kant's practical philosophy,
Heidegger emphasizes this point – 'to give this priority in everything, to will the ought of pure willing' (Heidegger, *Essence of Human Freedom*, trans. Ted Sadler [London: Continuum, 2002], p. 201).
39   Kant, 'The Contest of the Faculties', in *Kant's Political Writings*, ed. Hans Reiss (Cambridge:
Cambridge University Press, 1970), p. 181.
40   Rousseau, *Social Contract*, in *Rousseau's Political Writings*, eds. Alan Ritter and Julia Conaway
Bondanella (New York: Norton, 1988), pp. 4:2, 1:6.

interest, that is to say, the most equitable, so that it is necessary merely to be just to be assured of following the general will'.[41]

A general interest exists only if the will to pursue it is stronger than the distraction of particular interests. To say that a general will is 'strong' doesn't mean that it stifles dissent or imposes uniformity. It means that in the process of negotiating differences between particular wills, the willing of the general interest eventually finds a way to prevail. There is an inclusive general will in so far as those who initially oppose it correct their mistake and realize that 'if my private opinion had prevailed I would have done something other than what I had willed', i.e. something inconsistent with my ongoing participation in the general will.[42] So long as it lasts, participation in a general will, be it that of a national movement, a political organization, a social or economic association, a trade union, etc., always involves a resolve to abide by its eventual judgement, not as an immediate arbiter of right and wrong but as the process of collectively deliberating and *willing* what is right. Participation in a general will involves acceptance of the risk of finding yourself being, at any given moment, 'wrong with the people rather than right without them'.[43] By the same token, it's precisely in so far as it remains actively capable of seeking and willing the collective right that we can agree with Rousseau and Sieyès when they insist that, in the long run, a general will can neither err nor betray.[44]

After Robespierre, Saint-Just summarizes the whole Jacobin political project when he rejects 'purely speculative' or 'intellectual' conceptions of justice, as if 'laws were the expression of taste rather than of the general will'. The only legitimate definition of the general will is 'the material will of the people, its simultaneous will; its goal is to consecrate the active and not the passive interest of the greatest number of people'.[45]

Mobilization of the general will of the people must not be confused, then, with a merely putschist vanguardism. An abrupt appropriation of the instruments of government by a few 'alchemists of revolution' is no substitute for the deployment of popular power.[46] In spite of obvious stra-

---

41   Ibid., p. 2:4; Rousseau, 'Discourse on Political Economy', in *Rousseau's Political Writings*, p. 66.

42   Rousseau, *Social Contract*, p. 4:2; Louis Antoine de Saint-Just, *Œuvres complètes*, eds. Anne Kupiec and Miguel Abensour (Paris: Gallimard 'Folio', 2004), p. 482.

43   Jean-Bertrand Aristide, cited in J. P. Slavin, 'Haiti: The Elite's Revenge', *NACLA Report on the Americas* 25:3 (December 1991), p. 6.

44   Rousseau, 'Discourse on Political Economy', p. 66; *Social Contract*, pp. 2:3; 1:7 (translation modified).

45   Saint-Just, *Œuvres complètes*, p. 547.

46   See Marx and Engels, *'Les Conspirateurs', par A. Chenu'* (1850), in *Collected Works of Marx and Engels*, vol. 10, p. 318; Marx, 'Meeting of the Central Authority, September 15, 1850', in *Collected Works of Marx and Engels*, vol. 10, pp. 625–9; Engels, 'Introduction', in Marx, *Civil War in France*, p. 14.

tegic differences, Lenin is no more tempted than Luxemburg to substitute a Blanquist conspiracy for 'the people's struggle for power', via mobilization of the 'vast masses of the proletariat'.[47] It's not a matter of imposing an external will or awareness upon an inert people, but of people working to clarify, concentrate and organize their own will. Fanon makes much the same point, when he equates a national liberation movement with the inclusive and deliberate work of 'the whole of the people'.[48]

3. The will of the people is thus a matter of material power and active empowerment, before it is a matter of representation, authority or legitimacy. What divides society is its response to popular self-empowerment. This is as much a Marxist as it is a Jacobin insight. Any social 'transformation can only come about as the product of the – free – action of the proletariat', notes Lukács, and 'only the practical class consciousness of the proletariat possesses this ability to transform things'. Such a praxis-oriented philosophy did not die out after the political setbacks of the 1920s. Sartre took up the same theme in the early 1950s (before Badiou in the 1970s): as far as politics is concerned, a 'class is never separable from the concrete will which animates it nor from the ends it pursues. The proletariat forms itself by its day-to-day action. It exists only by action. It *is* action. If it ceases to act, it decomposes.'[49]

Will commands the initiation of action, not representation. An exercise in political will involves taking power, not receiving it, on the assumption that (as a matter of 'reason' or 'natural right') the people are always already entitled to take it. 'The oppressed cannot enter the struggle as objects,' Freire notes, 'in order *later* to become human beings.'[50] It makes no sense, as John Brown argued during his trial in 1859, to treat the imperatives of justice merely as recommendations that must bide their time: 'I am yet too young', Brown said on the eve of his execution, 'to understand that God is any respecter of persons.'[51] A similar impatience

---

47 V. I. Lenin, 'The Conference Summed Up' (7 May 1906); cf. Hal Draper, 'The Myth of Lenin's "Concept of The Party"' (1990); both available at www.marxists.org.

48 Frantz Fanon, *The Wretched of the Earth*, trans. Constance Farrington (New York: Grove Weidenfeld, 1968), pp. 155–6.

49 Lukács, *History and Class Consciousness*, p. 205; Sartre, *The Communists and Peace*, trans. Martha Fletcher (New York: Braziller, 1968), p. 89.

50 Paulo Freire, *Pedagogy of the Oppressed*, trans. Myra Ramos (London: Penguin, 1996), p. 50.

51 Cited in Arthur Jordan, 'John Brown's Raid on Harper's Ferry', *International Socialist Review* 21:1 (1960); available at www.marxists.org. 'The general will, to be truly so, must be general in its object as well as in its essence; it must come from all to be applied to all' (Rousseau, *Social Contract*, p. 2:4).

informs the strategic voluntarism of Che Guevara, who knew that it is pointless to wait 'with folded arms' for objective conditions to mature. Whoever waits for 'power to fall into the people's hands like a ripe fruit' will never stop waiting.[52]

As one of today's more eloquent proponents of a 'living communism' suggests, an inclusive popular politics must start with an unconditional assertion of the 'humanity of every human being'. Our politics, says S'bu Zikode, chairperson of the Durban shack-dwellers' movement Abahlali baseMjondolo, is rooted in the 'places that we have taken' and kept:

> We will no longer quietly wait for our humanity to be finally recognized one day. We have already taken our place on the land in the cities and we have held that ground. We have also decided to take our place in all [political] discussions and to take it right now. We take our place humbly, but firmly. We do not allow the state to keep us quiet in the name of a future revolution that does not come. We do not allow the NGOs to keep us quiet in the name of a future socialism that they can't build. We take our place as people who count the same as everyone else.[53]

Those who lack confidence in the people, by contrast, recommend the virtues of patience. It is always too early, from this perspective, for equality and participation. Only when they 'grow up' or 'progress' might today's people become worthy of the rights that a prudent society will withhold – forever. Between confidence in the people and confidence in historical progress, as Rousseau anticipated, there is a stark choice.

4. Like any form of free or voluntary action, the will of the people is grounded in the practical sufficiency of its exercise. Will is no more a 'substance' or object of knowledge than the *cogito* variously reworked and affirmed by Kant, Fichte and Sartre. A 'fundamental freedom' or 'practical exercise of reason' proves itself through what it does and makes, rather than through what it is, has or knows. Freedom demonstrates and justifies itself through willing and acting, or else not at all. We *are* free, writes Beauvoir, but freedom '*is* only by making itself be'. We are free in

---

52   Che Guevara, 'The Marxist-Leninist Party', in *Che: Selected Works of Ernesto Guevara*, eds Rolando E. Bonachea and Nelson P. Valdés (Cambridge MA: MIT Press, 1969), pp. 104–6.
53   S'bu Zikode, 'The Burning Issue of Land and Housing', 28 August 2008; available at www. diakonia.org.za.

so far as 'we will ourselves free',[54] and we will ourselves free by crossing the threshold that separates passivity and 'minority' from volition and activity. We will ourselves free across the distance that our freedom puts between itself and a previous unfreedom. We are free as self-freeing.

5. If it is to persist, a political association must be disciplined and 'indivisible' as a matter of course.[55] Internal difference and debate within an organized association is one thing; factional divisions or schisms are another. Popular freedom persists as long as the people assert it. 'In order that the social pact may not be an empty formula,' as Rousseau's notorious argument runs, 'it tacitly includes the commitment, which alone can give force to the others, that anyone who refuses to obey the general will shall be compelled to do so by the entire body; this means nothing else than that he will be forced to be free.' Preservation of public freedom, in Robespierre's arresting phrase, requires acknowledgement of the 'despotism of truth'. Collective freedom will endure, in short, only so long as the people can defend themselves against division and deception.[56]

'Virtue' is the name that Rousseau and the Jacobins gave to the practices required to defend a general will against deception and division. Virtue in this generic sense need not take the form of an exclusive patriotism. To practise virtue is simply to privilege collective over particular interests, and to ensure that society is governed 'solely on the basis of the common interest . . . Each person is virtuous when his private will conforms totally to the general will.' If then 'we wish the general will to be accomplished' we only need to encourage 'all the private wills to agree with it, or in other words . . . make virtue reign'.[57]

6. The practical exercise of will only proceeds, as a matter of course, in the face of resistance. To will is always to continue to will, in the face of difficulty or constraint. To continue or not to continue – this is the essential choice at stake in any militant ethics.[58] Either you will and do something, or you do not. Even as it discovers the variety of ways of doing

---

54   Simone de Beauvoir, *Ethics of Ambiguity*, trans. Bernard Frechtman (New York: Citadel Press, 1976), pp. 24–5, 130–1.

55   'For the same reason that sovereignty is inalienable, it is indivisible, for the will is general, or it is not' (Rousseau, *Social Contract*, 2:2; cf. Robespierre, *Œuvres*, vol. 7, p. 268).

56   Rousseau, *Social Contract*, 1:7; Robespierre, *Œuvres*, vol. 9, pp. 83–4.

57   Rousseau, *Social Contract*, 2.1; 'Discourse on Political Economy', pp. 69, 67, translation modified.

58   Cf. Beauvoir, *Ethics of Ambiguity*, pp. 27–8; Badiou, *Ethics*, trans. Peter Hallward (London: Verso, 2001), pp. 52, 91.

or not-doing, these are the alternatives a political will must confront: yes or no, for or against, continue or stop, where 'to stop before the end is to perish'.[59]

If for the Jacobins of 1793 'terror' comes to figure as the complement to 'virtue', it is above all as a consequence of their determination to overcome the resistance of the privileged and their political protectors. Terror in the Jacobin (as opposed to Thermidorian) sense is the deployment of whatever force is required to overcome those particular interests that seek to undermine or disempower the collective interest. The reason why the Jacobin terror continues to terrify our political establishment, in a way that the far more bloody repression of the 1871 Commune does not, has little to do with the actual amount of violence involved. From the perspective of what is already established, notes Saint-Just, 'that which produces the general good is always terrible'. The Jacobin terror was more defensive than aggressive, more a matter of restraining than of unleashing popular violence. 'Let us be terrible', Danton said, 'so that the people need not be'.[60]

7. By the same token, the practical exercise of will distinguishes itself from mere wish or fantasy through its capacity to initiate a process of genuine 'realization'.[61] After Fichte, Hegel complements the voluntarist trajectory initiated by Rousseau and Kant, and opens the door to Marx, when he identifies a free collective will – a will that wills and realizes its own emancipation – as the animating principle of a concrete political association. Thus conceived, the will is nothing other than 'thinking translating itself into existence . . . The activity of the will consists in cancelling and overcoming [aufzuheben] the contradiction between subjectivity and objectivity and in translating its ends from their subjective determination into an objective one.'[62] After Hegel, Marx will expand the material dimension of such concrete determination, without ever abandoning the idea that what is ultimately determinant are not given economic or historical constraints but free human action – the

59   Robespierre, Œuvres, vol. X, p. 572.
60   Saint-Just, 'Institutions républicaines' (1794), in Œuvres, p. 1141; Danton, 10 March 1793, cited in Sophie Wahnich, La Liberté ou la mort: Essai sur la terreur et le terrorisme (Paris: La Fabrique, 2003), p. 62.
61   Cf. Sartre, Being and Nothingness, p. 505; Gramsci, 'The Modern Prince', in Selections From the Prison Notebooks, pp. 175, n. 75.
62   G. W. F. Hegel, Elements of the Philosophy of Right, trans. H. B. Nisbet (Cambridge: Cambridge University Press, 1991), §4A, §28, translation modified.

ability of 'each single individual' to prescribe their own ends and make their own history.[63]

8. Realization of the will of (the) people is oriented towards the universalization of its consequences. As Beauvoir understood better than Sartre, I can only will my own freedom by willing the freedom of all; the only subject that can sustain the work of unending self-emancipation is *the* people as such, humanity as a whole. Kant, Hegel and Marx take some of the steps required to move from Rousseau's parochial conception of a people to its universal affirmation, but the outcome was again anticipated by Jacobin practice: 'the country of a free people is open to all the people on earth', and the only 'legitimate sovereign of the earth is the human race . . . The interest, the will of the people, is that of humanity.'[64]

9. A final consequence follows from this insistence on the primacy of political will: voluntary servitude is in some ways more damaging than external domination. If the will is 'determinant in the first instance' then the most far-reaching forms of oppression involve the collusion of the oppressed. This is the point anticipated by Étienne La Boétie, and then radicalized in different ways by Du Bois, Fanon and Aristide (and also Foucault, Deleuze and Žižek . . .): in the long run it is the people who empower their oppressors, who can harm them 'only to the extent to which they are willing to put up with them'.[65]

Of course, it wouldn't be hard to write a history of the twentieth century in such a way as to illustrate the apparent futility of political will, to say nothing of the idea of communism. The failure of German communism in the 1920s, the failure of 'Soviet man' in the 1930s, the failure of anti-colonial liberation movements in the 1950s and '60s, the failure of Maoism, the failure of 1968, the failure of anti-war and anti-globalization protests – all these seeming failures might seem to demonstrate one and the same basic point: the diffuse, systemic and hence insurmountable nature of contemporary capitalism, and of the forms of state and disciplinary power which accompany it.

---

63   Marx and Engels, *The German Ideology*, (London: Lawrence & Wishert, 1970), p. 55; cf. Marx, *Capital*, I, p. 739.
64   Saint-Just, *Œuvres*, p. 551; Robespierre, *Œuvres*, vol. 9, p, 469; vol. 7, p. 268.
65   Étienne La Boétie, *The Discourse of Voluntary Servitude*, trans. Harry Kurz (New York: Columbia University Press, 1942); available at www.constitution.org; translation modified.

Such a distorted history, in my opinion, would amount to little more than a rationalization of the defeats suffered in the last quarter of the twentieth century. Ever since the revolutionary upheavals in late eighteenth-century France and Haiti, the history of the modern world has been shaped above all by the determination of our ruling classes to pacify the people they rule. As Michel Foucault demonstrated in convincing detail, a wide range of counter-revolutionary strategies for criminalizing, dividing and then dissolving the will of the people – for restoring the people to their 'normal' condition as a dispersed and passive flock – were hastily developed during and after the French Revolution; in a useful intervention Naomi Klein has recently shown how, in the last couple of decades, similar strategies have been deployed at new levels of intensity and ferocity.[66] The result, so far, has been the preservation of popular passivity and deference on a confounding scale.

In the late 1940s Beauvoir already bemoaned our tendency to 'think that we are not the master of our destiny; we no longer hope to help make history, we are resigned to submitting to it'.[67] By the late 1970s such complaint, revalorized as celebration, had become the stuff of a growing consensus. This consensus has now been dominant, in both politics and philosophy, for more than thirty disastrous years. It's time to leave it behind.

---

66   Cf. Foucault, *Psychiatric Power*, trans. Graham Burchell (New York: Palgrave, 2006). In her *Shock Doctrine* (New York: Metropolitan Books, 2007), drawing on the paradigm illustrated by Ewen Cameron's notorious psychiatric experiments at the McGill University in the 1950s, Naomi Klein shows how 'disaster capitalists' systematically make use of natural disasters, military assault and psychological warfare in order to 'soften up' popular resistance to newly intense forms of exploitation or oppression. 'Shock' serves to isolate and disorientate people, paralysing their will and capacity to defend their own most essential interests.

67   Beauvoir, *Ethics of Ambiguity*, p. 139.

8   The Common in Communism

Michael Hardt

The economic and financial crisis that exploded in Fall 2008 resulted in an extraordinarily rapid sea-change in the realm of political imaginaries. Just as a few years ago talk of climate change was ridiculed and dismissed in the mainstream media as exaggerated and apocalyptic, but then almost from one day to the next the fact of climate change became the nearly universal common sense, so too the economic and financial crisis has rearranged the dominant views of capitalism and socialism. Until very recently, any critique of neo-liberal strategies of deregulation, privatization and the reduction of welfare structures – let alone of capital itself – was cast in the dominant media as crazy talk. Today, *Newsweek* proclaims on its cover, with only partial irony, 'We are all socialists now.' The rule of capital is suddenly open to question, from Left and Right, and some form of socialist or Keynesian state regulation and management seems inevitable.

We need to look, however, outside this alternative. Too often it appears as though our only choices are capitalism or socialism, the rule of private property or that of public property, such that the only cure for the ills of state control is to privatize and for the ills of capital to publicize, that is, exert state regulation. We need to explore another possibility: neither the private property of capitalism nor the public property of socialism but the common in communism.

Many central concepts of our political vocabulary, including communism as well as democracy and freedom, have been so corrupted that they are almost unusable. In standard usage, in fact, communism has come to mean its opposite, that is, total state control of economic and social life. We could abandon these terms and invent new ones, of course, but we would leave behind too the long history of struggles, dreams and aspirations that are tied to them. I think it is better to fight over the concepts themselves in order to restore or renew their meaning. In the case of communism, this requires an analysis of the forms of political organization that are possible today and, before that, an investigation of the nature of contemporary economic and social production. I will limit myself in this essay to the preliminary task of the critique of political economy.

One of the reasons that the communist hypotheses of previous eras are no longer valid is that the composition of capital – as well as the conditions and products of capitalist production – have altered. Most importantly, the technical composition of labour has changed. How do people produce both inside and outside the workplace? What do they produce and under what conditions? How is productive cooperation organized? And what are the divisions of labour and power that separate them along gender and racial lines and in the local, regional and global contexts? In addition to investigating the current composition of labour, we also have to analyse the relations of property under which labour produces. Along with Marx we can say that the critique of political economy is, at its heart, a critique of property. 'The theory of the Communists', Marx and Engels write in the *Manifesto*, 'may be summed up in the single sentence: Abolition of private property.'[1]

In order to explore the relationship and struggle between property and the common, which I consider to be central to communist analysis and proposition, I want to read two passages from Marx's 1844 *Economic and Philosophical Manuscripts*. By referring the *Manuscripts* I do not intend to pose the early Marx against the late, to celebrate Marx's humanism, or anything of the sort. These are arguments, in fact, that continue through-out Marx's work. Nor is it necessary to appeal to the master to renew the concept of communism. The *Manuscripts* provide an occasion for reading the common in communism, which is increasingly relevant today, but also for measuring the distance between Marx's time and our own.

In the first passage, titled 'The Relation of Private Property', Marx proposes a periodization that highlights the dominant form of property in each era. By the mid nineteenth century, he claims, European soci-eties are no longer primarily dominated by immobile property, such as land, but instead by mobile forms of property, generally the results of industrial production. The period of transition is characterized by a bitter battle between the two forms of property. In typical fashion Marx mocks the claims to social good made by owners of both types of property. The land-owner emphasizes the productivity of agriculture and its vital impor-tance for society as well as 'the noble lineage of his property, the feudal

---

1   Karl Marx and Friedrich Engels, *The Communist Manifesto* (London: Verso, 1998), p. 52.

reminiscences, the poetry of remembrance, his high-flown nature, his political importance, etc.'[2] The owner of movable property, in contrast, attacks the parochialism and stasis of the world of immobile property while singing his own praises. 'Movable property itself', Marx writes, 'claims to have won political freedom for the world, to have loosed the chains of civil society, to have linked together different worlds, to have given rise to trade, which encourages friendship between peoples and to have created a pure morality and a pleasing culture.'[3] Marx considers it inevitable that mobile property would achieve economic dominance over immobile property.

Movement inevitably triumphs over immobility, open and self-conscious baseness over hidden and unconscious baseness, *greed* over *self-indulgence*, the avowedly restless and versatile self-interest of *enlight-enment*, over the parochial, worldly-wise, artless, lazy and deluded *self-interest of superstition*, just as *money* must triumph over the other forms of private property.[4]

Marx, of course, mocks both of these property owners, but he does recognize that movable property, however despicable, does have the advantage of revealing 'the idea of *labour* as the sole *essence of wealth*'.[5] His periodization, in other words, highlights the increased potential for a communist project.

I want to analyse a parallel struggle between two forms of property today, but before doing that I should note that the triumph of movable over immobile property corresponds to the victory of profit over rent as the dominant mode of expropriation. In the collection of rent, the capitalist is deemed to be relatively external to the process of the production of value, merely extracting value produced by other means. The generation of profit, in contrast, requires the engagement of the capitalist in the production process, imposing forms of cooperation, disciplinary regimes, etc. By the time of John Maynard Keynes, profit has such dignity with respect to rent that Keynes can predict (or prescribe) the 'euthanasia of the rentier' and thus the disappearance of the 'functionless investor' in

---

2   Karl Marx, *Economic and Philosophical Manuscripts*, in *Early Writings*, trans. Rodney Livingstone and Gregor Benton (London: Penguin, 1975), p. 338.
3   Ibid., p. 339.
4   Ibid., p. 340.
5   Ibid., p. 343.

favour of the capitalist investor who organizes and manages production.[6] This conception of an historical movement within capital from rent to profit also corresponds to the purported passage in many analyses from primitive accumulation to capitalist production proper. Primitive accumulation might be considered, in this context, an absolute rent, expropriating entirely wealth produced elsewhere.

The passages from rent to profit and from the dominance of immobile to that of mobile property are both part of a more general claim by Marx that by the mid nineteenth century large-scale industry has replaced agriculture as the hegemonic form of economic production. He does not make this claim, of course, in quantitative terms. Industrial production at the time made up a small fraction of the economy even in England, the most industrialized country. And the majority of workers toiled not in the factories but in the field. Marx's claim instead is qualitative: all other forms of production will be forced to adopt the qualities of industrial production. Agriculture, mining, even society itself will have to adopt its regimes of mechanization, its labour discipline, its temporalities and rhythms, its working day, and so forth. E. P. Thompson's classic essay on clocks and work-discipline in England is a wonderful demonstration of the progressive imposition of industrial temporality over society as a whole.[7] In the century and a half since Marx's time, this tendency for industry to impose its qualities has proceeded in extraordinary ways.

Today, however, it is clear that industry no longer holds the hegemonic position within the economy. This is not to say that fewer people work in factories today than ten or twenty or fifty years ago – although, in certain respects, their locations have shifted, moving to the other side of the global divisions of labour and power. The claim, once again, is not primarily quantitative but qualitative. Industry no longer imposes its qualities over other sectors of the economy and over social relations more generally. That seems to me a relatively uncontroversial claim.

More disagreement arises when one proposes another form of production as successor to industry and hegemonic in this way. Toni Negri and I argue that immaterial or biopolitical production is emerging in that hegemonic position. By immaterial and biopolitical we try to grasp together the production of ideas, information, images, knowledges, code, languages,

6   John Maynard Keynes, *The General Theory of Employment, Interest and Money* (London: MacMillan, 1936), p. 376.
7   E. P. Thompson, 'Time, Work-Discipline, and Industrial Capitalism', *Past and Present* 38:1 (1967): 56–97.

social relationships, affects and the like. This designates occupations throughout the economy, from the high end to the low, from health-care workers, flight attendants and educators to software programmers and from fast food and call-centre workers to designers and advertisers. Most of these forms of production are not new, of course, but the coherence among them is perhaps more recognizable and, more important, their qualities tend today to be imposed over other sectors of the economy and over society as a whole. Industry has to informationalize; knowledge, code and images are becoming ever more important throughout the traditional sectors of production; and the production of affects and care is becoming increasingly essential in the valorization process. This hypothesis, of a tendency for immaterial or biopolitical production to emerge in the hegemonic position which used to be held by industry, has all kinds of immediate implications for gender divisions of labour and various international and other geographical divisions of labour, but I cannot treat them in this essay.[8]

If we focus on the new struggle between two forms of property implied by this transition we can return to Marx's formulations. Whereas in Marx's time the struggle was between immobile property (such as land) and moveable property (such as material commodities), today the struggle is between material property and immaterial property – or, to put it another way, whereas Marx focused on the mobility of property today the central issue is scarcity and reproducibility, such that the struggle can be posed as being between exclusive versus shared property. The contemporary focus on immaterial and reproducible property in the capitalist economy can be recognized easily from even a cursory glance at the field of property law. Patents, copyrights, indigenous knowledges, genetic codes, the information in the germplasm of seeds, and similar issues are the topics most actively debated in the field. The fact that the logic of scarcity does not hold in this domain poses new problems for property. Just as Marx saw that movement necessarily triumphs over immobility, so too today the immaterial triumphs over the material, the reproducible over the unreproducible, and the shared over the exclusive.

The emerging dominance of this form of property is significant, in part, because it demonstrates and returns to centre stage the conflict between the common and property as such. Ideas, images, knowledges, code, languages and even affects can be privatized and controlled as

---

8   On immaterial and biopolitical production, see Michael Hardt and Tony Negri, *Commonwealth* (Cambridge, MA: Harvard University Press, 2009), Chapter 3.

property, but it is more difficult to police ownership because they are so easily shared or reproduced. There is a constant pressure for such goods to escape the boundaries of property and become common. If you have an idea, sharing it with me does not reduce its utility to you, but usually increases it. In fact, in order to realize their maximum productivity, ideas, images and affects must be common and shared. When they are privatized their productivity reduces dramatically – and, I would add, making the common into public property, that is, subjecting it to state control or management, similarly reduces productivity. Property is becoming a fetter on the capitalist mode of production. Here is an emerging contradiction internal to capital: the more the common is corralled as property, the more its productivity is reduced; and yet expansion of the common undermines the relations of property in a fundamental and general way.

One could say, in rather broad terms, that neo-liberalism has been defined by the battle of private property not only against public property but also and perhaps more importantly against the common. Here it is useful to distinguish between two types of the common, both of which are the object of neo-liberal strategies of capital. (And this can serve as an initial definition of 'the common'.) On the one hand, the common names the earth and all the resources associated with it: the land, the forests, the water, the air, minerals and so forth. This is closely related to seventeenth-century English usage of 'the commons' (with an 's'). On the other hand, the common also refers, as I have already said, to the results of human labour and creativity, such as ideas, language, affects and so forth. You might think of the former as the 'natural' common and the latter as the 'artificial' common, but really such divisions between natural and artificial quickly break down. In any case, neo-liberalism has aimed to privatize both these forms of the common.

One major scene of such privatization has been the extractive industries, providing transnational corporations with access to diamonds in Sierra Leone or oil in Uganda or lithium deposits and water rights in Bolivia. Such neo-liberal privatization of the common has been described by many authors, including David Harvey and Naomi Klein, in terms that mark the renewed importance of primitive accumulation or accumulation by dispossession.[9]

---

9   See David Harvey, *A Brief History of Neoliberalism* (Oxford: Oxford University Press, 2005); and Naomi Klein, *The Shock Doctrine* (New York: Metropolitan Books, 2007). For an excellent analysis of neo-liberalism's focus on extractive industries in Africa, see James Ferguson, *Global Shadows: Africa in the Neoliberal World Order* (Durham: Duke University Press, 2006).

The neo-liberal strategies for the privatization of the 'artificial' common are much more complex and contradictory. Here the conflict between property and the common is fully in play. The more the common is subject to property relations, as I said, the less productive it is; and yet capitalist valorization processes require private accumulation. In many domains, capitalist strategies for privatizing the common through mechanisms such as patents and copyrights continue (often with difficulty) despite the contradictions. The music industry and computer industry are full of examples. This is also the case with so-called biopiracy, that is, the processes whereby transnational corporations expropriate the common in the form of indigenous knowledges or genetic information from plants, animals and humans, usually through the use of patents. Traditional knowledges concerning, for instance, the use of a ground seed as a natural pesticide, or the healing qualities of a particular plant, are turned into private property by the corporation that patents the knowledge. Parenthetically I would insist that piracy is a misnomer for such activities. Pirates have a much more noble vocation: they steal property. These corporations instead steal the common and transform it into property.

In general, though, capital accomplishes the expropriation of the common not through privatization per se but in the form of rent. Several contemporary Italian and French economists working on what they call cognitive capitalism – Carlo Vercellone most prominently – argue that just as in an earlier period there was a tendential movement from rent to profit as the dominant mode of capitalist expropriation, today there is a reverse movement from profit to rent.[10] Patents and copyrights, for example, generate rent in the sense that they guarantee an income based on the ownership of material or immaterial property. This argument does not imply a return to the past: the income generated from a patent, for instance, is very different from that generated from land ownership. The core insight of this analysis of the emerging dominance of rent over profit, which I find very significant, is that capital remains generally external to the processes of the production of the common. Whereas in the case of industrial capital and its generation of profit, the capitalist plays a role internal to the production process, particularly in designating the means of cooperation and imposing the modes of discipline, in the

---

10   See, for example, Carlo Vercellone, 'Crisi della legge del valore e divenire rendita del profitto', in Andrea Fumagalli and Sandro Mezzadra (eds), *Crisi dell'economia globale* (Verona: Ombre corte, forthcoming).

production of the common the capitalist must remain relatively external.[11] Every intervention of the capitalist in the processes of the production of the common, just as every time the common is made property, reduces productivity. Rent is a mechanism, then, to cope with the conflicts between capital and the common. A limited autonomy is granted the processes of the production of the common with respect to the sharing of resources and the determination of the modes of cooperation, and capital is still able to exert control and expropriate value through rent. Exploitation in this context takes the form of the expropriation of the common.

This discussion of rent points, on the one hand, to the neo-liberal processes of accumulation by dispossession in so far as primitive accumulation can be called a form of absolute rent. On the other hand, it casts in a new light the contemporary predominance of finance, which is characterized by complex and very abstract varieties of relative rent. Christian Marazzi cautions us against conceiving of finance as fictional, in opposition to the 'real economy', a conception that misunderstands the extent to which finance and production are both increasingly dominated by immaterial forms of property. He also warns against dismissing finance as merely unproductive in contrast to an image of productivity roughly tied to industrial production. It is more useful to situate finance in the context of the general trend from profit to rent, and the correspondingly external position of capital with respect to the production of the common. Finance expropriates the common and exerts control at a distance.[12]

Now I can bring to a close and review the primary points of my reading of this first passage from Marx's early manuscripts, in which he describes the struggle between two forms of property (immobile versus moveable) and the historical passage from the dominance of landed property to that of industrial capital. Today we are also experiencing a struggle between two forms of property (material versus immaterial or scarce versus reproducible). And this struggle reveals a deeper conflict between property as such and the common. Although the production of the common is increasingly central to the capitalist economy, capital cannot intervene in the production process and must instead remain external, expropriating value in the form of rent (through financial and other mechanisms). As a result the production and productivity of the common becomes an

---

11   See Marx's discussion of cooperation in Chapter 13 of *Capital*, vol. 1, trans. Ben Fowkes (London: Penguin, 1976), pp. 439–54.

12   See Christian Marazzi, *Capital and Language*, trans. Gregory Conti (New York: Semiotext(e), 2008).

increasingly autonomous domain, still exploited and controlled, of course, but through mechanisms that are relatively external. Like Marx, I would say this development of capital is not good in itself – and the tendential dominance of immaterial or biopolitical production carries with it a series of new and more severe forms of exploitation and control. And yet it is important to recognize that capital's own development provides the tools for liberation from capital, and specifically here it leads to the increased autonomy of the common and its productive circuits.

This brings me to the second passage from the *Manuscripts* that I want to consider, 'Private Property and Communism'. The notion of the common helps us to understand what Marx means by communism in this passage. 'Communism', he writes, 'is the positive expression of the abolition of private property.'[13] He includes that phrase 'positive expression' in part to differentiate communism from the false or corrupt notions of the concept. Crude communism, he claims, merely perpetuates private property by generalizing it and extending it to the entire community, as universal private property. That term, of course, is an oxymoron: if property is now universal, extended to the entire community, it is no longer really private. He is trying to emphasize, it seems to me, that in crude communism even though the private character has been stripped away, property remains. Communism properly conceived instead is the abolition not only of private property but of property as such. 'Private property has made us so stupid and one-sided that an object is only *ours* when we have it.'[14] What would it mean for something to be ours when we do not possess it? What would it mean to regard ourselves and our world not as property? Has private property made us so stupid that we cannot see that? Marx is searching here for the common. The open access and sharing that characterize use of the common are outside of and inimical to property relations. We have been made so stupid that we can only recognize the world as private or public. We have become blind to the common.

Marx does arrive at a version of the common (as the abolition of property) some twenty years later in volume 1 of *Capital*, when he defines communism as the result of capital's negative dialectic.

The capitalist mode of appropriation, the result of the capitalist mode of production, produces capitalist private property. This is the first

---

13 Marx, *Early Writings*, pp. 345–6.
14 Ibid., p. 351.

negation of individual private property, as founded on the labour of the proprietor. But capitalist production begets, with the inexorability of a law of Nature, its own negation. It is the negation of negation. This does not re-establish private property for the producer, but gives him individual property based on the acquisition of the capitalist era: i.e., on co-operation and the possession in common of the land and of the means of production.[15]

Capitalist development inevitably results in the increasingly central role of cooperation and the common, which in turn provides the tools for overthrowing the capitalist mode of production and constitutes the bases for an alternative society and mode of production, a communism of the common.

What I find dissatisfying about this passage from *Capital*, though, aside from its dialectical construction, is that the common Marx refers to – 'co-operation and the possession in common of the land and the means of production' – grasps primarily the material elements in question, the immobile and moveable forms of property made common. This formulation does not grasp, in other words, the dominant forms of capitalist production today. If we look back at the passage in the early *Manuscripts*, however, and try to filter out Marx's youthful humanism, we find a definition of communism and the common that does highlight the immaterial or, really, biopolitical aspects. Consider, first, this definition of communism, which Marx proposes after having set aside the crude notion: 'Communism is the positive supersession of private property as human self-estrangement, and hence the true appropriation of the human essence through and for man; it is the complete restoration of man to himself as a social, i.e. human, being.'[16] What does Marx mean by 'the true appropriation of the human essence through and for man'? Clearly he is working on the notion of appropriation against the grain, applying it in a context where it now seems strange: no longer appropriation of the object in the form of private property but appropriation of our own subjectivity, our human, social relations. Marx explains this communist appropriation, this non-property appropriation, in terms of the human sensorium and the full range of creative and productive powers. 'Man appropriates his integral essence in an integral way', which he explains in terms of 'all his human relations to the

15   Marx, *Capital*, vol. 1, p. 929.
16   Marx, *Early Writings*, p. 348.

world – seeing, hearing, smelling, tasting, feeling, thinking, contemplating, sensing, wanting, acting, loving'.[17] I think the term 'appropriation' here is misleading because Marx is not talking about capturing something that already exists, but rather creating something new. This is the production of subjectivity, the production of a new sensorium – not really appropriation, then, but production. If we return to the text we can see that Marx does, in fact, pose this clearly: 'Assuming the positive supersession of private property, man produces man, himself and other men'.[18] On this reading Marx's notion of communism in the early manuscripts is far from humanism, that is, far from any recourse to a pre-existing or eternal human essence. Instead the positive content of communism, which corresponds to the abolition of private property, is the autonomous human production of subjectivity, the human production of humanity – a new seeing, a new hearing, a new thinking, a new loving.

This brings us back to our analysis of the biopolitical turn in the economy. In the context of industrial production, Marx arrived at the important recognition that capitalist production is aimed at creating not only objects but also subjects. 'Production thus not only creates an object for the subject, but also a subject for the object.'[19] In the context of biopolitical production, however, the production of subjectivity is much more direct and intense. Some contemporary economists, in fact, analyse the transformations of capital in terms that echo Marx's formulation in the early manuscripts. 'If we had to hazard a guess on the emerging model in the next decades', posits Robert Boyer, for example, 'we would probably have to refer to the *production of man by man*.'[20] Christian Marazzi similarly understands the current passage in capitalist production as moving towards an 'anthropogenetic model'. Living beings as fixed capital are at the centre of this transformation and the production of forms of life is becoming the basis of added value. This is a process in which, when put to work, human faculties, competences, knowledges and affects – those acquired on the job but more importantly those accumulated outside work – are directly productive of value.[21] One distinctive feature of the work of head and heart, then, is that paradoxically the *object* of production

---

17   Ibid., p. 351.
18   Ibid., p. 349.
19   Marx, *Grundrisse*, trans. Martin Nicolaus (London: Penguin, 1973), p. 92.
20   Robert Boyer, *La croissance, début de siècle* (Paris: Albin Michel, 2002), p. 192.
21   Christian Marazzi, 'Capitalismo digitale e modello antropogenetico di produzione', in Jean-Louis Laville (ed.), *Reinventare il lavoro* (Rome: Sapere 2000, 2005), pp. 107–26.

is really a *subject*, defined, for example, by a social relationship or a form of life. This should make clear at least the rationale for calling this form of production *biopolitical*, since what are produced are forms of life.

If we return to Marx in this new light, we find that the progression of definitions of capital in his work actually gives us an important clue for analysing this biopolitical context. Although wealth in capitalist society first appears as an immense collective of commodities, Marx reveals that capital is really a process of the creation of surplus value via the production of commodities. But Marx develops this insight one more step to discover that in its essence capital is a *social relation* – or, to extend this even further, the ultimate object of capitalist production is not commodities but social relations or forms of life. From the standpoint of biopolitical production we can see that the production of the refrigerator and the automobile are only midpoints for the creation of the labour and gender relations of the nuclear family around the refrigerator and the mass society of individuals isolated together in their cars on the freeway.

I have highlighted the correspondence or proximity between Marx's definition of communism and the contemporary biopolitical turn of the capitalist economy, both of which are oriented towards the human production of humanity, social relations and forms of life – all in the context of the common. At this point I need to explain how I regard this proximity and why it is important. But before doing so let me add one more element to the mix.

Michel Foucault appreciates all the strangeness and richness of the line of Marx's thinking that leads to the conclusion that '*l'homme produit l'homme*' (using like Marx the gender-defined formulation). He cautions that we should not understand Marx's phrase as an expression of humanism. 'For me, what must be produced is not man as nature designed it, or as its essence prescribes; we must produce something that does not yet exist and we cannot know what it will be.' He also warns not to understand this merely as a continuation of economic production as conventionally conceived: 'I do not agree with those who would understand this production of man by man as being accomplished like the production of value, the production of wealth, or of an object of economic use; it is, on the contrary, destruction of what we are and the creation of something completely other, a total innovation.'[22] We cannot understand this produc-

---

22   Michael Foucault, 'Entretien' (with Duccio Tromadori), *Dits et écrits*, vol. 4 (Paris: Gallimard, 1994), pp. 41–95, quotation p. 74. Published in English as Michel Foucault, *Remarks on Marx* (New York: Semiotext(e), 1991), pp. 121–2. At this point in the interview Foucault is discussing his differences from the Frankfurt School.

tion, in other words, in terms of the producing subject and the produced object. Instead producer and product are both subjects: humans produce and humans are produced. Foucault clearly senses (without seeming to understand fully) the explosiveness of this situation: the biopolitical process is not limited to the reproduction of capital as a social relation but also presents the potential for an autonomous process that could destroy capital and create something entirely new. Biopolitical production obviously implies new mechanisms of exploitation and capitalist control, but we should also recognize, following Foucault's intuition, how biopolitical production, particularly in the ways it exceeds the bounds of capitalist relations and constantly refers to the common, grants labour increasing autonomy and provides the tools or weapons that could be wielded in a project of liberation.

Now we are in a position to understand the point of recognizing the proximity between the idea of communism and contemporary capitalist production. It is not that capitalist development is creating communism or that biopolitical production immediately or directly brings liberation. Instead, through the increasing centrality of the common in capitalist production – the production of ideas, affects, social relations and forms of life – are emerging the conditions and weapons for a communist project. Capital, in other words, is creating its own gravediggers.[23]

I have attempted to pursue two primary points in this essay. The first is a plea for the critique of political economy or, rather, a claim that any communist project must begin there. Such an analysis makes good on our periodizations and reveals the novelties of our present moment by conducting an investigation of not only the composition of capital but also class composition – asking, in other words, how people produce, what they produce, and under what conditions, both in and outside the

---

23 It would be interesting at this point to investigate the relation between this economic discussion of the common and the way the common functions in Jacques Rancière's notion of politics. 'Politics', he writes, 'begins precisely when one stops balancing profits and losses and is concerned instead with dividing the parts of the *common*' (*Disagreement*, trans. Julie Rose [Minneapolis: University of Minnesota Press, 1999], p. 5; *La mésentente* [Paris: Galilée, 1995], p. 24). The common, according to Rancière's notion, is the central and perhaps exclusive terrain of *partage*, that is, the process of division, distribution and sharing. 'Politics', Rancière continues, 'is the sphere of activity of a common that can only ever be contentious, the relationship between parts that are only parties and credentials or entitlements whose sum never equals the whole' (p. 14; pp. 34–5). Perhaps communism, as I conceive it here, is the only form that qualifies for Rancière's notion of politics: the *partage* of the common. I explore the role of the common in Rancière's thought briefly in 'The Production and Distribution of the Common', *Open: Cahier on Art and the Public Domain* 16 (2009): 20–31.

workplace, both in and outside relations of wage labour. And all this reveals, I maintain, the increased centrality of the common.

The second point extends the critique of political economy to the critique of property. And, specifically, communism is defined not only by the abolition of property but also by the affirmation of the common – the affirmation of open and autonomous biopolitical production, the self-governed continuous creation of new humanity. In the most synthetic terms, what private property is to capitalism and what state property is to socialism, the common is to communism.

Putting my two points together – that capitalist production increasingly relies on the common and that the autonomy of the common is the essence of communism – indicates that the conditions and weapons of a communist project are available today more than ever. Now to us the task of organizing it.

9   Communism, the Word
(Notes for the Conference)

Jean-Luc Nancy

Not the word before the notion, but the word as notion and as historical agent.

'Communism' is a word with a strange history. It is very difficult to trace its origin. Nevertheless, it is certain that the word 'communist' existed already in the fourteenth century. It referred to 'people having in common a property belonging to the category of "main morte" – that is, not being subject to the law of heritage'. A monastery belongs to the community of the monks, which is, as a community, independent from the individual monks. It seems that at the same time and even earlier, from the twelfth century, the same word designated some aspects of common law and was linked to the communal movement which became the beginning of a bourgeoisie.

Later, namely in the eighteenth century, the word appears in a text written by Victor d'Hupay de Fuveau in 1785 – four years before the French Revolution. It designates the project or the dream of founding a community of life – which precisely is supposed to replace that of the monks.

Here, for example, a quotation from d'Hupay:

This union and this community of a moral–economic regime would be feasible by small groups, in all states, without conflating the fortunes of each, by paying attention to the fair merits of a diversity of talents, something the Zealots of Plato's *Republic* had still not wished to acknowledge. It would strengthen the bonds of human friendship within each profession by excluding all inessential and external distinctions, abhorrent within the same class of Citizens: puerile rivalries that overwhelm and lead states as one to their ruin and to all manner of crimes. Such were the noxious abuses remedied by the simple Sumptuary Law of good King Idomeneus, model of our two Henrys. The Agapes of the first Christians led towards the same goal, by uniting men in this spirit of simplicity most suitable for the maintenance of peace and religion. It would therefore belong to a Prince who would like to deserve the title of Father of the Homeland (*Patrie*), that all those who encouraged the establishment of the Monks, become useless nowadays, place these new and true models of all states, each with their specific function, in the numerous Monasteries which, in depopulating every day, seem to be awaiting a better destination.

D'Hupay was a friend of Restif de la Bretonne's, who was the first to present 'communism or communauté' as a kind of government. In his autobiography (*Monsieur Nicolas*), he presents it as one among nine types of government and writes that it is only effective for some people of South America, who 'work together in the morning and play together in the afternoon' (this is not very different from what Marx says in *The German Ideology*).

A short time later, at the time of the French Revolution, Gracchus Babeuf, taking part in the first 'Commune insurrectionnelle de Paris', famously used the word 'communautariste' and the phrase 'communauté nationale' in the context of his thought about the 'Égaux'.

Alongside this explicit use of the word, other nouns designated the same thing. Such was, for example, the doctrine of the English Diggers of the sixteenth century, who spoke of the land as a 'common treasure'. The Diggers belong to the time of the first English Revolution, which ended with the creation of the first Republic under the name of *Commonwealth*, a term which at the time almost had the meaning of '*res publica*'.

Such historical data, however, are unable to give us the origin and the meaning – or, even better, the sense – of 'communism'. No history nor etymology can produce something like sense.

Nevertheless, we may understand something from this history. Something important has been at stake with this word, with its invention and with the attempt or need involved in it. Something which is still in front of us, which is still to be discovered, or which is still to *come*.

Communism – the word, again. The word as presence, as feeling, as sense (more than meaning).

To a certain extent, it seems strange that the inquiry or commentary about this word should be so rare. As if it were always considered as self-evident . . . It is, in a way – but in which way? This deserves a little more reflection.

Even if history is not enough to explain what we could call the 'destiny' of this word, something seems to be positive. *Community* – *koinônia*, *communitas* – emerges at times of profound social transformation or of great turmoil including the destructions of a social order. This was the case in the pre-Christian era, in the later stages of feudalism and, later still, at the time of the first industrial revolution. The first involved the transformation of the whole social and cultural structure of the ancient world, the final obliteration of what had opened the ancient world itself; the deconstruction of agrarian culture and theocracy. Such a deconstruction makes clear, or pushes into the foreground, what was hidden under or inside the construction: that is, the togetherness of people (even the togetherness of people with every other being such as animals, plants, even stars and stones). Before and out of the Greek – occidental – moment, togetherness comes first. We call this a '*holistic society*', supposing that such a society understands itself as a *holon*, a whole. To the whole we oppose the parts – as parts taken out of their whole – or a togetherness of several wholes – that is, of individuals. In both representations the same question arises: what becomes of togetherness when a whole is not given and perhaps is not even capable of being given in any way?

Thus arises *koinônia* or, I would say, the drive to it, the drive to *community*. It comes or it emerges, perhaps it constitutes itself, because what it calls, what it names or designates is not or is no longer given.

Certainly, many important features or trends of common life – or, to be more precise, of life in common – are already given with the first kind of mankind, since precisely this first type is not or has never been an individual but a group, a gathering of many. But as far as we can see, something of the togetherness is *given* – and is given with or through an aspect of the whole, of totality (which has nothing to do with what has been called *totalitarianism*).

If togetherness is given without this aspect, if it is given as a *society* – an association instead of, say, an integration like the family, the tribe, the clan – then the association as such raises a question about its own possibility and consistency: how is it possible to associate those who seem not to want it or even to reject it. Society then is what its members – the *socii* – have to accept and to justify. On the contrary, *communitas* or *communio*, is invented as the idea of what justifies by itself the presence and even the existence of its members.

Communism is togetherness – the *Mitsein*, the *being-with* – understood as pertaining to the existence of individuals, which means, in the existential sense, to their *essence*. *Society* means an unessential – even if necessary – link between individuals who are, in the final analysis, essentially separate.

(I will not enter into an analysis of the word *socialism*, neither in general nor in Marx's text. As we know, for several historical reasons but also – this is my belief – because of the strength and depth of the meaning of the word (of the image, of the symbol), *communism* alone took and retained the force of being more than a political choice, a political line and a party.)

This, for me, is the point: *communism* has more than, and something other than, a political meaning. It says something about property. Property is not only the possession of goods. It is precisely beyond (and/ or behind) any juridical assumption of a possession. It is what makes any kind of possession *properly* the possession of a subject, that is, properly its expression. Property is not *my* possession: it is *me*.

But *me*, *I*, never exists alone. It exists essentially *with* other existing beings. The *with* is no external link, it is no link at all. It is *togetherness* – relation, sharing, exchange, mediation and immediation, meaning and feeling.

The *with* has nothing to do with what is called *collective*. Collectivity means collected people, people taken together from anywhere to the nowhere of the collectivity or of the collection. The *co-* of *collective* is not the same as that of *communism*. This is not only a matter of etymology (*munire* versus *ligare*). It is a matter of ontology: the *co-* of collectivism is a mere external '*side by side*' which implies no relationship between the sides or between the parts of this '*partes extra partes*'.

The *co-* of communism is of another kind. It is, in the terms used by Heidegger about the *mit* of the *Mitsein*, not a *categorical* but an *existential* with (*mit*, *co-*). A categorical *with* means, in a more or less Kantian way, that it is merely formal and does no more than distinguish between *with* and *without* (you are here with me, but you could be here without me; it disturbs neither the fact you are here, nor the fact that you are you as I am me). An existential *with* implies that neither you nor me are the same when together or when separate. It implies that the *with* belongs to the very constitution or disposition or, as you may wish to say, to the *being* of us. There is more to it. Only in such a case can we speak of a '*we*' – or better, only in this case is it possible that a *we* comes to be spoken. Better still: if the *we* can only and each time be a *speech act*, then only a *we* existentially spoken may *perform* its significance (what exactly this significance is, is another matter. For now, I only note that it implies a relationship, not a mere *side-by-side*).

(Another parenthesis – apologies! It is not sure that there is, absolutely, something like 'a mere side-by-side'. Juxtaposition is already a relationship. But we may discuss this point later.)

By combining the various arguments I have employed so far, I can say that *communism* is the speech act of existence as it is ontologically being-in-common. This speech act claims (for) the ontological truth of the *common*, that is the relation – which ultimately is nothing else than *sense*.

(I will come back elsewhere to this identity of sense and relation – as well as to the identity of truth and the existential co-.)

Further: the truth of the common is property. Property does not mean only the possession or the belonging. To the contrary, one should rather say that possession or belonging may only be truly understood and determined if *property* is first understood.

Marx wanted to open the way for a property he calls *'individual property'*, as distinct from *'private property'* as from *'collective property'*. Private and collective both refer only to the realm and the categories of law. The law knows only formal and external links. *Individual* property means, on the other hand, property which is proper to the proper *subject* (we may call it 'personal' or even, as Marx does, 'individual').

Subject means the capacity of what we could call 'properness'. The way to enter a relationship or to engage in a link, an intercourse, a communication, which has nothing to do with possessing something (but may also be possible with things, objects). I am *proper* in so far as I commit myself as well as I communicate, that is, as the word makes clear, I am in the common (which in English can be the name for the common or communal place), I am made of it, by it, to it. Freud offers the best way to understand it. As he states, the *I* or the *ego* is only a small disk, almost a point, emerging at the surface of the large *it* which is the totality of the otherwise being of the world. Even in solitude, I am made of the whole world as it takes with 'me' or as 'me' a new singular point of sensitivity.

Communism, therefore, means the common condition of all the singularities of subjects, that is, of all the exceptions, all the uncommon points whose network makes a world (a possibility of sense). It does not belong to the political. It comes before any politics. It is what gives to politics an absolute prerequisite to open the common space to the common itself – neither to the *private* nor to the *collective*, neither to separation nor to totality – without permitting the political achievement of the common itself or an attempt to turn it into a substance. *Communism* is a principle of activation *and* limitation of politics.

At this point it becomes necessary to question the *-ism*. Any *-ism* implies a system of representation, and a kind of ideologization (both in the Marxian and the Arendtian meaning of *ideology*). *Cartesianism* is the ideologization of Descartes's original drive.

I do not want to go into the question of historical or so-called, so oddly called, *real* communism. *Communism* is still exposed to the risk of becoming an ideology and should lose its *-ism*. The word is *commun* without *-ism*. Not even *commun – common, kommune*, any thing that could be taken as something like a form, a structure, a representation – but *com*. The Latin preposition *cum* taken as the universal preposition, the presupposition of any existence.

This is not politics, it is metaphysics or, if you prefer, ontology. To be is to be *cum*. (At the very moment I am writing this, I am surrounded by a singing crowd of *fútbol aficionados* on a *plaza* in Madrid. There is a multitude of symbols, problems, feelings about the common.) But it asks politics this question: how can we think about society, government, law, not with the aim of achieving the *cum*, the *common*, but only in the hope of letting it come and taking its own chance, its own possibility of making sense – if, as I wish to suggest, any sense is necessarily *common sense* or, if not 'common sense' in the common meaning of the phrase, then with the meaning that any sense is made of communication, of sharing or exchange. But of an exchange which is not an exchange of possessions, but an exchange of property, where my property becomes proper by its own *commitment*. Sometimes this is called 'love', 'friendship', sometimes 'faithfulness'. Sometimes 'dignity', sometimes 'art', sometimes 'thought', sometimes even 'life' and 'sense of life' – under all those names lies nothing else than a commitment to the common.

If the question of communism is the question of property – namely, the question of neither collective nor private property but of individual as well as common property, then a double question arisis:

1. What does it mean to be both 'individual' and 'common'? How are we to understand 'the individuality of commonness' and 'the community of individualness'?

2. How are we to think of wealth and poverty in the realm of common-individual property?

I would like to answer the first question by arguing that it has to be taken in terms of the *singular-plural*, which has other implications than 'individual-common'. I do not want to address this matter here (I have already written on it elsewhere), other than to suggest that *singular-plural* avoids the jeopardy of the double substantiality which may be involved in 'individual-common'.

As far as wealth and poverty are concerned the answer is clear: wealth means to possess more than *common* life needs, poverty to have less. The first communist command is obviously that of justice: to give to the common what common life needs. This need is at the same time simple, evident (in a way, it is included in human rights – which nevertheless may be discussed from other points of view), and yet unclear: between the need and the desire or the wish, there is neither a simple nor clear difference.

It is then necessary to think differently. We shall not only take a first step towards 'needs' and their 'satisfaction' – even if, of course, we must insist on a level of elementary or minimal satisfaction. But we must also consider that infinity is involved in each need as its very essence. Need is to be understood as the impulse to get something (like bread, water or space) but also as a drive towards what is not a thing, and maybe is nothing other than infinity.

At this point we are again close to capitalism, that is, to infinity interpreted as the endless accumulation of things (which are all equivalent, as measured by the very possibility of accumulating them, whose name is money – money itself taken as the endless process of *making money*). Capitalism is endlessness instead of infinity, or infinity as the endless production of *capital* itself.

This has been, so to speak, a choice made by civilization. At one point (even if this point is extended over centuries) Western civilization opted for endlessness. This was the point at which infinity as the absolute given in each existence changed into infinity as an endless process towards accumulation.

Of course this choice has been connected with a change in the understanding of wealth.

Control, regulation of the market is not enough. The challenge concerns not only managing the system of production-consumption; it is also about the meaning of wealth. Wealth and poverty may have two quite different uses and meanings. One may be accumulation versus disaccumulation, or enrichment versus impoverishment. Another, what I would call glory versus humility. ('The Humble': the name of a virtue became the name of poor people.)

Perhaps glory and humility cannot be called wealth and poverty. They are related to each other not as the *plus* to the *minus* but as, say, a monk in his simple frock facing a golden altar. Or myself listening to Beethoven's quartets.

Possibly this relationship – whose proper name is *adoration* or *worship*, which names a kind of prayer as well as a form of love – never took place as such in society, or was always already mixed with or transformed into the opposition between wealth and poverty. Nevertheless, as a matter of fact, the couple *rich/poor* as such, and as philosophical as well as moral and religious theme or topic, was formed precisely at the time of pre-capitalism, in Antiquity, between Plato – and the critique of money-making Sophists – and Christ – with his strong rejection of wealth. That age was the first, and in a sense perhaps the last time of the critique of wealth. Wealth no longer thought in terms of its glory but, on the contrary, as the fake brightness *par excellence*.

Our civilization is schizophrenic; it thinks its own value, its main value (money) is fake.

The question of property is the question of the proper property, which belongs to the proper 'person': that is, of the proper 'wealth' (or 'glory' – or, this is the same in a way, the proper 'sense'). Such a proper property may only be *common*. As *private*, it makes no sense (sense for a single one being no sense at all); as *collective* it has the same effect, since the collective is a single – mechanical – unity, not the plurality of the common.

Common is the adequate word for the properness of being, if being means ontologically being 'in common'.

And this is not a 'hypothesis', not an additional speculation about 'being' or, much better, 'to be'. To be is impossible – absolutely impossible – if you think of it as a kind of mere 'thing', or as a kind of 'being' (which often takes the same meaning in our language). 'To be' is not a thing, is no-thing. It 'is' (if we may use this word), or it designates, precisely no thing, not any kind of thing. 'To be' cannot stay among other beings or things. 'To be' means the common character of all beings: that they are. This common character is not itself something else nor something more than the mere fact that 'they are'. They? Yes, all, every thing . . .

Therefore, 'common' has nothing to do with a 'commonness' which would be an attribute or a quality of beings. 'Common' means the opening of the space between beings (things) and the indefinite, maybe infinite, possibility that this space opens, reopens, changes, and modalizes. This space closes itself sometimes but never all the way to the limit of leaving a unique and sole 'being', which would disappear at the very moment of its isolation.

The common means space, spacing, distance and proximity, separation and encounter. But this 'meaning' is not a meaning. It opens precisely beyond any meaning. To that extent, it is allowed to say that 'communism' has no meaning, goes beyond meaning: here, where we are.

10   Communism:
Some Thoughts on the Concept and Practice

Antonio Negri

At the basis of historical materialism lies the claim that history is the history of class struggle. When the historical materialist investigates class struggle, she does so through the critique of political economy. The critique concludes that the *meaning* of the history of class struggle is communism, 'the real movement which abolishes the present state of things' (Marx, *The German Ideology*). It is a case of being *inside* this movement.

People often object to this claim that it is an expression of a philosophy of history. But I think the political meaning of critique should not be mistaken for a historical *telos*. In history the productive forces normally produce the social relations and institutions that contain and dominate them: this is evident in all historical determinations. So why would anyone regard as historical illusion, political ideology or metaphysical nonsense the possibility of subverting this situation and freeing the productive forces from the command of capitalist relations of production (following the meaning of class struggle in operation)? We will try to demonstrate that the opposite is the case.

1

Communists assume that history is always the history of class struggle. For some this position is untenable because history is determined and now so totally dominated by capital that such an assumption is ineffectual and unverifiable. But they forget that capital is always a *relation of power* (of force), that whilst it might be able to organize a solid and overbearing *hegemony*, this hegemony is always the function of a particular command inside a power relation. Neither the concept of capital nor its historical variants would exist in the absence of a proletariat which, whilst being exploited by capital, is always the living labour that produces it. Class struggle is the power relation expressed between the boss and the worker: this relation invests exploitation and capitalist command and is established in the institutions that organize the production and circulation of profit.

Others who claim that history cannot simply be reduced to class struggle assume the permanent subsistence of a 'use value'. They qualify this as the value of labour power or as the value of nature and of the environmental surroundings of human labour. This assumption is not only radically inadequate as an explanation of capitalist development, but is also certainly wrong as a description of the current form of capitalism.

Capital has conquered and enveloped the entire life-world, its hegemony is global. There is no room for *narodniki*! Class struggle develops here, 'from the premises now in existence', not under different circumstances: class relations are founded on these historical determinations (*historical determinism*) and the new *production of subjectivity* (of the boss and worker alike).

Firstly, it is of interest to note that there is no longer an 'outside' in this context, and that struggle (not only struggle, but the substance of subjects in struggle) is now totally 'inside'; there is no longer any semblance or reflection of 'use value'. We are completely immersed in the world of 'exchange value' and its brutal and ferocious reality.

Historical materialism explains how and why exchange value is so central to class struggle: 'In bourgeois society, the worker e.g. stands there purely without objectivity, subjectively; but the thing which *stands opposite* him has now become the *true community* [*das wahre Gemeinwesen*]', which the proletariat 'tries to make a meal of, and which makes a meal of him'.[1]

Yes, but in this alternative appropriation – that of the capitalists against that of the workers – capital definitely appears as a relation. Communism begins to take shape when the proletarian takes it as her objective to re-appropriate the *Gemeinwesen*, the community, to turn it into the order of a new society.

Therefore exchange value is very important, it is the common social reality, built and secured so that it can no longer be traced back to the simple circulation of labour, money and even capital. It is surplus value turned into profit, accumulated profit, rent from land and estates, fixed capital, finance, the accumulation of primary sources, machines and devices productive on earth and then launched into space, communication

---

1   Karl Marx, *Grundrisse*, Notebook V, trans. M. Nicolaus (London: Pelican, 1973), p. 496.

networks, and – finally and especially – money, the great common paradigm: '[Money] is itself the community [*Gemeinwesen*] and can tolerate none other standing above it.'[2] Here lies the historical determination. Exchange value is already given in a common form. As *Gemeinwesen*. It's here, it's the world, there is nothing else or other, no outside.

Take for instance the example of finance: who could conceive of doing without money in the form of finance? Money has become the common land where once the *Heimat* (Homeland) lay, the consistency of populations at the end of the 'Gothic period', when possession was organized into *commons*. Those *commons* and that land are now exchange value in the hands of capitalists. If we want this land back, we reclaim it in the conditions we find it in: at the apex of capitalist appropriation, soiled by exchange value; under no illusions of purity and innocence.

When Spinoza told us that in the Hebrew state in the year of the jubilee all debts were written off and the equality of citizens restored, or when Machiavelli insisted on the fact that the agrarian laws gave new life to the Roman Republic because the plebs' re-appropriation of the land also renewed the democratic process, they were holding onto the illusion that it was possible to go back to nature and democracy.[3]

But for us, determining the liberation of the labour force and being communists demands the re-appropriation of a common reality that is neither original nor democratically desirable, but rather something that stands opposed to us as power after we have reproduced it with effort and blood.

But let us not be discouraged. As Gramsci taught us in his reading of class struggle, historical materialism proposes to grasp the continuous *metamorphosis* or rather the anthropology of the character of the worker through different experiences of the proletarian use of technologies and capitalist social organization.

This introduces a new question, because as the worker changes herself in struggle, she imposes a real *metamorphosis* on capital. If there are epochs or cycles of struggle, their ontological consistency is measured against this anthropological basis. No nature, identity, gender or race can resist this movement of transformation and historical metamorphosis of the relationship between capital and workers. The multitudes are shaped and always re-qualified by this dynamics. This is also valid for the definition

---

2   Ibid., Notebook II, p. 223.
3   Niccolo Machiavelli, *Discourse on Livy*, Book I, Chapter 27 (London: Penguin, 2007), p. 99; Benedict de Spinoza, *A Theological-Political Treatise* (Cambridge: Cambridge, 2007), p. 216.

of time in class struggle. When class struggle appears as the production and transformation of subjectivity, the revolutionary process assumes a long-term temporality, an ontological accumulation of counter-power, the 'optimism' of the material force of proletarian 'reason', the desire that becomes solidarity, the love that is always rational, and following Spinoza, the related 'pessimism of the will'. '*Caution*!', he said, when the passions are mobilized towards the construction of political structures of freedom. Our guide is not the aleatory emergence of rebellions, these divine sparks of hope that can carve paths of light into the night, but the constant and critical effort and work of organization, the calculated risk of insurrection. Philosophical imagination can give colour to the real but cannot replace the effort of history-making: the event is always a result, never a starting point.

2

Being communist means being against the State. The State is the force that organizes, always normally yet always exceptionally, the relations that constitute capital and discipline the conflicts between capitalists and the proletarian labour force.

This being against the State is directed against all the modes of organization of *private* property and the *private* ownership of the means of production, as well as the *private* exploitation of labour power and the *private* control of capital's circulation. But it is also against the *public*, that is, the *state* and *national* configurations of all these operations of alienation of the power (*potenza*) of labour.

Being communist entails the recognition that the public is a form of alienation and exploitation of labour – of *common* labour, in our case. So what is the public? As the great Rousseau said, the public is the enemy of private property, what 'belongs [itself] to nobody' (Jean-Jacques Rousseau, *Second Discourse on the Origin of Inequality*). But it is just sophism to attribute to the State what actually belongs to everyone. The State says: 'The common does not belong to you, despite the fact that you made it, produced it in common, and invented it and organized it as common.' The State's manumission of the common, i.e. what we all produced and thus belongs to us, will go under the name of management, delegation and representation . . . the implacable beauty of public pragmatism.

Therefore communism is the enemy of socialism because socialism is the classical form of this second model of alienation of proletarian power (*potenza*), which also requires a distorted organization of the production of its subjectivity. The perversions of 'real socialism' have neutralized a century of class struggle and dispelled all the illusions of the philosophy of history. It is interesting to see how 'real socialism', despite initiating massive processes of collectivization, never questioned the disciplines of command, be they juridical, political, or pertaining to the human sciences. The institutional structure of socialism and its political polarities were produced by an ideology that arbitrarily opposed private to public – whilst these, following Rousseau, overlap one another – and sanctified a ruling class whose functions of command reproduced those of the capitalist *élite* whilst they claimed to be self-elected 'vanguards'!

Being against the State means, first of all, expressing the desire and ability to manage the entire system of production, including the division of labour and the accumulation and redistribution of wealth, in a radically democratic way – as a 'democracy of all'.

Here it is worth providing new definitions. Historical materialism is also an 'immanentism of subjectivity'. It declares that not only is there no 'outside' to the world we live in, but also that, 'from inside' this world, the workers, citizens and all subjects are ever-present elements of singular resistance and moments in the construction of a different form of common living.

They are present even when the most grievous and dreariest historical lull is suffocating us. Multitude is a class concept and the singularities that compose it are always nuclei of resistance in the relation of subjugation imposed by capital. The singular obeys because he must do so and cannot do otherwise, but always as a resistance, there, inside the power relation. The breaking of this relation is always a possibility, just as much as the maintenance of the relation of command. Here, outside of any philosophy of history, inside this common phenomenology, we perceive how central and essential the possible indignation against power, its order and abuses, and the refusal of wage labour (and/or of labour subjected to the end of reproducing capitalist society) are to the formation of another model of society and the extent to which they point to the present virtuality (virtual presence) of a different order, another prospect of life. These push towards rupture, and can do so because the rupture that is always possible can become real, or rather necessary (and we will come back to the characters of this rupture). There can be revolution.

The insistence on indignation, refusal and rebellion must be able to translate into *constituent power*. The struggle against the State and against all of the constitutions that organize and represent it must also contain the ability to produce new power by means of new knowledge. You can never grip a lightning bolt with bare hands, only the multitude, the history of rebelling class struggle, can do so. But the relation between the historical circumstances and the production of subjectivity keeps changing. As we said earlier, this is one of the realms of development of this continuous metamorphosis of the anthropology of the worker. The *technical* composition of the labour force is in constant motion and corresponds to an always adequate, and different, production of subjectivity. This is a *political* composition that must find concrete forms of expression and desire for revolution in its present circumstances.

The production of subjectivity and new political composition can also anticipate the historical and social conditions in which the revolutionary process is constructed, but there is always a dialectical link between the material determination and the revolutionary tension of collective desire: an elastic band that might snap but remains itself. As Lenin said, dual power is always short-lived, rebel power must hold back the time of history in subjective anticipation (the pushing forward of subjectivity). Constituent power is the key to anticipating and realizing revolutionary will against the State.

In traditional State theory, anarchy and dictatorship are the opposite extremes of all possible forms of sovereign command, but when we speak of *communist democracy* against the State, we do not do so on the grounds of a possible mediation between anarchy and dictatorship. On the contrary, we propose the overcoming of this alternative because revolutionary struggle not only has no outside but the inside that it defines knows a subversive power, that is, a 'below' that is opposed to the 'above' of sovereignty. Communist being is realized from this 'below', from the turning of constituent desires into expressions of power and alternative contents. So there can also be a revolution, as Gramsci taught, 'against *Das Kapital'*.

3

Being communist means building a new world where the exploitation of capital and subjection to the State are eliminated. Starting from our present circumstances, realistically, from the historical determinations that characterize our current condition, how do we move forward towards the realization of communism?

First of all, let us say that this determinism can be broken and overcome only by building a force that is superior to that of those in command. But how do we do that? As we said, political rupture seems necessary once indignation, refusal, resistance and struggle have produced a constituent power that wants to realize itself. Only force makes this move forward, this constituent rupture possible. From strikes, industrial sabotage, the breaking and piracy of systems of domination, migrant flight and mobility to riots, insurrections, and the concrete configurations of an alternative power: these are the first recognizable figures of a collective revolutionary will.

This shift is fundamental – communist imagination is exalted in the moment of rupture. Higher wages against labour exploitation, universal income against the financial crisis, a democracy of all against dictatorship: these are the outcomes of a history that produces constituent will. But this is not enough; even if the cause is insufficient it does not make it less necessary, less a *sine qua non*. It is not enough because there is no revolution without organization, just as the exaltation of the event was not enough, the resorting to myth, or the mystic reference to the bareness of bodies, to a threshold of poverty opposed to the ubiquity of oppression – none of this is enough because there still is no rational design that invests and involves the movements of rupture with the power of organization.

As Spinoza wrote: *'Cupiditas, quae ex ratione oritur, excessum habere nequit'* ('Desire which springs from reason cannot be excessive'),[4] which thus prohibits any definition of desire that arrests itself with (supposedly objective) limits. What I mean to say is that when we think about and experiment with this framework, no teleology or philosophy of history is at play, only a collective desire that, with force, builds up its organized surplus throughout the entire aleatory process of struggles: the surplus of communism in relation to the dull repetition of the history of exploitation. To this end, communism is closer to us today (which doesn't mean that it's around the corner) because the surplus labour extracted from labour power – as it changes with the cognitive metamorphosis – is only with difficulty translated and turned into that surplus value that the capitalist organizes into profit. Cognitive labour is terribly indigestible to capital.

But, as some tell us, there is no evidence to back up the claim that the relation between subjective excess and the communist project is given through the subversive and insurrectional movements of the multitude.

---

4   Spinoza, *Ethics*, Part IV, Proposition LXI (New York: Dover Publications, 1959), p. 229.

This is true. But we would respond that historical materialism and the immanence of the revolutionary project show us a subject that goes against capital and a multitude of singularities that organizes into anti-capitalist power (force), not formally, as a party, a mature and accomplished organization, but, by virtue of its existence, as a resistance that is stronger and better articulated the more the multitude is *a whole of singular institutions* in itself. The latter include forms of life, struggle, economic and union organization, strikes, the rupture of social processes of exploitation, experiences of re-appropriation, and nodes of resistance. At times they win in great clashes on issues that are central to the capitalist organization of society, at other times they lose, though always maintaining levels of antagonism that function as residues in new modes of subjectivation.

The multitude is a group of institutions that takes on different political compositions time after time and in relation to the tenor and vicissitudes of power relations. They are more than the elements of technical composition of the proletariat, and more than the aleatory and/or conjunctural organizations of the oppressed: they are actual moments of political recomposition and coagulates of the subversive production of communist subjectivity. *Cupiditates*![5] Instances of these are different and diversified relations between the expressions of a desire for emancipation (wage labour, social movements, political expressions) and the demand for political and/or economic reform.

From the standpoint of contemporary biopolitical society, the relation between *reform* and *revolution* is different from that in industrial societies. The transformation that has intervened is substantial and can easily be verified by an analysis of the generalization of the methods of *governance* in the exercise of sovereignty, in the current weakening of the classical forms of government. The flows, pressures and alterations of *governance* relations in post-industrial societies show a new terrain where the collision between movements and governments unfolds with alternate outcomes. But these consistently reveal the multiplication of assets for the struggle and organization of reform proposals and subversive tensions that give shape to and internally articulate the multitude. Here we start glimpsing the new *institutions of the common*.

This process is set off from below. It is a movement that is affirmed with force. Rather than dialectics, what describes it is its will to affirmation. It is not teleological, unless we charge the materialist theory and subversive

---

5   Passions, longings, desires, eagerness! (Translator's note)

practice of Machiavelli with ethical and historical finalism. Instead, the multitude is immersed in a process of *transition* that began when 'one divided into two', for as we said earlier, it is difficult to turn the surplus labour of the cognitive proletariat into profit and the latter reveals itself as revolutionary surplus (excess). Rather than a transition from one stage or mode of production to another, this is a change that unfolds inside the multitude itself; it exposes and acts on the web that links the anthropological metamorphoses of subjects to the changes in society and politics, and thus to the possibility of communist emancipation. The society we live in has been really and fully subsumed in capital. We call this command *capitalist biopower*. But if biopower is the product of the activity of capital even when its hegemony is global, this still needs to be based on a relation: the capital relation, always contradictory and possibly antagonistic, placed inside the biopolitical realm where life itself is put to work and all of its aspects are invested by power; but also where resistance is manifest and the proletariat is present in all of the figures where social labour is realized; where cognitive labour power expresses the excess of value, and the multitude is formed. This multitude is not disarmed, because all of these processes that traverse it also describe its institutional articulations and accretion of resistance and subjective emergences.

As we have said, the multitude is a totality of desires and trajectories of resistance, struggle and constituent power. We also add that it is a totality made of institutions. Communism is possible because it already exists in this transition, not as an end, but as a condition; it is the development of singularities, the experimentation of this construction and – in the constant wave of power relations – it is tension, tendency and metamorphosis.

4

What is a communist ethics? As we have seen, it is an ethics of struggle against the State because it moves from the indignation towards subjection and the refusal of exploitation. On the node of indignation and refusal lies the second element of the definition of a communist ethics, which is that of militancy and the *common* construction of struggle against exclusion and poverty, alienation and exploitation.

These two elements (struggle and common militancy) already open onto a new plane: that of a whole of singularities that, withdrawing from solitude, work to make themselves multitude – a multitude that looks for the common against privacy. Does this mean to achieve a democracy? For almost three centuries we have conceived of democracy as the administration of the public good, the institutionalization of the State's appropriation of the common. If we seek democracy today, we need to radically rethink it as the common management of the common. This management entails a redefinition of (cosmopolitan) space and (constituent) temporality. It is no longer a case of defining the form of a social contract where everything is everyone's and thus belongs to no one: everything, as it is produced by everyone, belongs to all.

This shift will only occur in the name of organization. The whole history of the communist movements regarded the issue of organization as fundamental, because organization is a collective-being-against, a principle of institution, and thus the very essence of making-multitude. The facts of the crisis of neo-liberalism, the cultures of individualism, the natural refusal of solitude of human beings who are born and grow up in society, the recognition that solitude is death, manifest themselves as an organization of resistance against the new reduction to solitude which, in individualist morality, capital tries to re-impose upon subjects.

The first three elements of a communist ethics are: revolt against the State, common militancy, and production of institutions. Clearly these are traversed by two fundamental passions: the passion that pushes from natural neediness and economic poverty towards a power of labour and science freed from capital's command; and the passion of love that from the refusal of solitude leads to the political constitution of the common (unsurprisingly, religion, bourgeois aesthetics and all New Age ideologies try to recuperate, mystify and neutralize these passions). By coming together, developing new forms of common coexistence in resistance and organization the constituent power of communism is invented. This concept of constituent power has nothing to do with the constitutional structures that capital and its State have organized. At this point, the power (*potenza*) of labour power, the invention of the multitude and the constituent expression of the proletariat on the one hand, and capitalist power, the disciplinary arrogance of the bourgeoisie and the repressive vocation of the State on the other, are not homologous. Because the constituent ethics of communism runs much deeper and invests the biopolitical dimension of historical reproduction, and as class struggle makes historical being, it is now going to spread inside the determinations of our age onto the whole set of biopolitical *dispositifs*. Here communist ethics touches upon the great issues of life (and of death) and takes on the character of great dignity when it appears as the generous and creative articulation of the power (*potenza*) of the poor and the common desire for love, equality and solidarity.

We have now come to the point where the idea of a practice of 'use value' re-emerges. This use value is no longer *outside* but *inside* the history made by struggles. It is no longer a remembrance of nature or the reflection of a presumed origin, nor an instance in time or an event of perception, but an expression, a language and a practice.

Finally, under no circumstances is it an identity, a reflection on the concrete character assumed as the point of insertion into a universal, but a mixture, a communal, multitudinal, hybrid and mongrel construction, the overcoming of everything that was otherwise known as identity in the dark centuries that precede us. The man emerging out of this ethics is a multicoloured Orpheus, a poverty that history returns to us as wealth rather than origin, as desire-to-come rather than misery. This is the new use value: the *common*. Our existence signals a series of common conditions that we keep wanting to emancipate by withdrawing them from capitalist alienation and State command. Use value is the newly acquired form of the technical composition of labour, as well as the common political *dispositif* that lies at the foundation of the practices of constitution of the world in history. The new use value consists in these *dispositifs* of the common that are opening up new paths for the organization of struggle and the forces of destruction of capitalist command and exploitation.

other forms of egalitarian invention that demonstrated the collective power of emancipated men and women.

I said: we can add. This means: we can draw a deduction from the thesis of the communism of intelligence to forms of collective implementation of this communism. This is where the difficulty appears. How far can the communist affirmation of the intelligence of anybody coincide with the communist organization of a society? Jacotot entirely denied such a possibility. Emancipation, he said, is a form of action that can be transmitted from individuals to individuals. As such it is strictly opposed to the logic of social bodies which is a logic of aggregation governed by laws of social gravitation similar to the laws of physical gravitation. Anybody can be emancipated and emancipate other persons so that the whole of mankind be made of emancipated individuals. But a society can never be emancipated.

This is not only the personal conviction of a maverick individual. Nor is it a mere question of opposing individual emancipation to collective emancipation. The question is: how can the collectivization of the capacity of anybody coincide with the global organization of a society? How can the anarchical principle of emancipation become the principle of a social distribution of tasks, positions and powers? It is about time, I think, to differentiate this problem from the worn-out sermons on spontaneity and organization. Emancipation certainly means disorder, but this disorder has nothing spontaneous about it. Conversely, organization may simply mean the spontaneous reproduction of existing forms of social discipline. What a discipline of emancipation may mean appeared to be a problem for those who, in the century of Jacotot, set out to construct communist colonies, like Cabet, or simply communist parties, like Marx and Engels. Communist communities, like the Icarian community led by Cabet in the United States, failed. They did not fail, as the opinion goes, because individuals could not submit to the common discipline. On the contrary, they failed because the communist capacity could not be privatized. The sharing of the capacity of anybody could not be turned into the virtue of the private communist man. The temporality of emancipation – I mean the temporality of the exploration of collective power – could not coincide with the timetable of an organized society giving to everyone his or her function. Other communities around them did much better. The reason for their success is that they were not made up of communists. They were made up of men and women obeying a religious discipline. But the Icarian community was made up of communists. Therefore the communism of this community was split from the outset into two parts: a communist organization of everyday life ruled by the Father of the Community, and an egalitarian assembly embodying the communism of the communists. After all, a communist worker is a worker asserting his capacity to talk and to make laws about common affairs instead of merely doing his own job as a 'useful' worker. We must bear in mind that this problem had been sorted out very long ago in Plato's *Republic*: for Plato, workers, meaning the people with iron souls, cannot be communist; only the legislators who have gold in their soul can and must let go of material gold and live, as communists, on the production of non-communist workers. In such a way the Republic can be properly defined as the power of communists over workers. It is an old solution, but it still works in the case of the communist state I mentioned earlier, with the help of a solid troop of guardians.

Cabet had no guardians at all. As for Marx and Engels, they decided to disband the Communist Party they had created and to wait for the evolution of the productive forces to produce true communist proletarians – instead of those silly asses who thought they were their equals, though they did not catch anything of their theory. Communism, they said, is not the gathering of emancipated individuals, attempting to experience collective life as a response to selfishness or injustice. It is the full implementation of a form of universality already at work in the capitalist organization of production and the bourgeois organization of forms of life, of a collective rational power already existing, if in the form of its contrary: the particularity of private interests. The collective forces of communism already existed. What was needed was only the form of their collective and subjective reappropriation.

The only problem was of course the *only* itself. But, as we know, the difficulty could be overturned, thanks to two axioms. Firstly there is a dynamic intrinsic to the actualization of those collective forces. The power of the 'unseparate' which is at work in them tends to burst the forms of capitalist 'privateness'. Secondly, it does so even more as that dynamic shatters all other forms of community, all the forms of 'separate' communities, embodied in the State, religion or traditional social bonds, in such a way that the problem of the *only* was overturned: the collective reappropriation, meant by communism, turned out to be the *only* form of possible community still remaining after the collapse of all other communities.

So the tension between communists and community could be settled. The point is that this settlement tends to erase the heterogeneity of the logic of emancipation with respect to the logic of development of the social order. It tends to erase what is at the core of emancipation, namely the affirmation of the communism of intelligence or the capacity of anybody to be where she can't be and do what she cannot do. It tends on the contrary to predicate the possibility of communism on the presupposition of her impotence. Now this declaration of impotence is a twofold one. At a first level it makes the creation of a communist subjectivity the consequence of a disempowerment created by the historical process. The proletariat is the class of society which is no longer a class of society but the product of the decomposition of all classes. As such it has nothing to lose except its chains. And what it has to acquire for its empowerment, namely the awareness of its situation, is something that it is *forced* to acquire by the disempowering process. In other words the competence of the proletarian (or the gold of knowledge) belongs to him only as the product of the experience of the 'iron' condition, the experience of factory work and factory exploitation.

But, on the other hand, the condition of the iron man was set up as a condition of ignorance determined by the mechanism of ideological dissimulation. The iron man, which means the individual caught in the mechanism of exploitation, can only see this process upside down, mistaking subjection for freedom and freedom for subjection. That's why his competence cannot be his competence. It is the knowledge of the global process – with its core, the knowledge of ignorance – a knowledge only accessible to those who are not caught up in the grip of the machine, namely the communists as such.

So when we say that the communist hypothesis is the hypothesis of emancipation, we must not forget the historical tension between the two hypotheses. The communist hypothesis is possible on the basis of the hypothesis of emancipation, meaning the collectivization of the power of anyone. It is possible on the basis of the egalitarian presupposition. At the same time the communist movement – meaning the movement defining the creation of a communist society as its goal – has been permeated from its inception by the opposite presupposition: the inegalitarian presupposition with its various aspects: the pedagogical/progressive hypothesis of the division of intelligence; the counter-revolutionary analysis of the French Revolution as the outbreak of individualism, destroying the forms of social solidarity; the bourgeois denunciation of the autodidactic and anarchic appropriation of words, images, ideas and aspirations by the common people, and so on. The hypothesis of emancipation is a hypothesis of confidence. But the development of Marxist science and of the communist parties mixed it up with its contrary, a culture of distrust based on a presupposition of incompetence.

Not surprisingly, this culture of distrust restaged the old Platonic opposition between the communist and the worker. It did so in a specific form, the form of a double bind, disqualifying the communist impulse in the name of the worker's experience and the worker's experience in the name of the knowledge of the communist avant-garde. Alternatively the worker played the part of the egoistic individual, unable to look beyond the here and now of immediate economic interest, or the part of the expert trained by the long and irreplaceable experience of work and exploitation. The communist in turn played either the part of the individualist anarchist, eager to see his aspirations become real at the risk of overtaking the slow march of the process, or the part of the knowing militant entirely devoted to the cause of the collective. The repression of the golden communist by the iron worker and of the iron worker by the golden communist has been performed by all communist state powers – from the New Economic Policy to the Cultural Revolution – and internalized by Marxist science as well as by leftist organizations. Let us remember, for instance, how my generation moved from the Althusserian assertion of the power of science unveiling the inescapable illusions of the agents of production, to the Maoist enthusiasm for the re-education of the intellectuals by the workers and work factory, at the risk of confusing the re-education of intellectuals through manual labour with the re-education of dissidents through hard labour.

I think that this is one of the major issues at stake if something new is to be thought of, or something forgotten to be revived, under the name of communism. There is not much point, I think, in reviving the idea of communism on the sole basis of the argumentation that indeed it caused a lot of deaths and did many horrible things, but that, after all, capitalism and the so-called democracies also have much blood on their hands. It is the same kind of calculation that compares the number of Palestinian victims of the Israeli occupation with the number of Jewish victims of the holocaust, or the victims of the Nazi holocaust with the millions of Africans subjected to slavery and deportation, the victims of French republican colonization, the Indians massacred in democratic America, etc. This way of making comparisons and hierarchies between evils ends up toppling over into its opposite: the erasing of the differences, the negation of all historical singularities in the name of the equivalence of exploitation with exploitation which is the last word of a certain kind of Marxist nihilism.

I don't think much time should be devoted to this debate. Nor do I think that it is worth reviving the discussion on spontaneity and organization and the ways to take over state power. The history of communist parties and states can certainly teach us how to build strong organizations and how to take over and keep state power. It does not teach as much about what communism as the power of anybody may look like. So I would agree with Alain Badiou that what counts for us as the history of communism or the history of emancipation is above all the history of communist moments, which used to be moments of vanishing or disruption of state powers and of the influence of instituted parties. A moment is not only a vanishing point in time. It is also a *momentum*: the weight that tips the scales, producing a new balance or imbalance, an effective reframing of what the 'common' means, a reconfiguration of the universe of the possible. Nor is it the time of a mere chaotic whirling of unbound particles. Communist moments display higher forms of organization than the routine of bureaucracy. But this organization is always the organization of a dis-order with respect to the 'normal' distribution of places, functions and identities. Communism is thinkable for us as the tradition created around a number of moments, famous or obscure, when simple workers and ordinary men and women proved their capacity to struggle for their rights and for the rights of everybody, or to run factories, companies, administrations, armies, schools, etc., by collectivizing the power of the equality of anyone with everyone. If something has to be reconstructed under the name of communism, it is a form of temporality singularizing the connection of those moments. Now this reconstruction entails a reviving of the hypothesis of confidence in that capacity, a hypothesis that has been more or less suppressed and eventually destroyed by the culture of distrust in the communist states, parties and discourses.

This linkage between the issue of temporality and the question of what a communist subjective affirmation may mean is certainly central in the contemporary forms of re-assertion of the idea of communism. But it seems to me that the discussion has often been pre-empted by some problematic evidences concerning the logic of the capitalist process. This has happened in two main ways. On the one hand, communism has been strongly reasserted as a consequence of the transformations of capitalism itself. The development of the forms of immaterial production has been presented as demonstrating the connection between two formulas of the

Communist Manifesto, the statement that 'everything solid melts into air' and the statement that the capitalists are their own gravediggers. What capitalism mostly produces today, instead of goods available for private appropriation, is a network of human communication where production, consumption and exchange are no longer separated but match up in the same collective process. So, the content of capitalist production is said to break through the capitalist form, and increasingly turns out to be the same as the communist power of cooperative immaterial labour. Here the latent opposition between the 'iron worker' and the 'golden communist' tends to be sorted out by the historical development of capitalism to the advantage of the latter: in that sense, the less work and workers we have, the more communism we have. The most disturbing point for me is that this victory of the communist over the worker appears more and more as the victory of the communism of Capital over the communism of the communists. In his book *Goodbye Mr Socialism* Antonio Negri cites a statement made by another theorist that the financial institutions, notably the pension funds, are the only institutions presently able to give us the measure of accumulated and unified labour, such that today the capitalist institution could be said to embody the reality of collective labour: a communism of Capital that should be turned into a communism of the multitudes. In his presentation at this conference, Antonio Negri very clearly made the point that this capitalist communism is an appropriation of the common by Capital, which means an expropriation of the multitudes from the common. Now, the point is: how far can we name it communism at all? How far can we assert the rationality of this process? At issue in what is called 'crisis' today is precisely this rationality. The current 'crisis' is in fact the failure of the capitalist utopia that has reigned for the twenty years following the collapse of the Soviet Empire: the utopia of the perfect self-regulation of the free market and of the possibility of organizing all forms of human life according to the logic of that market. A rethinking of communism today must take into account the unheard-of situation of the failure of the capitalist utopia.

The same situation forces us to question another form of contemporary Marxist discourse. I am thinking of the pervasive description of a final state of capitalism producing the triumph of a global petite bourgeoisie embodying the Nietzschean prophecy about the 'last man': a world entirely devoted to the service of goods, the cult of the commodity and the spectacle, the obedience to the superego injunction of 'jouissance', the narcissistic consumption of forms of self-experimentation, etc. This global triumph of so-called mass individualism is given in those narrations the name of democracy. Democracy then appears as the lived world built by the domination of Capital and the increasing capitalist destruction of forms of community and universality. This narrative can thus construct a simple alternative: either democracy – meaning the despicable reign of the 'last man' – or a 'beyond democracy' for which communism turns out to be the suitable name.

The point is that many people share the diagnosis without sharing the conclusion: among them, right-wing intellectuals bemoaning the democratic destruction of the social bond and the symbolic order; old-style sociologists opposing good social criticism to bad post-'68 'artistic criticism'; new-style sociologists scoffing at our ineptitude in coping with the reign of global abundance; and philosophers calling us to the revolutionary task of saving Capitalism by instilling into it a new spiritual content. In this context the seemingly good alternative (democratic quagmire or communist surge) soon appears problematic: when you have described the infamous reign of global democratic narcissism, you may conclude that therefore we need communism to get out of this mire. But the question then arises: with whom, with what subjective forces, can you imagine building this communism? So the communist summons is at risk of turning into a Heideggerian prophecy calling on us to reverse as we are on the edge of the abyss, or to engage in forms of action designed mainly to hit the enemy and jam the economic machine. The point is that the sabotage of the economic machine is more efficiently implemented by American traders and Somalian pirates. Unfortunately this efficient type of sabotage creates no space for any communism.

A reconsideration of the communist idea today entails the attempt to disentangle the temporality of its forms of possibility from those temporal plots: the plot which discovers the inherence of communism in capitalism, or the plot which treats communism as the last chance for those on the edge of the abyss. Those two temporal plots are still dependent on the two forms of encroachment of the inegalitarian logic on the logic of emancipation: the progressive logic of Enlightenment, giving to Capitalism the privilege of the schoolmaster educating the ignorant workers and levelling the way from the old inequality to the future communism; and the reactive anti-Enlightenment logic identifying the forms of modern lived experience with the triumph of bourgeois individualism over community. The project of reviving the idea of communism makes sense if it involves the task of re-examining those forms of encroachment and the way they still determine our descriptions of the present. It should involve a reconsideration of the mainstream descriptions of the contemporary world: contemporary forms of capitalism, the explosion of the labour market, the new precariousness of labour and the destruction of systems of social solidarity, all create forms of life and experiences of work that are possibly closer to those of nineteenth-century artisans than to the universe of hi-tech workers and the global petite bourgeoisie given over to the frenetic consumption described by so many contemporary sociologists. Now, the point is not simply about empirical accuracy. It is about the very connection between forms of analysis of the historical process and ways of mapping the possible. We should have learned at last how problematic all strategies based on the analysis of social evolution may be. Emancipation can be neither the accomplishment of a historical necessity, nor the heroic reversal of this necessity. It has to be thought out of its un-timeliness, which means two things: first the absence of historical necessity for its existence, second its heterogeneity with respect to forms of experience structured by the time of domination. The only communist legacy that is worth examining is the multiplicity of forms of experimentation of the capacity of anybody, yesterday and today. The only possible form of communist intelligence is the collective intelligence constructed in those experimentations.

One may object that I define communism in terms not much different from my own definition of democracy. I can answer first that, in my understanding of emancipation, one has to question the classical statement opposing communism to democracy conceived as either the State organization of bourgeois domination, or the lived world framed by the power of the commodity. It is certainly true that democracy can name different things, but the same goes for communism. And the fact is that the combination of the faith in historical necessity with the culture of distrust produces a specific kind of communism: communism as the appropriation of the productive forces by the State power and its management by a 'communist' elite. Again, this is a possible future for capitalism. I don't think it is a future for emancipation. The future of emancipation can only mean the autonomous growth of the space of the common created by the free association of men and women implementing the egalitarian principle. Must we simply call it 'democracy', or is it helpful to call it 'communism'? I see three reasons for the use of the latter: first, it emphasizes the principle of the unity and equality of intelligences; second, it emphasizes the affirmative aspect of the process of collectivization of this principle; third, it stresses the self-superseding capacity of the process, its boundlessness, which entails its ability to invent futures that are not yet imaginable. On the contrary, I would reject the term if it meant that we knew what this capacity can achieve in terms of global transformation of the world, along with the path leading to this point. What we know is what this capacity is able to achieve now, in terms of dissensual forms of collective struggle, life and thinking. The rethinking of communism entails above all the investigation of the potential of collective intelligence intrinsic to the construction of those forms. This investigation supposes the full restoration of what I have called the hypothesis of confidence.

12   Did the Cultural Revolution End Communism? Eight Remarks on Philosophy and Politics Today

Alessandro Russo

1

Sociology today, especially political sociology, which often restricts itself to the inanity of counting and recounting electoral results, is affected by a peculiar theoretical paralysis concerning the question of subjectivities. A sociological workshop on the 'Idea of communism' would hence be unthinkable. This is thus a rare occasion for me to listen to philosophers discussing their views on political subjectivity. The fact that outstanding philosophers should declare here that, despite all their theoretical differences, they share the *Idea* that communism is a fundamental term for philosophy makes this meeting no ordinary academic ritual, but a special event in contemporary philosophy, in particular with regard to its relationship with politics.

As far as politics is concerned, we all know very well how problematic the existence of the very name of communism has been for at least three decades. On the one hand, it has been the object of a profound abjuration, above all among the ranks of the old communist bureaucrats, and yet, on the other hand, the same name stills appears on the insignia of one of the greatest powers in the world, although its literal sense is rather dubious. We cannot believe that the *Manifesto of the Communist Party* of 1848 and the *Statute of the Chinese Communist Party* of 2008 have much in common.

Given this situation, we might think that what we are witnessing here is a migration of the name of communism from politics to philosophy. This conclusion would, however, be far too hasty. The discontinuity between politics and philosophy is a problem that has long been discussed by many of the participants in this conference. Jacques Rancière, for instance, has written of a *mésentente* between politics and philosophy, which is much more than a misunderstanding. It is rather a disagreement, sometimes perhaps even a bitter disagreement. Alain Badiou has developed decisive features of his philosophical system by exploring its basic intransitivity with politics, as well as with the other 'conditions' of philosophy itself. Slavoj Žižek has recently tested his personal proximity to, and distance from, Mao's philosophical texts, trying to disentangle the political and the philosophical issues. In brief, many of us consider that a principle of separation between politics and philosophy is vital for both, but, at the same time, that philosophy without politics cannot exist.

Thus, my first understanding of the 'communist hypothesis' – my hypothesis on this hypothesis, I would say – is that it is the name for an 'ethics of philosophy' concerning its 'political condition'. I have read the thesis that 'from Plato onwards, Communism is the only political *Idea* worthy of a philosopher' as *a philosophical declaration on philosophy*. I am eager to listen to the other speakers, who will clarify this point, but at the moment I consider this thesis above all *a declaration in defence of philosophy*. A defence against whom and what? Against, of course, its perennial adversary, the *doxa*, but also against a peculiar contemporary target, that is to say, *de-politicization*. I mean here not the lack of opposition *amicus/hostis*, but the interdiction that the present regime of opinion imposes on any possible political invention and on the very conception of politics as an invention of thought. Under the rule of present 'opinion' no politics is conceivable outside the logic of state power. Declaring the 'Idea of communism' manifests the radical opposition of philosophy to the enchainment of politics in the 'cavern' of 'governance'.

Today's de-politicization is in fact lethal for philosophy because, in suppressing one of its fundamental conditions, it radically debilitates philosophy itself and aims to make it a scholarly *doxa*, in order, finally, to suppress it. Vice versa, the desire of a philosopher cannot exist, I believe, without contrasting the de-politicization and, at the same time, without scrutinizing the field of politics in search of possible egalitarian inventions. So, my hypothesis is that for the philosopher one of the conditions for not renouncing his own desire is to promote the hypothesis that politics *can only be* an invention for everybody, as absolutely egalitarian as philosophy itself.

2

Might communism, for the same reason, be a hypothesis for politics? The question requires a very different perspective, because the principle of separation between philosophy and politics, which is essential to both, implies that in each of them the same names may have very different destinies. As a name in philosophy, communism can be conceived as being in continuity with a Platonic Idea, albeit materialistically reforged. However, as a name in politics, communism is entangled with a peculiar 'epoch' – that initiated by Marx's *Manifesto* – and it has also been overwhelmed by an 'epochal change', as the statement of our conference says. Yet, where to locate this change, and ultimately how to contemplate this epoch, requires further discussion.

Politics, or rather the only politics worthy of being discussed here, articulates a singular desire to invent forms of mass self-liberation, and deploys its capacities in a register of unceasing subjective discontinuities. It can rely neither on eternal ideas, nor on perennial adversaries. Politics is one of the rarest and most discontinuous modes of subjectivity, or, as Sylvain Lazarus has quite literally discovered, it exists only in given 'sequences', of which the major features are a general brevity and a strong intellectual singularity. Not only is politics a singular mode of rationality, but also each political sequence has its own intellectual stake, that is to say that, in the end, each sequence has its own politics. Out of this invention and reinvention, there are only simulacra of politics; merely the perennial fights among rulers, or would-be rulers, for domination over the ruled.

The theory of politics as a rare, intermittent phenomenon poses a series of new questions which cannot be solved in terms of the previous conceptions of politics as the 'history of class struggle', or as reflecting objective conditions over subjective processes. If politics is a field of intrinsically subjective discontinuities, if it exists only in discrete sequences determined by the singular issues at stake, then how is it possible to think, for instance, of the relationships between two different sequences? And, how can we consider the relationship between a political sequence, which is generally short, and the long phases of de-politicization? Moreover, how is it possible, from this perspective, to rethink the very category of 'epoch' and of epochal change while avoiding the vague teleology of conventional historicism?

A problem of periodization has to be discussed as far as the issue of epochal change is concerned. The statement of the conference cites the year 1990 as the crucial turning point: 'a certain epoch was over'. There can be no doubt about this, but what was the nature of that change? And what were its driving forces? The early '90s, as is well known, marked above all a major change in the twentieth-century state regimes, that is to say, the collapse of the Soviet Union and of almost all the communist party-states. China is, of course, a vast exception that requires special investigation. But, what finally determined that collapse? Not coups d'états, not real military defeats, not disastrous economic crises, nor even popular revolts. Those states were 'ruined' – one of Machiavelli's favourite terms – seemingly in the most ordinary conditions. The undoing of a set of state apparatuses was so sudden, unexpected and unprecedented that highly fantastic explanations are still widespread, such as the threat of 'star wars', the prayers of the pope, the cult of a certain black Madonna in Poland, or the innate superiority of democracy over totalitarianism.

3

The path of research I would propose lies elsewhere: the 1990s should be investigated as the belated result, in terms of state apparatuses, of a series of decisive political events going back to more than two decades earlier. In other words, the end of the communist party-states, though actually *not only* of the communist parties, cannot be contemplated without a profound reconsideration of the political singularities of the 1960s. I am aware that the relationship between the political events of the late '60s and the collapse of the socialist states in the early '90s is far from self-evident. More than two decades separate the Cultural Revolution in China and the end of the USSR, or May 1968 and the fall of the Berlin Wall. The vast difference in the ideological atmosphere, the structure of public opinion, the geopolitical framework, the balance of forces and so on, create the effect of an incommensurable distance between the two situations. The early '90s thus appear as the mark of a patent epochal change, whereas the '60s are, in this perspective, ostensibly the empty prolongation of an old political world, although they were inexplicably crowded with all sorts of subjective unrests. The question of the delayed effects of the '60s on the '90s requires, therefore, a series of argumentative steps, the first of which inevitably concerns the nature of the Cultural Revolution.

The Cultural Revolution I refer to here was not exclusive to China. It was rather the epicentre of a political sequence disseminated in very different national circumstances, from the mid '60s to the late '70s; it was a worldwide political configuration, we might say. The problem is how might we consider those disparate political subjectivities as belonging to the same configuration, and in what sense does all this concern an 'epochal change'? The relationship between this 'political configuration' and the 'epoch' is particularly entangled, since the 1960s–1970s were the moment of the radical destabilization of previous accepted visions of history conceived as the major set of interpretive categories for politics. We must actually examine two overlapping terminations: that, in the late '70s, of a political configuration and that of an 'epoch'.

I propose to consider the 1960s–1970s as the political sequence that brought an epochal space of political knowledge to an end. We could call it the end of a 'political *épistème*', to borrow a well-known category of Foucault's, with, however, one difference that I shall point out. A prerequisite for examining the twofold termination is to disentangle the singular forms of political intellectuality which appeared in that world-wide sequence from the political culture that constituted the 'language of the situation', as Badiou was to call it. The peculiar feature of the Cultural Revolution was a dramatic confrontation between political thought and political knowledge.

All the forms of political subjectivity that appeared in that configuration were deeply permeated with its political culture, whose key categories were 'party', 'class struggle' and 'proletariat'. Let us call it the 'modern revolutionary *épistème*'. Nevertheless, the processes of their real existence – their rise, growth, decline and exhaustion – were determined by the degree of critical self-distancing from the basic elements of that politi-cal culture, or by the intensity of a self-authorization to think politically beyond the boundaries of the 'revolutionary *épistème*'. It is in the light of the insoluble tension, in that sequence, between political subjectivities and political culture, and finally between thinking and knowledge, that I propose to examine the 'twofold termination', that is to say, of a 'political configuration' and of an 'epoch'.

Three dimensions composed the general area of political knowledge in which the revolutionaries of the '60s arose. In actual fact, it was their arrival on the scene that revealed the modern political *épistème* as a three-dimensional structure. Three pillars of that political culture became the major critical issues at stake for all the political subjectivities of that configuration: (i) the party-state, as the sole seat for politics; (ii) the class-based vision of politics and the state; and (iii), the most decisive, the political value of the inclusion of the figure of the worker into the state.

The mutual consistency of the three elements was formed through a series of processes and phases that lasted for almost two centuries. The most important, however, is that their consistency can be grasped only from the point of view of their radical inconsistency, that is to say from the singular political configuration of the 1960s–1970s. In that sequence, the opposition of the new political subjectivities to the party-states, to their bureaucratic conservatism and finally to their anti-political attitude, soon involved the other two dimensions of the general area of modern political culture: the vision of 'class' and the political existence of the 'worker'. The whole process was very tortuous indeed, and detailed research has still largely to be carried out, but the key passages can be described as the subsequent entering into an unprecedented political turbulence of the three above-mentioned epistemic pillars: the 'party', the 'class' and the 'worker'.

4

I will draw most of my examples from the Chinese Cultural Revolution because, although it is the least seriously studied component of that decade, it was the moment when the key elements of the whole configuration were fully displayed. In this sense China was the political epicentre of the 1960s. The local 'culture', the 'habits' and the 'traditions', the 'socio-economic conditions', and all the determinations that constituted China as a particular social and cultural area, were obviously present in the Chinese political events of those years, but say nothing about their immense influence on a worldwide level. The political singularity of the Cultural Revolution, in being indifferent to any particular 'Chinese' determination, was the condition of its universality in the configuration of the 1960s–1970s.

The height of tension was from the outset the confrontation between new self-organized forms of political subjectivity and the party-state, which had been the organizational principle of politics for the whole of the twentieth century. In China, the rise of independent organizations, although they existed only in embryonic forms and exhausted their political originality in under two years, nonetheless constituted the crucial novelty. From 1966 to 1968 several thousands of these organizations existed, most of them printing their own independent periodicals and publications. It should also be recalled that this immense archive has barely been skimmed by historical research, and only a few basic elements of their development are actually known.

Be that as it may, the fact that their existence proved in the end to be an insoluble question in the framework of that political culture was not the particular consequence of a 'totalitarian' regime: in the mid '60s, all over the world, the party-state was the only conceivable place where politics could be organized. In 1966 in China, to admit or deny the possibility that an unlimited plurality of political seats could fully exist outside the CCP caused an irreversible split, which influenced all the following developments decisively. As is well known, Mao warmly welcomed the 'Red Guards' as a possible source of the revitalization of the organizational principles, whereas Liu Shaoqi and Deng Xiaoping saw in them only an element of disorder that should be firmly opposed by drawing 'a line of distinction between the internal and the external', as they said. The demarcation line was, of course, between the party-state as the sole legitimate seat of politics and the claim of the 'Red Guards' to exist as independent entities able to formulate political declarations. The problem was, however, that the real content of these political declarations was, in the last analysis, the claim to exist as independent political bodies capable of formulating political declarations.

The tautology is only apparent since, beyond a number of cultural clichés everybody used at the time, including 'class', 'revolution', 'proletariat' and so forth, which made any difference in the respective positions unintelligible, the first 'demarcation line' concerned the existence of an unlimited plurality of political sites versus the uniqueness of the party-state. The crucial content of those political disputes was the basic condition of politics itself, of its organizational conditions. It was not, indeed, an issue restricted to China: at the core of the political configuration of the 1960s–1970s lay a whole series of vast mass disputes over the political worth of the party-states.

Besides the controversy about the 'demarcation line' between the party and the independent organizations, the principal theoretical-political obstacle that the new organizations encountered was the set of categories around 'class' and 'class struggle'. In those years, the most widespread attitude was to radicalize the 'class' vision, in order to contrast the 'revisionism', or the anti-political attitude, of the party-states. 'Never forget class struggle', Mao said. However, the class-based vision was not only unable to re-politicize, it also revealed that it was in itself a serious factor in de-politicization. In some cases, the reference to the 'class' doctrine, especially in its most extremist version, was even deliberately used to create confusion.

Several examples from China's '60s can be cited showing how important it was to maintain a distance from the class-based vision, and, vice versa, how seriously the latter hindered the development of new forms of political subjectivity. Soon after the *Decision in Sixteen Points*, which stated in early August 1966 that independent organizations were welcome, the most essential divergence became to what degree the freedom to create 'Red Guard' organizations, and to participate in them, could be extended. The 'class' criterion, it should be noted, was one of the main arguments for restricting their existence. In the earliest groups of 'Red Guard' organizations, for example, which were mostly controlled by the sons and daughters of high cadres in the party-state, the prevailing attitude was to admit and to privilege the political activism mainly, and often exclusively, of students with a 'good' class background.

That 'class' vision was particularly obtuse, as in the case of a so-called 'theory of lineage' (*xue tong lun*), according to which the sons and daughters of parents belonging to the 'bad classes' were decidedly anti-revolutionary and, conversely, those with a 'good class' pedigree, which obviously included the 'revolutionary cadres', were innate revolutionaries. This was, needless to say, a degeneration of the historical-political 'class' vision, but it exercised a true influence for a while and was a significant symptom of how the 'class' reference worked in the regime of opinion in the socialist state. This aberrant 'biological classism' was defeated after bitter confrontations, because in the end the explosion of political activism among students could not be contained by means of these disciplinary tricks. However, the worst effects of the 'born-red theory' continued to poison the ideological atmosphere in the following years.

Scholarly research on the Cultural Revolution is an almost barren field, and has, moreover, been severely restricted in China by the 'radical negation' that the government imposes on the events. However, a close analysis of what the current historical narrative invariably describes as manifestations of purely irrational violence might show that they were often entangled with a series of hindrances set up on purpose to constrain the extension of political activism among students. The 'class' reference, while brutally distorted, was one of the most frequently used snares. Other notorious examples were the episodes of hooliganism on the part of the early 'Red Guard' organizations against 'bourgeois' households, including those of renowned artists and writers, which became easy targets (in some cases the police bureaus themselves provided the students with the addresses) and were used to channel political activism away from the real issue at stake, which was in fact about the degree to which independent organizations might exist.

What finally decided the course of events was the question whether, along with students, workers might also form their own independent political organizations. The reference to the class-based vision of politics was obviously omnipresent, and was also used as a pretext to restrain the independent organizations, but in this case the controversies involved a set of fundamental theoretical and organizational elements and were therefore much tenser and more oriented towards real alternatives. The massive appearance of the workers on the political scene of the Cultural Revolution, however, not only did not clarify the 'class' issue, but was also the factor in a decisive impasse, and finally in the undoing, of the entire network of references of the very category of 'working class' in the 'revolutionary *épistème*'.

When in Shanghai, in the autumn of 1966, the first groups of workers declared that they had formed organizations of 'Revolutionary Rebel Workers', or 'Red Guards', independent of the party-state, they created a serious predicament for the entire leadership of the CCP. Even the Maoist leaders in Beijing, the 'Group in Charge of the Cultural Revolution', who at that time de facto governed the central organs of the party-state, were not able to express a clear-cut attitude immediately. For its part, the Shanghai Party Committee was definitely against them and fostered instead another organization called the 'Scarlet Guards'. Most of the members of the latter were workers too, but their political programme declared above all that the 'Revolutionary Rebels' should not be allowed to exist, because they were anti-revolutionary and enemies of the 'working class'. For the 'Scarlet Guards', a name clearly claiming a brighter 'red', the only organizational condition of the workers was to remain firmly within the forms established by the leadership of the party-state.

The opposing organizations soon attracted several hundred thousand members, and within a few weeks virtually the entire 'working class' of Shanghai became involved in the dispute. The unrest produced in January the collapse of the Shanghai Party Committee and the Municipal Committee, which had been unable to deal with the situation other than with measures that had only served to increase the confusion, such as an unexpected distribution of bonuses among workers in order to quell the protest. This all finally led to the collapse of their authority, in the sense of the loss of their capacity to ensure obedience. In actual fact, it was an 'abdication', rather than a dismissal from above.

But, what really set the two camps in opposition? And why was it so inextricably difficult for the party authorities to deal with the situation?

Among the great political events of the twentieth century, the Shanghai January Storm is probably the least studied. This is in part a consequence of the severe censorship concerning research on the Cultural Revolution imposed by the Chinese government after 1976, but the most fundamental reason is undoubtedly theoretical. The intensity of the contrast between 'Red' and 'Scarlet' cannot be explained by any conceptualization in terms of 'class analysis', in the sense both of conventional historical materialism and of academic political sociology. All the research on the topic, to tell the truth very scanty indeed, which has analysed the division between the two camps as a consequence of socio-economic conditions (for instance, temporary workers against tenured workers), as well as the outcome of the influence of opposing factions in the CCP leadership (Maoists versus 'moderates'), has hardly produced any convincing results. When examined carefully, the socio-economic status of the workers in the different organizations turns out to be frequently quite similar, while the influence of the divisions among the party leaders was very controversial and contradictory. In the case of the 'Scarlet Guards' the patronage of the local party authorities was evident, but it was not, I believe, a decisive factor.

The split was essentially subjective, not the reflection of 'objective' socio-economic conditions, or of bureaucratic forces. Masses of workers were affected by a widespread anxiety concerning nothing less than the figure of the worker in contemporary politics. For the 'Revolutionary Rebel Workers' the capacity to organize their own political entities in order to 'carry out the Cultural Revolution' was truly decisive, while for the 'Scarlet Guards' it was totally unthinkable that workers should form independent organizations. The 'line of demarcation' was in this case, too, between the uniqueness of the party-state and the unlimited plurality of independent political organizations, with the added complication that the figure of the worker was placed at a key point in the consistency of the party-state, an issue, moreover, which was not restricted to China, or to communist parties alone. If the student organizations had been perceived as a challenge to the stability of the party-state and had created an irreversible political split in the leadership of the CCP, the existence of independent worker organizations constituted a far more radical danger, since it affected the fundamental nucleus of the very existence of the socialist state.

5

I do not intend here to extend this very short conceptual history of the Cultural Revolution any further. The point is that the political configuration of the 1960s, seen from its Chinese epicentre, brought to a close an entire network of political knowledge. It proved the political exhaustion of the three basic concepts that structured the consistency of that area of knowledge; namely, it proved that (i) *the party-states* were anti-political; (ii) *the class-based vision of politics*, albeit in a radical version, was not able to revitalize parties, but was, on the contrary, a serious hindrance to the development of new political subjectivities; (iii) *the inclusion of the political figure of the worker in the state* was falsely political, but had evolved rapidly into new disciplinary forms both in the factory and in the state order.

It is clear, however, that these three 'basic concepts' of the modern political *épistème* were not limited to the communist party-states. The political parties were peculiar institutional novelties in all forms of state in the twentieth century. As Sylvain Lazarus argued, all the 'regimes of the century' – socialist, parliamentary and also fascist – were built around the crucial role of the party-state. Something similar must be argued about the class-based vision. Class and class struggles were concepts that were not Marxist inventions, but, as Marx himself acknowledged, were invented by the 'bourgeois historians and economists', including Ricardo, Guizot, Thierry, Mignet and so on. The main inventor of the thesis 'all history is the history of class struggle' was Guizot rather than Marx. A class-based vision, in different forms, then became a basic orientation of all the forms of the modern state from the nineteenth century. Marx said that his particular new concept was not the class struggle, but the theory of the end of the classes through the 'dictatorship of the proletariat'. Even the political value of the worker was not exclusive to the socialist state. It was the same, in different forms and degrees, in the parliamentary states, too. The 'welfare state', for instance, would not have been conceivable without a certain 'inclusion' of the worker into the state, through leftist parties, trade unions and so forth. In brief, the termination of the modern political *épistème* was not limited to the socialist state.

The 'epochal passage' in actual fact concerned all forms of the twentieth-century state. In the statement of the conference it is said that the '90s saw the failure not only of the socialist states, but also above all of the 'democratic left'. My point is that the collapse of the socialist states, whose roots go back to the Chinese Cultural Revolution, namely to the radical impasse of the relationship between the working class and the Communist Party, initiated a crisis on a worldwide level, which radically affected the 'party' as the general form of the organization of the state.

6

If we say that the Cultural Revolution brought the modern revolutionary *épistème* to an end, what can be said about the name 'communism'? The question in the title of my presentation needs to be clarified. In fact, the CR did not *put an end to* the name 'communism'. The Cultural Revolution, rather than *ending* communism, *divided* it into two, to quote Mao's favourite philosophical motto. The result of the Cultural Revolution, and, needless to say, of the radical impasse that concluded the last ten years of Maoism in China, was a split of the name 'communism' into two, or in other words, it produced the division of the name 'communism' into *a name in philosophy* and *a name in politics*. As a name in philosophy 'communism' does exist, as we can see at this conference. We cannot say that the Cultural Revolution actually ended communism as a philosophical ιδέα. It is the name for a desire of the philosopher, a desire that perhaps the present conditions of de-politicization make even more acute.

What is to be said about politics? If one considers the discontinuous character of politics, 'communism', rather than being a name for a singular political thought, has been the name in a political culture to which different political sequences have referred. Communism was the name for the maximum extension of an area of political knowledge in the sense discussed above. It was the name for the very consistency of the 'modern revolutionary *épistème*', to which different singular political configurations, existing in different times and places, referred from the nineteenth century to the 1970s.

Can 'communism', then, be a name in politics today? There is a problem that I have briefly mentioned above: communism still exists as the name for a powerful party-state. Thus, if a political creation today, a new political organization aiming to invent forms of mass self-liberation, refers to the name 'communism', a problem soon arises: how is one to deal with the Chinese Communist Party? Is it the same 'communism'? If the answer is 'Yes', then the problem is solved, but some of us would have several objections. Furthermore, I am afraid, the Chinese Communist Party would also have many objections. However, if it is not the same 'communism', any political organization that should decide to refer to the

masses'. We might adopt formulas that are less inscribed in the language of the 'people's war', but politics absolutely must find new forms of relationship with philosophy today.

The basic conditions for this reinvention are, of course, that the previous political-philosophical 'sutures' should not be repeated, and that the principle of separation between politics and philosophy be stressed. The most decisive condition, however, is that the new relationships must be built starting not from the *philosophia perennis*, but from the contemporary issues at stake for philosophy as well as for politics. It goes without saying that there are different philosophies and philosophers, but there are at least two issues that constitute, I believe, essential novelties for the entire field of contemporary philosophy, which politics cannot renounce if it is to establish a new intellectual *vis-à-vis*: a new exploration of the theory of the subject and a materialist rethinking of the theory of the state.

In contemporary philosophy, namely in French philosophy, which has constituted its core at least since the '60s, a new exploration of the terrain of the subject and subjectivity has begun; it departs radically from previous conceptions, both those affiliated with the transcendental subject, and those of the dialectics between the objective and the subjective. Alain Badiou is certainly the philosopher who has explored in greatest depth the new logical possibilities of a theory of the subject, strengthened by a radical reconstruction of the edifice of ontology, and placing the question within the framework of a field of theories of subjective singularities. The very idea of the 'conditions of philosophy', above all of mutually independent conditions, is a great rational resource, a truly emancipatory perspective – not only for philosophy, but also for all single modes of thought, including politics, and for their mutual relationships, including undoubtedly the relationships with philosophy itself.

The other major stake in contemporary philosophy, which political thought cannot avoid considering carefully, is the question of the peculiar materiality of the state. The previous conceptions of the state as embodying an ideal of sovereignty or even of justice, as well as of the state as reflecting an external and more structural materiality, finally converged in situating the state in the sphere of mere 'ideality', where it was extremely difficult to establish a rational delimitation of its obscure objectivity. In contemporary thought, every great philosophical figure, from Sartre on, has been deeply concerned with the issue of the permanence of the figure of the state as a result of a sort of structural objectivity intrinsic to the subjective world itself, or rather of a radical communitarian deficit of the speaking being. Although very different paths of research have been opened by different philosophers, such as Althusser's theory of 'state apparatuses', Foucault's 'governmentality', Badiou's 'state of the situation', or Hardt and Negri's concept of 'empire', they compose, despite all the divergences, a philosophical configuration that provides rich intellectual references to renew the vision of the state in radical fashion.

All possible contemporary political inventions should definitely engage in a new intellectual proximity with philosophy as far as these issues are concerned. Moreover, these philosophical explorations into subjectivity and into the state clearly have a background in the most burning political issues. Mao said, as is well known, that correct ideas neither come from heaven, nor are they innate, but they come from various forms of 'practice'. Many of the contemporary philosophical ideas on subjective singularities and on the peculiar materiality of the state are strongly enmeshed with 'social practices', and all the above-mentioned philosophical figures have been involved in political militancy. In actual fact, the process of the close of the 'communist *épistème*' has been, for these philosophical meditations, much more than a major source. It has often deeply affected personal intellectual itineraries, creating a singular 'political condition' for contemporary philosophy. The fact that, after its closure as a political name, 'communism' arises once again as an outstanding name in philosophy, however paradoxical this might seem, is actually a sign that philosophy cannot renounce a particular political concern pivoting on the very concept of equality. It is starting from the declaration of this concern that political thought should reassess its long-term 'disagreement' with philosophy and establish a new terrain for intellectual friendship.

13   The Politics of Abstraction:
Communism and Philosophy

Alberto Toscano

What might it mean to be a communist in philosophy, or to treat communism as a philosophical idea? A scandal or an anachronism for its detractors, such a question is not likely to sit well with communism's relatively sparse and beleaguered partisans, for whom speculative abstraction might stand as the nemesis of concrete politics. This essay seeks to foreground what I'd like to call the politics of abstraction – signalling both the political contests over the conceptual definition of communism and the often polemical characterization of communism as an abstract politics – in order to reconsider the manner in which philosophy is caught up in the very emergence of the idea of communism. Communism develops both *from* and *against* philosophy. To rethink the idea of communism today is also to rethink this double movement, of immanence and separation, inheritance and refusal.

A philosophical reflection on communism is immediately confronted with two apparently opposed retorts. From the standpoint of its most dogged opponents, communism is a political pathology of abstraction, a violent denial of worldly differences and customs, paying no heed to the density of history and the inertia of nature. It is the doomed attempt to philosophize the world into something other than what it is. In Hegel's vocabulary, communism is a figure of *fanaticism*. That is, to quote *The Philosophy of History*, 'an enthusiasm for something abstract – for an abstract thought which sustains a negative position towards the established order of things. It is the essence of fanaticism to bear only a desolating destructive relation to the concrete.'[1] In a world of differences, hierarchies and stratifications, how could an intransigent politics

---

1   G. W. F. Hegel, *The Philosophy of History* (New York: Dover, 1956), p. 358. This passage is taken from Hegel's discussion of Islam, whose politics of abstraction he elsewhere treats as analogous with those of the French Revolutionary Terror. See Hegel, *Lectures on the Philosophy of Religion, Vol. III: The Consummate Religion* (Berkeley: University of California Press, 1985), p. 218. I deal with these passages, as well as with the twentieth-century polemical analogies between Islam and communism, in *Fanaticism: The Uses of an Idea* (London and New York: Verso, 2010).

of egalitarianism be anything other than fanatical? Such views, which first gained momentum in reaction to the French Revolution – especially in Burke and his epigones – have continued to shadow the various instantiations of what Badiou calls 'generic communism'. This was (and remains . . .) the case in the literature of Cold War anti-totalitarianism, for which the desolations and destructions of Stalinism are to be referred, in the last instance, not to the logic of political and class struggles, or to the bellicose encirclement of the Soviet Union, or indeed to the baleful mechanics of bureaucratization, but to the fundamentally 'ideocratic' character of political rule in historical communism. Abstract thought is to blame – as the notion of 'ideocracy' intimates.[2] As a very minor contemporary example, consider these lines from a recent British review of Badiou's *The Meaning of Sarkozy*: 'So when he quotes Mao approvingly and equivocates over the rights and wrongs of the Cultural Revolution, it is hard not to feel a certain pride in workaday Anglo-Saxon empiricism, which inoculates us against the tyranny of pure political abstraction.'[3]

But this reproach of abstraction[4] is also – and this is my second point – internal to communist thinking itself, especially and above all in its Marxian variant. As early as his 1843 correspondence with Arnold Ruge, published in the *Deutsch-Französische Jarbucher*, Marx cast doubt on the emancipatory powers of a communism – the sort associated with the likes of Weitling or Cabet – which operated as a 'dogmatic abstraction'. As he remarks, it is precisely

> the advantage of the new movement that we do not anticipate the world with our dogmas but instead attempt to discover the new world through the critique of the old. Hitherto philosophers have left the keys to all riddles lying in their desks, and the stupid, uninitiated world had only to wait around for the roasted pigeons of absolute science to fly into its open mouth.

This is why the partisans of the new movement do not 'confront the world with new doctrinaire principles and proclaim: Here is the truth, on your knees before it! It means that we shall develop for the world new principles from the existing principles of the world.'[5] Is this profes-

---

2   The term, employed by the historian Martin Malia in *The Soviet Tragedy*, is (rather sympathetically) criticized in Claude Lefort, *Complications: Communism and the Dilemmas of Democracy*, trans. Julian Bourg (New York: Columbia University Press, 2007).

3   Rafael Behr, 'A Denunciation of the "Rat Man"', *Observer*, 1 March 2009.

4   See Peter Osborne, 'The Reproach of Abstraction', *Radical Philosophy* 127 (2004).

5   Karl Marx, *Early Writings*, trans. Rodney Livingstone and Gregor Benton (London: Penguin, 1975), pp. 207 and 208.

sion of critical and political immanence a mere abdication of philosophy? Far from it. Marx's problem, and the problem of communist politics and communist theory, will remain that of a *non-dogmatic anticipation*. And the character and modalities of this anticipation will mutate in accordance with the conjuncture that confronts it.

Taking Marx's 'Introduction to a Critique of Hegel's Philosophy of Right' as emblematic in this respect, it is possible to suggest that the anticipatory function of philosophy is inversely proportional to the revolutionary maturity of the situation in which it intervenes. Marx's plea for radicalization is insistently contextualized in terms of German *backwardness*. What is perhaps most arresting about this text is precisely how the most generic of programmes, universal social emancipation, is meticulously and strategically situated in a very *singular* political predicament. Having lyrically encapsulated the results of the critique of religion, which he regards as having been 'essentially completed' for Germany, Marx is confronted with the obstacles preventing the prolongation of the unmasking of religious abstraction into the vanquishing of social and political abstraction, of 'the criticism of heaven . . . into the criticism of earth, the *criticism of religion* into the *criticism of law* and the *criticism of theology* into the *criticism of politics*'. But the retrograde character of the German situation impairs the force of critique as generative, immanent negativity. In Marx's caustic words: 'Even the negation of our present political situation is a dusty fact in the historical junk room of modern nations. If I negate powdered wigs, I am still left with unpowdered wigs.'[6] Or, as we may echo today: 'If I negate subprime mortgages, I still have mortgages.'

What is the critical philosopher to do when faced with an anachronistic regime that, as Marx puts it, 'only imagines that it still believes in itself'?[7] The German anachronism is double: on the one hand, the farce of restoration without revolution in practice; on the other, the anticipation of the future in theory. It is the latter which alone is worthy of the kind of immanent critique that would be capable of extracting, out of the productive negation of the purely speculative image of 'ideal history',[8] the weapons for a genuine overturning of the status quo. In other words, the radicalism of philosophy – that is, of philosophy's existence as the self-criticism of philosophy – is dictated by the paradoxical coexistence

6   Ibid., p. 245.
7   Ibid., p. 247.
8   Ibid., p. 249.

of practical backwardness and theoretical advance. In order to be properly radicalized, the situation surveyed by Marx is thus *compelled* to pass through philosophy. Neither a practical repudiation of philosophy nor a philosophical overcoming of practice are possible: '*You cannot transcend philosophy without realizing it*', nor can you '*realize philosophy without transcending it*'.[9] It is important to stress that though these may appear as universally binding postulates, they are specified by Germany's anomalous retardation, its admixture of political anachronism (the powdered wigs) and philosophical anticipation (Hegel's *Philosophy of Right* as the most advanced articulation of the modern state, a state which of course does not actually exist in Germany). This anomaly even permits Marx to hint at Germany's comparative revolutionary advantage, as when he asks: 'can Germany attain a practice *à la hauteur des principes*, that is to say, a revolution that raises it not only to the *official level* of modern nations, but to the *human level* that will be their immediate future?'[10]

Notwithstanding Marx's faith in theoretical emancipation and his conviction that theory is not a mere collection of ideas but 'an *active* principle, a set of *practices*',[11] philosophy's practical conversion appears thwarted by the absence of the '*passive* element' or '*material* basis' for revolutionary praxis. This basis would ordinarily be found in the domain of civil society, in the sphere of needs: 'A radical revolution can only be the revolution of radical needs, but the preconditions and seedbeds for such needs appear to be lacking.' In other words, the 'theoretical needs' that emerge from the immanent critique of philosophy do not translate into 'practical needs'. The sheer immaturity and disaggregation of the German polity means that the 'classical' model of partial and political revolution is inoperative. But Marx could not countenance a praxis simply determined at the level of essence or of philosophy. As he unequivocally put it: 'It is not enough that thought should strive to realize itself; reality must itself strive towards thought.'[12] This embryonic version of Marx's later 'method of the tendency'[13] dictates that radical emancipation find its

---

9   Ibid., p. 250.

10   Ibid., p. 251.

11   'Marx, far from rejecting the importance of "ideas" (or "theory") in history, assigns them a leading role, or even, perhaps, makes them history's driving force, on condition – and it is, evidently, this condition which marks his break with idealism – that the "theory" in question is not a collection of ideas but an *active* principle, a set of *practices*' (Stathis Kouvelakis, *Philosophy and Revolution: From Kant to Marx*, trans. G. M. Goshgarian [London and New York: Verso, 2003], p. 324).

12   Marx, *Early Writings*, p. 252.

13   See Antonio Negri, 'Crisis of the Planner State', in *Books for Burning*, ed. Timothy S. Murphy (London and New York: Verso, 2005), pp. 26–30.

objective or *positive* possibility' in 'the formation of a class with *radical chains*', the proletariat – that the impossible become real.[14]

The aim of this brief excursus is to stress that, even as critical attention shifts from the limits of the political state to the mode of production and its laws of motion, the demand for a *non-dogmatic* anticipation will continue to define Marx's work, as will the need to reassert the difference between the approach of the 'new movement' and that of dogmatic foresight, especially when the latter takes the form of 'philosophical fantasies' of a truth which would serve as the standard against which to judge social change – Marx and Engels's main accusation, in the *Communist Manifesto*, against utopian socialism. This figure of philosophical anticipation, initially framed in terms of reality striving towards thought, and later enveloped and surpassed in the critical knowledge of capitalism's tendencies, has significant repercussions on our very idea of communism. The specificity of communism stems from its intrinsic and specific temporality, from the fact that, while never simply non- or anti-philosophical, it is an idea that contains within it, inextricably, a tension towards realization, transition, revolution.

I want briefly to draw the consequences of this argument in terms of four interlinked dimensions of the notion of communism that challenge the philosophical sufficiency or autonomy of the concept: equality, revolution, power and knowledge. These are dimensions that contemporary radical thought sometimes defines *by contrast* with the historical vicissitudes of communist politics and its associated critique of political economy. Thus, *economic* equality is sometimes treated as the counterpart to equality as a *philosophical* principle or axiom; power, especially state power, is regarded as a dimension external to philosophical questioning about communism; *knowledge* is juxtaposed to *truth* and revolution is regarded as an, at best, enigmatic and, at worst, obsolete model of emancipatory change.

Let's begin with equality. The affirmation of equality, both as a political maxim and as a social objective, lies of course behind the age-old view of communism as a dangerous levelling force, a violent abstraction unleashed on a world of embedded customs and refractory differences. But communism – in its own words, so to speak – has also, at different times, articulated its *own* criticism of equality as abstraction. Consider the *Critique of the Gotha Programme*, and the commentary on that document in Lenin's *The State and Revolution*. Faced with a truly 'economistic' theory

---

14   Marx, *Early Writings*, p. 256.

of justice (the social-democratic ideal whereby equality signifies fair distribution, the equal right of all to an equal product of labour), Marx retorts – in passages whose significance for the *concept* of equality have yet, one might contend, to be fully assumed – that the notion of equality implied by this distributionist vision of communism is still steeped in the very abstractions that dominate bourgeois society. Speculating about a communist society that *emerges from* capitalist society – and is thus, not just its negation, but its *determinate* negation – Marx notes that the abrogation of exploitation and the capitalist appropriation of surplus value would *not yet* end the forms of injustice that inhere in the domination over social relations by the abstraction of value. In a nascent communist society, distribution is still 'governed by the *same* principle as the exchange of commodity equivalents: a given amount of labour in one form is exchanged for the same amount in another'.

Equality in such an embryonic, transitional communism is still beholden to the domination of a standard, *labour*, which is itself the bearer of inequalities – of capacity, productivity, intensity, and so on. The equal right so blithely invoked by the social democrat is thus '*in its content one of inequality, just like any other right*', since a 'right can by its nature only consist in the application of an equal standard' to *unequal* individuals.[15] In other words, a political and philosophical notion of equality as a right, grounded on the idea of an abstract and universal measure or standard, still bears the birthmarks of a form of social measurement based on the value of labour. In Lenin's gloss, 'the mere conversion of the means of production into the common property of the whole of society . . . *does not remove* the defects of distribution and inequality of "bourgeois right" which *continues to dominate* in so far as products are divided "according to work"'.[16]

What philosophical lessons are to be drawn from these remarks for our idea of communism? First of all that, to the extent that communism is the *determinate* and not the simple negation of capitalism – i.e. inasmuch as it is not a 'dogmatic abstraction' – the problem of its realization is inherent to its concept. The communist problem of equality is the problem of an equality, to quote Lenin, '*without any standard of right*'[17] – that is, an equality which does not perpetuate the inequalities generated under

---

15   Karl Marx, 'Critique of the Gotha Programme', in *Karl Marx: A Reader*, ed. Jon Elster (Cambridge: Cambridge University Press, 1986), p. 165.
16   V. I. Lenin, *The State and Revolution* (Beijing: Foreign Languages Press, 1976), p. 114.
17   Ibid., p. 115.

capitalism by the domination of social relations by the measures of value, the labour-standard in particular. Such a 'non-standard' equality can only be envisaged as an outcome of revolution and transition.

From a philosophical standpoint, we could wonder whether the very notion of equality is still at work here. Rather than either affirming the principled equality of human beings or promising their eventual levelling, communist 'equality' implies creating social relations in which inequalities would be rendered inoperative, no longer subsumed as unequal under an equal standard or measure of right. This idea of equality beyond right and value is of course in its own way profoundly abstract – but it demonstrates, first, how the philosophical contribution of communism involves a struggle against a certain type of abstraction (the kind which is derivative of the capitalist form of value and the standards the latter imposes), and second, how the question of realization is intrinsic to the idea of communism. In effect, I think it would be more appropriate, when it comes to Marx and Lenin's discussions of equality, to speak of a problem rather than an idea of communism, in line with Deleuze's definition of a problem in his *Bergsonism* and with reference to Marx, as something that 'always has the solution it deserves, in terms of the way in which it is stated (i.e., the conditions under which it is determined as a problem), and of the means and terms at our disposal for stating it. In this sense, the history of man, from the theoretical as much as the practical point of view is that of the construction of problems'.[18]

In what concerns the concept of equality, we can thus see how a communist philosophy or theory might 'anticipate' a communist politics, not in the sense of producing its own futurological standard against which to measure instances of communism, but by delineating the problems and lines of solution that communism calls for. As I hope to have suggested with reference to the concept of equality, while communism should not be envisaged in terms of ossified programmatic principles or anachronistic refrains, it can be usefully conceived in terms of problems that orient their own resolution. Communism, to quote an evocative and minimal definition from Engels's *Principles of Communism*, is 'the doctrine of the conditions for the liberation of the proletariat'. Precisely because doctrine and conditions are not immobile, communism is never exempt from the need to formulate its protocols of realization. This has important consequences for the philosophical debate about communism, which cannot but also be

---

18   Gilles Deleuze, *Bergsonism*, trans. Hugh Tomlinson and Barbara Habberjam (New York: Zone Books, 1991), p. 16.

a debate about communist *power*. By power I mean the collective capacity both to prefigure and to enact the principles of communism. Too often, in recent discussions, responding both to the grim vicissitudes of communist politics in the short twentieth century and to meanings given to the idea of power in the social and political sciences (from Weber's domination to Foucault's governmentality), there has been a tendency to think that the philosophy and politics of communism need to separate themselves from power, to think a dimension of politics removed from questions of force, control and authority. But precisely because communism cannot be separated from the problem – rather than the programme – of its realization, it can also not be separated from the question of power.

This is a vast debate, to which it is impossible to do justice in a few lines, but I think a couple of points can nonetheless be made. First of all, for the problem of communism and power to be even posed without falling into the usual traps, we need to overcome the apparent antinomy between communism as the name for a form of political *organization* with social transformation as its aim, and communism as a form of social and economic *association* with social equality as its *practice*. It is the least one can say that in the twentieth century the relations between crafting the means for the conquest of power and enacting the transformation of everyday life have been immensely problematic, and that the very notion of a 'politics of producers', to use the Marxian formulation, has been overwhelmed by historical conflicts that have left the legacies of commune, council and soviet, with some rare exceptions, in a state of abeyance. But the problem – of thinking together these two aspects of communist practice, organization and association – remains. To reify them in the separation between politics and the economy is deeply unsatisfactory, precisely because, as I indicated *vis-à-vis* equality, the problem of moving beyond right and beyond value is inextricably a political and an economic problem; indeed, it directly upsets the very distinction between the two. In trying to overcome the antinomy between organization and association, between the instruments and the everyday practice of communism, we are obliged to address the question of power. But we cannot blithely reduce this question to the dimension of the state. The rather sterile doctrinal disputations over the evils and virtues of the seizure of state power tend to obscure the far greater challenge posed by thinking revolutionary politics in terms of the *splitting* of power – not just in the guise of a face-off between two (or more) social forces in a situation of non-monopoly over violence and political authority, but in the sense of a fundamental asymmetry in the *types* of power. That is why the problems posed by the notion of 'dual power' remain, as various political conjunctures around the world suggest, of such political, and indeed philosophical, significance – despite the fact that they cannot be conceived in ways congruent with their Leninist formulation in the interregnum between the February and October revolutions.[19]

The urgent challenge of dual power lies in the asymmetry that it introduces into the very concept of power. Power is not a homogeneous element to be accumulated, but a name for heterogeneous and conflicting forms of practice. Thus the power wielded by the soviets is incommensurable with that of their bourgeois counterparts, however 'democratic' they may be, because its source lies in popular initiative and not in parliamentary decree; because it is enforced by an armed people and not a standing army; and because it has transmuted political authority from a plaything of the bureaucracy to a situation where all officials are at the mercy of the popular will, and its power of recall. With its paragon in the Commune, this power is both *organizational*, in the sense that it incorporates strategic objectives, and *associative*, in that it is inseparable from the transformation of everyday life – but more to the point, because it is in and through the practice of association that the political capacity to organize is built up. The notion of a 'prefigurative communism' has its place here.[20] This is especially significant today because finding the means to make the communist hypothesis exist, to adopt Badiou's formulation, means finding efficacious ways of fostering such a political capacity.

Perhaps the most difficult problem for a philosophy concerned with – to repeat a term introduced at the outset – the *non-dogmatic anticipation* of communism, involves linking this subjective demand to build power qua political capacity with the question of the knowledge of the tendencies that traverse the conjuncture of contemporary capitalism. If – and these I think are preconditions for the intelligibility of communism as a concept distinct from those of equality or emancipation – communism is to be understood as a determinate negation of capitalism and its concrete forms of abstract domination, and as concerned with the 'conditions of liberation' that Engels spoke of, what role for knowledge? After all, the communist notion of revolution – regardless of the particular form it might take – lies at the intersection between the presence of a political

---

19   See Alberto Toscano, 'Dual Power Revisited: From Civil War to Biopolitical Islam', *Soft Targets* 2.1 (2007), available at www.softtargetsjournal.com.
20   See Carl Boggs, 'Marxism, Prefigurative Communism, and the Problem of Workers' Control', *Radical America* 11.6 (1977) and 12.1 (1978).

capacity or force and the idea that, from the partisan perspective of that organized capacity, it is possible to know and to anticipate practically the real tendencies in the world that communism seeks – determinately and determinedly – to negate. Without some such articulation of power and knowledge, the notion of communist revolution is unintelligible.

But what does it mean to demand that communist politics find or create its concrete foothold in real dynamics without, as the young Marx seemed to do, postulating a worldly logic whereby 'reality strives towards thought'? If a communist philosophy is preoccupied with the preparation and anticipation of politics, what relation does it bear to those forms of anticipatory knowledge – the kind of partisan knowledge that the later Marx sought to produce – which seek to delineate the contemporary field of realization for the problems of communism? Is it the case that, as Mario Tronti has noted about Marx's partisan epistemology, 'science as struggle is an ephemeral knowledge'?[21] If the idea or the problem of communism is inseparable, as I believe, from the problem of its realization – with the important consequences that this has for philosophy's relationship to communism – then the question of how to connect the prospects of communism to a partisan knowledge of the real and its tendencies, without mistaking these tendencies for a preformed logic or a philosophy of history, becomes crucial. This task is especially urgent in a world such as ours – a world which, to recall Marx, 'only imagines that it still believes in itself'. In 1842, in the *Rheinische Zeitung*, Marx wrote: 'The fate which a question of the time has in common with every question justified by its content, and therefore rational, is that the question and not the answer constitutes the main difficulty. True criticism, therefore, analyses the questions and not the answers. Just as the solution of an algebraic equation is given once the problem has been put in its simplest and sharpest form, so every question is answered as soon as it has become a real question.'[22] This is our task today, to turn the question of communism into a real question. We might then get the answers we deserve.

---

21   Mario Tronti, *Cenni di castella* (Fiesole: Cadmo, 2001), p. 19.
22   Karl Marx and Friedrich Engels, *Collected Works*, vol. 1 (Moscow: Progress Publishers, 1975), pp. 182–3.

14   Weak Communism?

Gianni Vattimo

1. The chapter title seems a banality. Communism is today weaker than ever as a political force.

2. This expression wishes to have another meaning, not completely different from the weakness of contemporary political communism. It suggests that communism ought to be weak in order to rediscover a meaningful presence among the political forces it encounters in society even before entering the electoral arena.

3. The weakness I am referring to is a theoretical weakness necessary to correct those 'metaphysical' claims which characterized communism in its original Marxist formulation. Communism should become theoretically 'weak', not simply because it has now lost its historical battle with capitalism. I am not claiming that had Lenin and Stalin been less metaphysical (in appealing to the laws of history, to the proletariat's almost holy mission, to economic development guaranteed by a planned economy), then the really existing communism that resulted from the October Revolution would still be alive and might even have triumphed over its enemies.

4. That things turned out as they did was an effect of a play of forces (and of weaknesses) that cannot be reduced to such a simple explanation, depending only minimally on theory. Thinking about a weak communism means rejecting not only Marx's message, but also Lenin's definition of communism as 'soviet power plus electrification' (assuming it was ever like this) in order to develop a definition that better corresponds to the actual situation (with all the vagueness that inevitably accompanies that expression).

5. Soviet communism was a 'metaphysical' communism because it was a war communism (pitted against counter-revolution, against Hitler,

against imperial capitalism). It also had to adopt many models of capitalism, beginning with the ideal of development at all costs, which under Stalin led to the imposition of many restrictions on freedom. (I should make it clear that when I talk about metaphysics, I am referring principally to the term in its Heideggerian sense, that is, as a violent imposition which claims objective evidence: with respect to truth, the human ideal, the 'natural' laws of society, the economy, and so forth.)

6. The present crisis of capitalism perhaps represents a second moment which completes the fall of the Berlin wall. Real capitalism is becoming discredited in the same way that real communism was in 1989. These are two aspects of the same dissolution of metaphysics – that is, of a world centred on capitalist industrialization (parallel and speculative) and on its communist variant. To see these events as aspects of the dissolution of metaphysics – a perspective which may seem overly abstract – is a way to grasp them in their radicalism. Interpreting the fall of the Berlin wall only in terms of a demand for freedom in Eastern Europe, or the recent bail-out of banks and corporations only as a crisis of capital, leads to needless attempts to 'repair' the 'metaphysical' system in its two main aspects: traditional humanism and technological-industrial capitalism.

7. Weak communism is what ought to take the place of these two violent and authoritarian models. 'Soviet power plus electrification' is the slogan of communism. Its arrival must include a good dose of anarchism; this is where the ideas of weakness comes from. It is useless to think of revolution as the immediate and violent taking of power – capitalism is infinitely stronger than that.

8. On the other hand, the revolutionary ideal must be saved from the corruption it has been subjected to in 'democratic' regimes. The history of the European left in recent years, especially in Italy, shows that whenever the left comes into power it fatally loses its transformative energy. Apart from gathering support and raising money for electoral campaigns, the left must also make compromises to achieve a good electoral result. Without any dogmatic revolutionary thought, we must reflect on this experience. Formal democracy always exposes the opposition to the risk of becoming an accomplice, as has always happened with trade unions. As a result, today the left is called upon to help save the banks, that is, the capitalist system, for the good of the workers, and so on. The problem for

communism now is to find a form of subversive political action without renouncing the few benefits of liberal and democratic society. Parliament and the streets, for example, can act in tandem. The myth of democracy has blocked us for too long.

9. We need an undisciplined social practice which shares with anarchism the refusal to formulate a system, a constitution, a positive 'realistic' model according to traditional political methods: for example, winning elections (who believes in them any longer?). Communism must have the courage to be a 'ghost' – if it wishes to recuperate an authentic reality.

15   How to Begin From the Beginning

Slavoj Žižek

When, in 1922, after winning the Civil War against all odds, the Bolsheviks had to retreat into the 'New Economic Policy' (NEP), which allowed a much wider scope for the market economy and private property, Lenin wrote a wonderful short text entitled 'On Ascending a High Mountain'. He uses the simile of a climber who has to return to the valley, after a first failed attempt to reach a new mountain peak, as a way of describing what it means to make a retreat in the revolutionary process. When we are retreating,

> the voices from below ring with malicious joy. They do not conceal it; they chuckle gleefully and shout: 'He'll fall in a minute! Serve him right, the lunatic!' Others try to conceal their malicious glee. They moan and raise their eyes to heaven in sorrow, as if to say: 'It grieves us sorely to see our fears justified! But did not we, who have spent all our lives working out a judicious plan for scaling this mountain, demand that the ascent be postponed until our plan was complete? And if we so vehemently protested against taking this path, which this lunatic is now abandoning (look, look, he has turned back! He is descending! A single step is taking him hours of preparation! And yet we were roundly abused when time and again we demanded moderation and caution!), if we so fervently censured this lunatic and warned every-body against imitating and helping him, we did so entirely because of our devotion to the great plan to scale this mountain, and in order to prevent this great plan from being generally discredited!'

After enumerating the achievements and the failures of the Soviet state, Lenin then goes on to emphasize the necessity of fully admitting to mistakes:

> Those Communists are doomed who imagine that it is possible to finish such an epoch-making undertaking as completing the foundations of

socialist economy (particularly in a small-peasant country) without making mistakes, without retreats, without numerous alterations to what is unfinished or wrongly done. Communists who have no illusions, who do not give way to despondency, and who preserve their strength and flexibility 'to begin from the beginning' over and over again in approaching an extremely difficult task, are not doomed (and in all probability will not perish).[1]

This is Lenin at his Beckettian best, echoing the line from *Worstward Ho*: 'Try again. Fail again. Fail better.' Lenin's climbing simile deserves a close reading. His conclusion – 'to begin from the beginning over and over again' – makes it clear that he is not talking merely of slowing down progress in order to fortify what has already been achieved, but precisely of *descending back to the starting point*: one should 'begin from the beginning', not from the peak one may have successfully reached in the previous effort. In Kierkegaard's terms, a revolutionary process is not a gradual progress, but a repetitive movement, a movement of *repeating the beginning* again and again. And this, exactly, is where we find ourselves today, after the 'obscure disaster' of 1989. As in 1922, the voices from below ring with malicious joy all around us: 'Serves you right, you lunatics who wanted to force your totalitarian vision on society!' Others try to conceal their glee, moaning and raising their eyes to heaven in sorrow, as if to say: 'It grieves us sorely to see our fears justified! How noble your vision of creating a just society was! Our hearts beat with you, but our reason told us that your noble plans would finish only in misery and new unfreedoms!' While rejecting any compromise with these seductive voices, we definitely have to 'begin from the beginning', that is, not to 'build further upon the foundations' of the revolutionary epoch of the twentieth century (which lasted from 1917 to 1989), but to 'descend' to the starting point and follow a *different* path. It is against this background that one should read Badiou's re-affirmation of the communist idea:

The communist hypothesis remains the right hypothesis, as I have said, and I do not see any other. If this hypothesis should have to be abandoned, then it is not worth doing anything in the order of collective action. Without the perspective of communism, without this Idea, nothing in the historical and political future is of such a kind as to

---

1   V. I. Lenin, 'Notes of a Publicist: On Ascending a High Mountain . . .', in *Collected Works*, vol. 33 (Moscow: Progress Publishers, 1965), pp. 204–11.

interest the philosopher. Each individual can pursue their private business, and we won't mention it again . . . But holding on to the Idea, the
existence of the hypothesis, does not mean that its first form of presentation, focused on property and the state, must be maintained just as it
is. In fact, what we are ascribed as a philosophical task, we could say
even a duty, is to help a new modality of existence of the hypothesis to
come into being. New in terms of the type of political experimentation
to which this hypothesis could give rise.[2]

One should be careful not to read these lines in a Kantian way, conceiving communism as a 'regulative Idea', thereby resuscitating the spectre
of an 'ethical socialism' with equality as its a priori norm-axiom. One
should rather maintain the precise reference to a set of social antagonisms
which generate the need for communism – Marx's good old notion of
communism not as an ideal, but as a movement which reacts to actual
social antagonisms, is still fully relevant. If we conceive communism as an
'eternal Idea', this implies that the situation which generates it is no less
eternal, that the antagonism to which communism reacts will always exist
– and from here, it is only one small step to a 'deconstructive' reading of
communism as a dream of presence, of abolishing all alienating re-presen-
tation, a dream which thrives on its own impossibility. How, then, are we
to break out of this formalism in order to formulate antagonisms which
will continue to generate the communist Idea? Where are we to look for
this Idea's new mode?

It is easy to make fun of Fukuyama's notion of the End of History,
but most people today *are* Fukuyamaean: liberal-democratic capitalism is
accepted as the finally found formula of the best possible society, all one
can do is try to make it more just, tolerant, etc. Consider what happened
recently to Marco Cicala, an Italian journalist: when, in an article, he used
the word 'capitalism', the editor asked him if this was really necessary –
could he not replace the word with a synonym, such as 'economy'? What
better proof of the total triumph of capitalism than the virtual disappearance of the very term in the last two or three decades?

A simple but pertinent question arises here: if liberal-democratic
capitalism obviously works better than all known alternatives, if liberal-
democratic capitalism is, if not the best, then at least the least bad form
of society, then why do we not simply resign ourselves to it in a mature

2   Alain Badiou, *The Meaning of Sarkozy*, trans. David Fernbach (London and New York: Verso,
2008), p. 115.

way, even accept it wholeheartedly? Why insist, against all hope, on the communist Idea? Is not such an insistence an exemplary case of the narcissism of the lost Cause?

This deadlock is hardly new – the great defining problem of Western Marxism was the lack of a revolutionary subject: why is it that the working class does not complete the passage from in-itself to for-itself and constitute itself as a revolutionary agent? This problem provided the main *raison d'être* for its reference to psychoanalysis, evoked precisely to explain the unconscious libidinal mechanisms which prevent the rise of class consciousness, mechanisms inscribed into the very being (social situation) of the working class. In this way, the truth of the Marxist socio-economic analysis could be saved, and there was no reason to give ground to the 'revisionist' theories about the rise of the middle classes, etc. For this same reason, Western Marxism was also engaged in a constant search for other social agents who could play the role of the revolutionary agent, as understudies to replace the indisposed working class: Third World peasants, students, intellectuals, the excluded . . .

Again, then, it is not enough to remain faithful to the communist Idea – one has to locate it in real historical antagonisms which give this Idea a practical urgency. The only *true* question today is: do we endorse the predominant naturalization of capitalism, or does today's global capitalism contain antagonisms powerful enough to prevent its indefinite reproduction? There are four such antagonisms: the looming threat of *ecological* catastrophe, the inappropriateness of the notion of *private property* for so-called 'intellectual property', the socio-ethical implications of *new techno-scientific developments* (especially in biogenetics), and, last but not least, *new forms of apartheid*, new Walls and slums. There is a qualitative difference between the last feature – the gap that separates the Excluded from the Included – and the other three, which designate the domains of what Hardt and Negri call the 'commons', the shared substance of our social being, the privatization of which involves violent acts which should also, where necessary, be resisted with violent means:

– *the commons of culture*, the immediately socialized forms of 'cognitive' capital, primarily language, our means of communication and education, but also the shared infrastructure of public transport, electricity, post, etc. (if Bill Gates were to be allowed a monopoly, we would have reached the absurd situation in which a private individual would literally own the software texture of our basic network of communication);

– *the commons of external nature*, threatened by pollution and exploitation (from oil to rain forests and the natural habitat itself);
– *the commons of internal nature* (the biogenetic inheritance of humanity); with new biogenetic technology, the creation of a New Man in the literal sense of changing human nature becomes a realistic prospect.

What the struggles in all these domains share is an awareness of the potential for destruction, up to and including the self-annihilation of humanity itself, if the capitalist logic of enclosing the commons is allowed a free run. Nicholas Stern was right to characterize the climate crisis as 'the greatest market failure in human history'.[3] So when Kishan Khoday, a UN team leader, recently wrote, 'There is an increasing spirit of global environmental citizenship, a desire to address climate change as a matter of common concern to all humanity',[4] one should give all weight to the terms 'global citizenship' and 'common concern' – the need to establish a global political organization and engagement which, neutralizing and channelling market mechanisms, expresses a properly communist perspective.

It is this reference to the 'commons' which justifies the resuscitation of the notion of communism: it enables us to see the progressing 'enclosure' of the commons as a process of proletarization of those who are thereby excluded from their own substance. Today's historical situation not only does not compel us to drop the notion of proletariat, of the proletarian position – on the contrary, it compels us to radicalize it to an existential level well beyond Marx's imagination. We need a more radical notion of the proletarian subject, a subject reduced to the evanescent point of the Cartesian *cogito*, deprived of its substantial content.

For this reason, the new emancipatory politics will no longer be the act of a particular social agent, but an explosive combination of different agents. What unites us is that, in contrast to the classic image of proletarians having 'nothing to lose but their chains', we are in danger of losing *everything*: the threat is that we will be reduced to an abstract empty Cartesian subject deprived of all substantial content, dispossessed of our symbolic substance, our genetic base heavily manipulated, vegetating in an unlivable environment. This triple threat to our entire being makes us all in a way proletarians, reduced to 'substanceless subjectivity', as Marx put it in the *Grundrisse*. The figure of the 'part of no-part' confronts us with the truth of our own position, and the ethico-political challenge is

---

3   Quoted in *Time* magazine, 24 December 2007, p. 2.
4   Quoted in ibid.

to recognize ourselves in this figure – in a way, we are all excluded, from nature as well as from our symbolic substance. Today, we are all potentially a *homo sacer*, and the only way to defend against actually becoming so is to act preventively.

This proletarianization alone, however, is not sufficient if we want to be counted as communists. The ongoing enclosure of the commons concerns the relations of people to the objective conditions of their life-process, as well as relations between people: the commons are privatized at the expense of the proletarianized majority. There is nevertheless a gap between these two aspects – the commons can also be restored to collective humanity without communism, in an authoritarian-communitarian regime; the de-substantialized, 'rootless' subject, deprived of its substantial content, can also be counteracted in the direction of communitarianism, by finding its proper place in a new substantial community. In this precise sense, Negri was on the mark with his anti-socialist title *Goodbye Mr Socialism*: communism is to be opposed to socialism, which, in place of the egalitarian collective, offers a solidary organic community – Nazism was national socialism, not national communism. There can be a socialist anti-Semitism, there cannot be a communist one. (If it appears otherwise, as in Stalin's last years, it is only as an indicator of a lack of fidelity to the revolutionary event.) Eric Hobsbawm recently published a column with the title: 'Socialism failed, capitalism is bankrupt. What comes next?' The answer is: communism. Socialism wants to solve the first three antagonisms without the fourth one, without the singular universality of the proletariat. The only way for the global capitalist system to survive its long-term antagonism and simultaneously to avoid the communist solution, will be to reinvent some kind of socialism – in the guise of communitarianism, populism, capitalism with Asian values, or whatever. The future will be communist . . . or socialist.

This is why we should insist on the qualitative difference between the last antagonism, the gap that separates the Excluded from the Included, and the other three: it is only the reference to the Excluded that justifies the term communism. There is nothing more 'private' than a State community which perceives the Excluded as a threat and worries how to keep them at a proper distance. In other words, in the series of the four antagonisms, that between the Included and the Excluded is the crucial one: without it, all others lose their subversive edge. Ecology turns into a problem of sustainable development, intellectual property into a complex legal challenge, biogenetics into an ethical issue. One can sincerely fight to preserve the environment, defend a broader notion of intellectual property, oppose the copyrighting of genes, without confronting the antagonism between the Included and the Excluded. What's more, one can even formulate some of these struggles in terms of the Included being threatened by the polluting Excluded. In this way, we get no true universality, only 'private' concerns in the Kantian sense of the term. Corporations like Whole Foods and Starbucks continue to enjoy favour among liberals even though they both engage in anti-union activities; the trick is that they sell products with a progressive spin: one buys coffee made with beans bought at above fair market value, one drives a hybrid vehicle, one buys from companies that provide good benefits for their staff and customers (according to the corporation's own standards), etc. In short, without the antagonism between the Included and the Excluded, we may well find ourselves in a world in which Bill Gates is the greatest humanitarian fighting poverty and diseases and Rupert Murdoch the greatest environmentalist, mobilizing hundreds of millions through his media empire.

It is thus crucial to insist on the communist-egalitarian emancipatory Idea, and insist in a very precise Marxian sense: there are social groups which, on account of their lacking a determinate place in the 'private' order of social hierarchy, stand directly for universality; they are what Rancière calls the 'part of no-part' of the social body. All truly emancipatory politics is generated by the short circuit between the universality of the 'public use of reason' and the universality of the 'part of no-part' – this was already the communist dream of the young Marx: to bring together the universality of philosophy with the universality of the proletariat. From Ancient Greece, we have a name for the intrusion of the Excluded into the socio-political space: democracy. Our question today is: is democracy still an appropriate name for this egalitarian explosion? The two extremes here are, on the one hand, the cursory dismissal of democracy as the mere illusory form of appearance of its opposite (class domination), and, on the other, the claim that the democracy we have, the really-existing democracy, is a distortion of true democracy – along the lines of Gandhi's famous reply to a British journalist who asked him what he thought about Western civilization: 'I think it would be a good idea.' Obviously, the debate which moves between these two extremes is too abstract: what we need to introduce as the criterion is the question of how democracy relates to the dimension of universality embodied in the Excluded.

There is, however, a recurrent problem we encounter here: the passage from the Jacobins to Napoleon, from the October Revolution to Stalin, from Mao's Cultural Revolution to Deng Xiaoping's capitalism. How are we to read this passage? Is the second phase (Thermidor) the 'truth' of the first revolutionary phase (as Marx sometimes seems to claim), or is it just that the revolutionary eventual series has exhausted itself? Let us focus briefly on the Cultural Revolution, which we can read at two different levels. If read as a part of historical reality (being), it can easily be submitted to a 'dialectical' analysis which perceives the final outcome of a historical process as its 'truth': the ultimate failure of the Cultural Revolution bears witness to the inherent inconsistency of the very project ('notion') of Cultural Revolution. It is the explication-deployment-actualization of these inconsistencies (in the same way that, for Marx, the vulgar, non-heroic, capitalist daily life of profit-seeking is the 'truth' of Jacobin revolutionary heroism).

If, however, we analyse it as an Event, as an enactment of the eternal Idea of egalitarian Justice, then the ultimate factual result of the Cultural Revolution, its catastrophic failure and reversal into the recent capitalist explosion, does not exhaust the real of the Cultural Revolution: the eternal Idea of the Cultural Revolution survives its defeat in socio-historical reality; it continues to lead the underground spectral life of the ghosts of failed utopias which haunt future generations, patiently awaiting its next resurrection. This brings us back to Robespierre, who expressed in a touching way the simple faith in the eternal Idea of freedom which persists through all defeats, without which, as was clear to him, a revolution 'is just a noisy crime that destroys another crime', the faith most poignantly expressed in his very last speech on 8 Thermidor 1794, the day before his arrest and execution:

> But there do exist, I can assure you, souls that are feeling and pure; it exists, that tender, imperious and irresistible passion, the torment and delight of magnanimous hearts; that deep horror of tyranny, that compassionate zeal for the oppressed, that sacred love for the homeland, that even more sublime and holy love for humanity, without which a great revolution is just a noisy crime that destroys another crime; it does exist, that generous ambition to establish here on earth the world's first Republic.[5]

Does the same not hold even more for the last big instalment in the life of this Idea, the Maoist Cultural Revolution? Without this Idea which

---

5   Maximilien Robespierre, *Virtue and Terror* (London and New York: Verso, 2007), p. 129.

sustained the revolutionary enthusiasm, the Cultural Revolution was to an even greater degree 'just a noisy crime that destroys another crime'. One should recall here Hegel's sublime words on the French Revolution, from his *Lectures on the Philosophy of World History* – which, of course, did not prevent him from coldly analysing the inner necessity of this explosion of abstract freedom turning into its opposite, the self-destructive revolutionary terror; however, one should never forget that Hegel's critique is immanent, accepting the basic principle of the French Revolution (and of its key supplement, the Haitian Revolution). And one should do exactly the same apropos the October Revolution (and, later, the Chinese Revolution): it was the first case in the entire history of humanity of a successful revolt on the part of the exploited poor – they were the zero-level members of the new society, they set the standards. The revolution stabilized itself into a new social order, a new world was created and miraculously survived for decades, amid unthinkable economic and military pressure and isolation. This was effectively 'a glorious mental dawn. All thinking beings shared in the jubilation of this epoch.' Against all hierarchic orders, egalitarian universality directly came to power. This is what the Hegelian approach clearly sees: far from reducing the revolutionary explosion to its final outcome, it fully acknowledges its universal 'eternal' moment.

The communist Idea thus persists: it survives the failures of its realization as a spectre which returns again and again, in an endless persistence best recapitulated by Beckett's already-quoted words: 'Try again. Fail again. Fail better.' This brings us to the crux of the matter. One of the mantras of the postmodern left is that one should finally leave behind the 'Jacobin–Leninist' paradigm of centralized dictatorial power. Perhaps, the time has come to turn this mantra around and admit that a dose of this 'Jacobin–Leninist' paradigm is precisely what the left needs today: today, more than ever, one should insist on what Badiou calls the 'eternal' Idea of communism or the communist 'invariants' – its other 'four fundamental concepts' at work from Plato through the medieval millenarian revolts to Jacobinism, Leninism and Maoism: strict *egalitarian justice*, disciplinary *terror*, political *voluntarism*, and *trust in the people*. This matrix is not 'superseded' by any new postmodern or postindustrial or post-whatever-you-want dynamics. However, till now, till the present historical moment, this eternal Idea functioned as, precisely, a Platonic Idea which persisted, returning again and again after every defeat. What is missing here – to put it in philosophico-theological terms – is the privileged link of the Idea to a singular historical moment (in the same way that, in Christianity, the whole eternal divine edifice stands and falls with the contingent event of the birth and death of Christ). There is something unique in today's constellation: many perspicuous analysts have noted that contemporary capitalism poses a problem for this logic of a resistance which persists – let me quote Brian Massumi's clear formulation of how contemporary capitalism has already overcome the logic of totalizing normality and adopted the logic of the erratic excess:

the more varied, and even erratic, the better. Normalcy starts to lose its hold. The regularities start to loosen. This loosening of normalcy is part of capitalism's dynamic. It's not a simple liberation. It's capitalism's own form of power. It's no longer disciplinary institutional power that defines everything, it's capitalism's power to produce variety – because markets get saturated. Produce variety and you produce a niche market. The oddest of affective tendencies are okay – as long as they pay. Capitalism starts intensifying or diversifying affect, but only in order to extract surplus-value. It hijacks affect in order to intensify profit potential. It literally valorizes affect. The capitalist logic of surplus-value production starts to take over the relational field that is also the domain of political ecology, the ethical field of resistance to identity and predictable paths. It's very troubling and confusing, because it seems to me that there's been a certain kind of convergence between the dynamic of capitalist power and the dynamic of resistance.[6]

Throughout the age of Really Existing Socialism, the secret hope of 'democratic socialists' was placed in the direct democracy of the 'soviets', workers' councils as the form of self-organization of the people; and it is deeply symptomatic how, with the decline of Really Existing Socialism, this emancipatory shadow which haunted it all the time has also disappeared. Is this not the ultimate confirmation of the fact that the council-version of 'democratic socialism' was just a spectral double of the 'bureaucratic' Really Existing Socialism, its inherent transgression with no substantial positive content of its own, i.e., unable to serve as the permanent basic organizing principle of a society? This is a profoundly Hegelian lesson of 'abstract negation': the end of a constellation is not the

---

6   Brian Massumi, 'Navigating Movements', in Mary Zournazi (ed.), *Hope* (New York: Routledge, 2002), p. 224.

victory of its counter-force, but also the defeat of that counter-force.

Of course, egalitarian-emancipatory 'de-territorialization' is not the same as the postmodern-capitalist version, but it nonetheless radically changes the terms of the emancipatory struggle: the enemy is no longer the established hierarchic order of a State. How, then, are we to revolutionize an order whose very principle is constant self-revolutionizing? Rather than, or more than, a solution to the problems we are facing today, communism is thus itself the name of a problem: of the difficult task of breaking out of the confines of the market-and-state frame, for which no quick formula is at hand: 'It's just the simple thing that's hard, so hard to do', as Brecht put it in his 'In Praise of Communism'.

The Hegelian answer is that the problem/deadlock is its own solution – not in the simple/direct sense that capitalism is already in itself communism, that only a purely formal reversal is needed. My surmise is: what if contemporary dynamic capitalism, precisely in so far as it is 'worldless', a constant disruption of all fixed order, opens up the space for a revolution which will break the vicious cycle of revolt and its reinscription, i.e., which will no longer follow the pattern of an evental explosion after which things return to normal, but will assume the task of a *new 'ordering' against the global capitalist disorder*? Out of revolt we should move on shamelessly to enforcing a new order. (Is this not one of the lessons of the ongoing financial meltdown?) This is why the focus on capitalism is crucial if we want to reactualize the communist Idea: today's 'worldless' dynamic capitalism radically changes the very coordinates of the communist struggle – the enemy is no longer the State to be undermined from its point of symptomal torsion, but a flux of permanent self-revolutionizing.

Consequently, I want to propose two axioms concerning the relationship between the State and politics. 1) The failure of the Communist State – Party politics is above all and primarily the failure of anti-statist politics, of the endeavour to break out of the constraints of State, to replace statal forms of organization with 'direct' non-representative forms of self-organization ('councils'). 2) If you do not have an idea of what you want to replace the State with, you have no right to subtract/withdraw from the State. Instead of withdrawing into a distance from the State, the true task should be to make the State itself work in a non-statal mode. The alternative 'either struggle for State power (which makes us the same as the enemy we are fighting) or withdraw into a posture of resistance from a distance towards the State' is a false one, because both its terms share the same premise: that a State-form, as we know it, is here to stay, so that all we can do is take over the State or maintain a distance towards it. Here, one should shamelessly repeat the lesson of Lenin's *The State and Revolution*: the goal of revolutionary violence is not to take over State power, but to transform it, radically changing its functioning, its relation to its base, etc. Therein resides the key component of the 'dictatorship of the proletariat' – Bulent Somay is right to point out that what qualifies the proletariat for this position is ultimately a *negative* feature: all other classes are (potentially) capable of reaching the status of the 'ruling class', in other words, of establishing themselves as the class controlling the state apparatus:

> what makes the working class into an agency and provides it with a mission is neither its poverty, nor its militant and pseudo-military organization, nor its proximity to the (chiefly industrial) means of production. It is only its structural inability to organize itself into yet another ruling class that provides the working class with such a mission. The proletariat is the only (revolutionary) class in history that abolishes itself in the act of abolishing its opposite.[7]

One should draw from this insight the only appropriate conclusion: the 'dictatorship of the proletariat' is a kind of (necessary) oxymoron, *not* a State-form in which the proletariat is the ruling class. We effectively have the 'dictatorship of the proletariat' only when the State itself is radically transformed, relying on new forms of popular participation. This is why there is more than hypocrisy in the fact that, at the highest point of Stalinism, when the entire social edifice was shattered by purges, the new constitution proclaimed the end of the 'class' character of Soviet power (voting rights were restored to members of classes previously excluded), and that the socialist regimes were called 'people's democracies' – a sure indication that they were not 'dictatorships of the proletariat' . . . But, again, how to achieve such a 'dictatorship'?

Peter Sloterdijk (definitely not one of us, but also not a complete idiot) remarked that if there is one person to whom they will build monuments a hundred years from now it is Lee Quan Yew, the Singapore leader who invented and realized so-called 'capitalism with Asian values'. The virus of this authoritarian capitalism is slowly but surely spreading around the globe. Before setting in motion his reforms, Deng Xiaoping visited Singapore and expressly praised it as a model for all of China to follow.

---

7   Bulent Somay, personal letter (28 January 2007). I am all the more content to quote this passage since his letter is deeply critical of me.

This change has a world-historical meaning: till now, capitalism seemed inextricably linked with democracy – there were, of course, from time to time recourses to direct dictatorship, but, after a decade or two, democracy once again imposed itself (recall only the cases of South Korea and Chile). Now, however, the link between democracy and capitalism has been broken.

Why this resurgence of direct (non-democratic) authority? Above and beyond cultural differences, there is an inner necessity for this resurgence in the very logic of today's capitalism. That is the central problem we are facing today: how does the late-capitalist predominance (or even hegemonic role) of 'intellectual labour' affect Marx's basic scheme of the separation of labour from its objective conditions, and of the revolution as the subjective re-appropriation of those objective conditions? Spheres such as the internet, production, exchange and consumption are inextricably intertwined, potentially even identified: my product is immediately communicated to and consumed by another. Marx's classic notion of commodity fetishism in which 'relations between people' assume the form of 'relations between things' has thus to be radically re-thought: in 'immaterial labour', 'relations between people' are 'not so much hidden beneath the veneer of objectivity, but are themselves the very material of our everyday exploitation',[8] so we can no longer talk about 'reification' in the classic Lukácsian sense. Far from being invisible, social relationality in its very fluidity is directly the object of marketing and exchange: in 'cultural capitalism', one no longer sells (and buys) objects which 'bring' cultural or emotional experiences, one directly sells (and buys) such experiences.

While one has to acknowledge that Negri is here on the trail of this key question, his answer seems too short; his starting point is Marx's thesis in the *Grundrisse* on the radical transformation of the status of 'fixed capital':

The development of fixed capital indicates to what degree general social knowledge has become a direct force of production, and to what degree, hence, the conditions of the process of social life itself have come under the control of the general intellect and been transformed in accordance with it. To what degree the powers of social production have been produced, not only in the form of knowledge, but also as immediate organs of social practice, of the real life process.[9]

---

8   Nina Power, 'Dissing', *Radical Philosophy* 154 (March–April 2009): 55.
9   Karl Marx, *Grundrisse*, trans. Martin Nicolaus (Harmondsworth: Penguin, 1973), p. 706.

With the development of general social knowledge, the 'productive power of labour' is thus 'itself the greatest productive power. From the standpoint of the direct production process it can be regarded as the production of fixed capital, this fixed capital being man himself.'[10] And, again, since capital organizes its exploitation by appearing as 'fixed capital' against living labour, the moment the key component of fixed capital is 'man himself', its 'general social knowledge', the very social foundation of capitalist exploitation is undermined, and the role of capital becomes purely parasitic: with today's global interactive media, creative inventiveness is no longer individual, it is immediately collectivized, part of 'commons', such that any attempt to privatize it through copyrighting becomes problematic – more and more literally, 'property is theft' here. So what about a company like Microsoft that does precisely this – organizing and exploiting the collective synergy of creative cognitive singularities? The only remaining task seems to be to imagine how cognitive workers will 'eliminate bosses, because an industrial control over cognitive work is completely *dépassé*'.[11] What new social movements signal is that 'the wage epoch is over, and that we have passed from the confrontation between work and capital concerning wages to the confrontation between the multitude and the State concerning the instauration of the citizen's income'.[12] Therein resides the basic feature of 'today's social revolutionary transition': 'One has to bring capital to recognize the weight and importance of the common good, and if capital is not ready to do it, one has to compel it to do so.'[13] Note Negri's precise formulation: not abolish capital, but compel it to recognize the common good, i.e., one remains within capitalism – if ever there was a utopian idea, this is it. Here is how Negri describes the proximity of today's biopolitical capitalism to the direct assertion of the productivity of the multitude:

> The picture is one of a circulation of commodities, webs of information, continuous movements, and radical nomadism of labour, and the ferocious exploitation of these dynamics . . . but also of constant and inexhaustible *excess*, of the biopolitical power of the multitude and of its excess with regard to the structural controlling ability of dominant institutions. All of the available energies are put to work, society is put to work . . . Within this exploited totality and injunction to work

---

10   Ibid.
11   Toni Negri, *Goodbye Mr Socialism* (Rome: Feltrinelli, 2006), p. 234.
12   Ibid., p. 204.
13   Ibid., p. 235.

lies an intransitive freedom that is irreducible to the control that tries
to subdue it. Even though freedom can run against itself ... lines of
flight still open up in this ambivalence: suffering is often productive
but never revolutionary; what is revolutionary is excess, overflow, and
power.[14]

What we find here is the standard post-Hegelian matrix of the productive flux which is always in excess with regard to the structural totality
which tries to subdue and control it. But what if, in a parallax shift, we
perceive the capitalist network itself as the true excess over the flow of
the productive multitude? What if, while the contemporary production
of multitude directly produces life, it continues to produce an excess
(which is even functionally superfluous), the excess of Capital? Why do
immediately produced relations still need the mediating role of capitalist
relations? What if the true enigma is: why does the continuous nomadic
'molecular' movement need a parasitic 'molar' structure which (decep-
tively) appears as an obstacle to its unleashed productivity? Why do we,
the moment we abolish this obstacle/excess, lose the very productive flux
constrained by the parasitic excess? This also means that we should turn
around the topic of fetishism, of 'relations between people appearing as
relations between things': what if the direct 'production of life' celebrated
by Hardt and Negri is falsely transparent, what if, in it, the invisible 'relations between (the immaterial, true) things (of Capital) appear as direct
relations between people'?

How did we come to this? The 1968 protests focused their struggles
against (what were perceived as) the three pillars of capitalism: factory,
school, family. As a result, each domain was subsequently submitted to
post-industrial transformation: factory-work is increasingly outsourced
or, in the developed world at least, reorganized on the basis of post-Ford-
ist non-hierarchical interactive team-work; permanent flexible privatized
education is increasingly replacing universal public education; multiple forms of flexible sexual arrangements are replacing the traditional
family.[15] The left lost in the very moment of its victory: the immediate
enemy was defeated, but replaced by a new form of even more direct
capitalist domination. In 'postmodern' capitalism, the market is invad-
ing new spheres which were hitherto considered the privileged domain
of the State, from education to prisons and security. When 'immaterial

---

14   Toni Negri, 'On Rem Koolhaas', *Radical Philosophy* 154 (March–April 2009): 49.
15   See Daniel Cohen, *Trois leçons sur la société post-industrielle* (Paris: Seuil, 2006).

work' (education, therapy, etc.) is celebrated as the kind of work which directly produces social relations, one should not forget what this means within a commodity-economy: that new domains, hitherto excluded from the market, are now commodified – when in trouble, we no longer talk to a friend but pay a psychiatrist or counsellor to take care of the problem; not parents but paid babysitters or educators take care of children, etc. We are thus in the midst of a new process of the privatization of the social, of establishing new enclosures.

To grasp these new forms of privatization, we need to critically transform Marx's conceptual apparatus. Because he neglected the social dimension of 'general intellect', Marx didn't envisage the possibility of *the privatization of the 'general intellect' itself* – this is what lies at the core of the struggle for 'intellectual property'. Negri is right here: within this framework, exploitation in the classic Marxist sense is no longer possible – which is why it has to be enforced more and more by direct legal measures, i.e., by a non-economic force. This is why, today, the exploitation increasingly takes the form of rent: as Carlo Vercellone put it, post-industrial capitalism is characterized by the 'becoming-rent of profit'.[16] And this is why direct authority is needed: it is needed in order to impose the (arbitrary) legal conditions for extracting rent, conditions which are no longer 'spontaneously' generated by the market. Perhaps therein resides the fundamental 'contradiction' of today's 'postmodern' capitalism: while its logic is deregulatory, 'anti-statal', nomadic/deterritorializing, etc., its key tendency towards the 'becoming-rent-of-profit' signals the strengthening role of the State whose (not only) regulatory function is ever more omnipresent. Dynamic de-territorialization coexists with and relies on increasingly authoritarian interventions of the State and its legal and other apparatuses. What can be discerned at the horizon of our historical becoming is thus a society in which personal libertarianism and hedonism coexist with (and are sustained by) a complex web of regulatory state mechanisms. Far from disappearing, the State is today gaining in strength.

In other words, when, due to the crucial role of the 'general intellect' (knowledge and social cooperation) in the creation of wealth, forms of wealth are increasingly 'out of all proportion to the direct labour time spent on their production', the result is not, as Marx seems to have expected, the self-dissolution of capitalism, but the gradual relative transformation of the profit generated by the exploitation of the labour force

---

16   See Carlo Vercellone (ed.), *Capitalismo cognitivo* (Rome: manifestolibri, 2006).

into rent appropriated by the privatization of the 'general intellect'. Take the case of Bill Gates: how did he become the richest man in the world? His wealth has nothing to do with the production costs involved in the products Microsoft sells (one can even argue that Microsoft pays its intellectual workers relatively high salaries). It is not the result of his success in producing good software at lower prices than his competitors, or in higher levels of 'exploitation' of his hired intellectual workers. If this were the case, Microsoft would have gone bankrupt long ago: people en masse would have chosen programmes like Linux, which are both free and, according to specialists, better than Microsoft's. Why, then, are millions still buying Microsoft? Because Microsoft has succeeded in imposing itself as an almost universal standard, (almost) monopolizing the field, a kind of direct embodiment of the 'general intellect'. Gates became the richest man on earth within a couple of decades by appropriating the rent received from allowing millions of intellectual workers to participate in that particular form of the 'general intellect' that he privatized and controls. Is it true, then, that today's intellectual workers are no longer separated from the objective conditions of their labour (they own their PCs, etc.), which is Marx's description of capitalist 'alienation'? Superficially yes, but more fundamentally *no*: they remain cut off from the social field of their work, from the 'general intellect' – because the latter is mediated by private capital.

And the same goes for natural resources, the exploitation of which is one of the great sources of rent today, accompanied by the permanent struggle over who is to receive that rent – the people of the Third World or Western corporations. The supreme irony is that in order to explain the difference between labour power (which, when put to work, produces surplus value over and above its own value) and other commodities (the value of which is consumed in their use and which thus involve no exploitation), Marx mentions as an example of an 'ordinary' commodity *oil*, the very commodity which is today a source of extraordinary 'profits'. Here also, it is meaningless to link the rise and fall of oil prices to rising or falling production costs or the price of exploited labour – the production costs are negligible, the price we pay for oil is a rent we pay to the owners of this resource because of its scarcity and limited supply.

It is as if the three components of the production process – intellectual planning and marketing, material production, the providing of material resources – are more and more autonomized, emerging as three separate spheres. In its social consequences, this separation appears in the guise of the 'three main classes' of today's developed societies, which are precisely *not* classes but three fractions of the working class: intellectual labourers, the old manual working class, and the outcasts (unemployed, or living in slums and other interstices of the public space). The working class is thus split into three, each part with its own 'way of life' and ideology: the enlightened hedonism and liberal multiculturalism of the intellectual class, the populist fundamentalism of the working class, and the more extreme, singular forms of the outcast fraction. In Hegelese, this triad is clearly the triad of the universal (intellectual workers), particular (manual workers), and singular (outcasts). The outcome of this process is the gradual disintegration of social life proper, of a public space in which all three fractions could meet – and 'identity' politics in all its forms is a supplement for this loss. Identity politics acquires a specific form in each of the three fractions: postmodern multicultural identity politics in the intellectual class, regressive populist fundamentalism in the working class, half-illegal initiatic groups (criminal gangs, religious sects, etc.) among the outcasts. What they all share is recourse to a particular identity as a substitute for the missing universal public space.

The proletariat is thus divided into three, each part played off against the others: intellectual labourers full of cultural prejudices against the 'redneck' workers; workers who display a populist hatred of intellectuals and outcasts; outcasts who are antagonistic to society as such. The old call 'Proletarians, unite!' is thus more pertinent than ever: in the new conditions of 'post-industrial' capitalism, the unity of the three fractions of the working class *is* already their victory.[17]

---

17   Maximilien Robespierre, *Virtue and Terror* (London and New York: Verso, 2007), p. 129.

Index

Abstraction 1, 58, 195–7, 199, 201;
  dogmatic 196, 200
Agamben, Giorgio 57, 78, 80, 95, 120–1
Althusser, Louis 36, 41, 172;
  critique of humanism 65, 86;
  figure for explaining Stalinism 16, 9–31;
  For Marx 42;
  state apparatuses 7, 194;
  will 119
Anarchism 37, 39, 54, 62, 172, 206, 207
Antigone 86, 88–9
Arendt, Hannah 95, 119, 122n;
  Arendtian meaning of ideology 150
Aristide, Jean-Bertrand 115, 124n, 129

Babeuf, François-Noël (Gracchus) 3, 113,
  146
Badiou, Alain ix, 16, 36, 58–61, 64, 80n,
  86, 113–5, 118, 120–1, 125, 173, 180,
  183, 193, 217;
  The Century 35, 46n;
  communism and the State 50–3;
  communist hypothesis 14, 50, 52–3,
    94–5, 167, 203, 210–1;
  The Communist Hypothesis 59;
  Ethics 81, 127n;
  event 78, 95, 100;
  Infinite Thought 34, 39;
  The Meaning of Sarkozy 13n, 51, 52, 196,
    210–1;
  Metapolitics 36n, 41n, 60–1, 95n, 99;
  *Of an Obscure Disaster: On the End of the
    Truth of State* 34, 59–60;
  Of Ideology 47, 52, 59;
  power and rebellion 47;
  rights 81–2, 97–9;
  Saint Paul 78;
  See also Saint Paul;
  'state of the situation' 7, 194;
  Theory of Contradiction 40–1;
  Theory of the Subject 50–1, 52

Bandung Conference 69, 71
Beauvoir, Simone de 118, 126–7, 129, 130
Benjamin, Walter 70, 72, 74, 76, 80, 85n,
  98
Biopolitical 140, 142, 164;
  capitalism 222;
  dispotifs 164;
  production 134–5, 139, 141–4;
  society 162;
  turn in the economy 141–2
Blanqui, Louis Auguste 10, 38, 125
Bloch, Ernst 85, 86
Bolivia viii, 54, 55n, 57n, 59, 62, 64n, 115,
  136
Bosteels, Bruno 3n
Burke, Edmund 97, 123, 196

Chávez, Hugo 115
China
  Communist Party of 20, 21, 190;
  Cultural Revolution 1, 2, 13, 17, 20–1,
    39, 46n, 47, 50, 52n, 172, 182–90,
    196, 216–7;
  ideological struggle in 20, 38, 220;
  People's War of Liberation in 2;
  resistance in viii;
  Shanghai Commune 15
Christianity 79, 91–2, 101, 121, 145–5,
  147, 218
Colonialism 29, 98;
  Anti-colonialism/post-colonialism 71,
    75, 129
Commons ix, 136, 157, 212–3, 214, 222
Communist Manifesto
  See Marx, Karl and Friedrich Engels
Communist Party-states 182, 189, 219
Constituent power 63, 92, 95, 159, 160–4
Constituted power 48, 92
Crisis
  Current financial vii, ix, 14, 24, 33–4,
    53, 81, 131, 161, 174;

ecological 77, 213;
in Communism 23, 190;
of capitalism 58, 174, 206

Deleuze, Gilles 47, 48, 55, 119, 123, 129,
    201;
    and Felix Guattari 46, 47
Derrida, Jacques 35, 87, 90n, 119, 123;
    Spectres of Marx 87
Dictatorship of the proletariat 18, 19, 20,
    21, 27, 50, 52, 106, 189, 220
Draper, Hal 116n, 125n

Eagleton, Terry 80n
Ecuador 64n, 115
Empire 26, 48–9, 81–2, 194;
    Roman 73;
    Soviet 174;
    See also Hardt, Michael and Antonio
        Negri *Empire*
Engels, Friedrich 20, 27, 32, 38, 124n,
    201, 203;
    See also Marx, Karl and Friedrich
        Engels
England
    Industrial production 134;
    Revolution 73, 146

Fanon, Frantz 75, 79, 125, 129
First International 116
Foucault, Michel 46, 48, 56, 120, 129, 130,
    142–3, 183, 194, 202
France
    Communist Party of 22, 30, 167;
    Revolution 2, 43, 52, 73, 81, 84, 92, 97,
        98, 120, 123, 130, 145, 171, 195n,
        196, 216–7
Freud, Sigmund 36, 40, 123, 149

General will 60, 118, 120–7
Germany 68, 197–8;
    communism in 93
Gramsci, Antonio 118, 128n, 157, 160
Greece
    Ancient 215;
    communism in 93;
    resistance in vii
Guattari, Felix 34, 46n, 47;
    See also Deleuze, Gilles and Felix
        Guattari

Habermas, Jurgen vii, 72
Haiti 112, 124n, 130;
    Revolution 3n, 217, 70, 130, 217;

See also Aristide, Jean-Bertrand
Hallward, Peter 3n, 86
Hardt, Michael 55n;
    and Antonio Negri 46n, 47–9, 81–2,
        134, 194, 212, 223;
    Empire 46n, 48, 81–2
Hegel, Georg Wilhelm Friedrich 4n, 5,
    22, 37n, 55, 68, 72, 89, 113, 115, 121,
    128, 129, 195, 197, 198, 217
Hegelian
    dialectic of progress 72;
    Hegelians (Young) 45;
    Hegelian–Marxist 72;
    Post-Hegelian 223
Heidegger, Martin 16, 29, 35, 87, 88, 119,
    123n, 148
Hobbes, Thomas 123
Human Rights 70n, 94–6, 151;
    Law 99;
    liberal theories of 71;
    Marxist debates over 81–6;
    Universal Declaration of 93–4
Hume, David 123

Industrial Revolution 147
Intellectual property 221–5
Iran
    Revolution 13n, 76, 79
Islam 75, 78–80, 103, 195n

Jacobin 44, 121–2, 124, 125, 127–9,
    216
Jacobin–Leninist 217

Kant, Immanuel 8, 67, 92–3, 106, 113,
    121, 123, 126, 128, 129
Kantian
    Act of Will 107;
    regulative Idea 50, 59, 114, 211
Klein, Naomi 77n, 130, 136

Lacan, Jacques 4, 5, 7, 8, 40, 41, 50
Laclau, Ernesto 55, 97–8
Lefort, Claude 81, 196n
Lenin, Vladimir 10, 16, 50, 67, 68n, 86,
    114, 125, 205, 209–10;
    ABC of Marxism 49, 52;
    distinctions from Marx 36;
    labour and equality 200–1;
    left-wing communism 33–4, 36–40, 53,
        54–5, 65;
    the party 19, 51–2, 52n, 61, 125n, 192;
    philosophy 22–3;
    revolution 9, 37–8, 55;

the state 9, 19–23, 28, 51, 52n;
State and Revolution 9, 19, 199, 200, 220;
What Is to Be Done? 19, 61,192;
will 160
Leninism 34, 114, 217;
See also Marxism–Leninism–Maoism
Leninist
Party 19, 51, 52n;
Post-Leninist 52n;
See also Marxist–Leninist and
Jacobin–Leninist
Liberal
Democrats 39, 71;
multiculturalism 226;
theories of rights (critiques of) 71, 81–3,
93, 95, 97;
universalism 81
Liberal Democracy
benefits of 207;
compatibility with capitalism 81, 215;
compatibility with military intervention
41;
legitimation through 'end of history' and
'least bad' alternative 81, 211
Liberation theology 75, 78, 121
Linera, Álvaro García 54–64
Lukács, Georg 67, 118, 125, 221
Luxemburg, Rosa 10, 125

Mao Zedong 8, 16, 33, 46n, 47, 50, 69, 12,
114, 115, 180, 190, 196, 216;
critique of Stalin 10;
leftists 39;
the party 21–3, 25;
the state 20–2, 25;
support for the Red Guards 185;
See also Revolutionary Rebel Workers;
theory and practice 192–3, 194
Maoism 34, 38, 217;
failure of 129;
in Nepal 13n;
See also Marxism–Leninism–Maoism
Maoist
China 38;
See also China, Cultural Revolution;
Ex-Maoist 40, 49;
re-education of intellectuals 172;
Union of French Communists Marxist–
Leninist 41
Marx, Karl 10, 16, 48, 50, 89, 148;
Capital 112, 113, 140, 116, 129n, 138n,
139–40, 160;
Economic and Philosophical Manuscripts
108, 132, 138–41;

Eighteenth Brumaire of Louis Bonaparte
72–3, 105;
Grundrisse 57, 105, 116n, 213, 221;
history 67, 72–3, 104, 116, 118, 189;
human nature 65;
humanism 132, 140–2;
industrial production, shifting qualities
of 134, 221–5;
intellectual property 221–5;
Latin America 61n;
League of Communists 60;
money 106;
the party 52, 58n, 60–1;
property 132–5, 138–9, 149;
revolution 197–8, 221;
rights 82–5, 94;
as Saint Paul 78;
the state 9, 18–21, 26, 61n, 61;
theory and practice 22–23, 30, 197–201,
204;
theory of communism 104–6, 111,
112–3, 115–7, 139–41, 196–7, 211,
216
Marx, Karl and Friedrich Engels 17–9, 37,
41, 45, 61, 124n, 169, 170, 199;
Communist Manifesto 14, 15, 17–9, 33,
40, 45, 47, 57, 61, 113, 115–6, 132,
174, 179, 181, 199;
German Ideology 33, 41, 73, 128–9, 146,
155
Marxism 50–1, 114, 203n;
contemporary leftism 34, 39;
Hegelianism 5, 72, 192;
Indigenism in Latin America 54, 57n,
62n, 64n;
Maoist Union of French Communists
Marxist–Leninist 41–2;
metaphysics 205;
revolutionary subject 212–4
Marxist
contradiction, idea of 40–6;
idea of communism 101–3, 108–9;
ideology 150;
intellectuals 81;
materialism 76;
paradoxical struggle with rights 85–6;
political action v Jacobin action 121–9;
theory 68, 114, 174
Marxism–Leninism–Maoism 40
Marxist–Leninist 40, 41, 126n
May 1968 Uprising 13, 15, 22, 40, 52, 53,
129, 175, 182, 223
Montesquieu, Charles de Secondat, baron
de 123

Morales, Evo 54, 64n;
    See also Bolivia
Muslim Brotherhood 76

Negri, Antonio 34, 46, 47, 50n, 51n, 55n,
    57, 61, 63, 64, 119, 174, 198n, 214,
    221–4;
    See also Hardt, Michael and Antonio
    Negri
Nietzsche, Friedrich Wilhelm 35, 46, 74,
    77, 87n, 119, 123, 174

Paris Commune 19, 52, 61, 116–7, 128,
    146
'Part of no-part' 213–5

Qutb, Sayyid 75–9

Rancière, Jacques 9n, 36, 44, 55–6, 65,
    81–2, 94–7, 143n, 179, 215
Rebel Workers 187–8;
    subject 54, 212;
    surplus 163, 223
Red Guards
    See Revolutionary Rebel Workers
Revolution 22, 25, 26, 36 n7, 38, 50, 85,
    89, 185, 199, 201, 206, 219;
    and Constitutionalization 92–3, 98–9;
    revolution v reform 35, 162;
    See also revolutions by individual
    country
Revolutionary
    episteme 183, 187, 190;
    event 214–6;
    excess
    See Revolutionary Surplus
    nationalism 102;
    politics 3, 6, 8, 9, 10, 78, 191, 192, 202
Robespierre 10, 112, 122, 124, 127–9, 216,
    226
Rousseau, Jean-Jacques 65, 121–8, 158,
    159
    Social Contract 65, 123–5, 127n
Russo, Alessandro 22

Saint Paul 73, 78, 86, 91, 106, 121
Sartre, Jean-Paul 79, 116, 118, 120, 122,
    125, 126, 128n, 129, 193;
    Post-Sartrean 119

Shakespeare, William 101, 103, 105, 108
Situationists 39
Slavery 70, 112, 172
Social contract 92, 164
Soviet Union
    See Union of Soviet Socialist Republics
Spinoza, Benedict de 123, 157, 158, 161
Stalin, Joseph 10, 30, 33, 50, 61, 68, 69,
    112, 115, 205, 206, 214, 216
Stalinism 16, 34, 196, 220
Stalinist party/state 20, 25, 30

Third Republic 26
Thompson, E. P. 134
Tocqueville, Alexis de 123
Toscano, Alberto 80n
Toussaint L'Ouverture, François-
    Dominique 10, 112
Trotsky, Leon 34, 39, 68–9

Union of Soviet Socialist Republics
    (USSR) 33, 59, 69, 78, 182, 196, 209;
    communism of 34, 64, 129, 205;
    Communist Party of 191;
    fall of viii, 40, 50, 174, 182, 189–90;
    revolution 19, 67, 68n, 97, 203, 205,
    216–17;
    See also Lenin, Vladimir; Joseph Stalin;
    and Leon Trotsky
United States of America
    civil rights movement 79;
    communism in 93, 169;
    election of Barack Obama viii;
    revolution and abolition of slavery 112

Venezuela viii;
    See also Chávez, Hugo

Welfare State vii, 26, 189,
Wittgenstein, Ludwig 105, 123

Xiaoping, Deng 185, 191, 216, 220

Young Hegelians
    See Hegelians, Young

Žižek, Slavoj x, 4, 33, 36, 80n, 81, 86, 91,
    113–5, 121, 123, 129, 180